ABOUT THE EDITORS

LINDA FAIRSTEIN is the bestselling author of a series of crime novels featuring Manhattan prosecutor Alex Cooper, including *Death Dance* (2006) and *Bad Blood* (2007). She is the former chief prosecutor of the Manhattan District Attorney's Office's pioneering Special Victims' Unit. She is married to Justin Feldman and lives in Manhattan and on Martha's Vineyard.

OTTO PENZLER is the proprietor of the Mysterious Bookshop, the founder of the Mysterious Press, the creator of Otto Penzler Books, and the editor of many books and anthologies.

THOMAS H. COOK is the author of twenty-one books—two works of nonfiction and nineteen novels, including *The Chatham School Affair*, which won the Edgar Allan Poe Award for Best Novel.

The Best American Crime Reporting

2007

The Best American CRIME REPORTING

Editors

2002: NICHOLAS PILEGGI

2003: JOHN BERENDT

2004: JOSEPH WAMBAUGH

2005: JAMES ELLROY

2006: MARK BOWDEN

The Best American
CRIME REPORTING

2007

Guest Editor
LINDA FAIRSTEIN

Series Editors
OTTO PENZLER AND
THOMAS H. COOK

AN ECCO BOOK

HARPER PERENNIAL

NEW YORK • LONDON • TORONTO • SYDNEY

HARPER ● PERENNIAL

THE BEST AMERICAN CRIME REPORTING 2007. Copyright © 2007 by Otto Penzler and Thomas H. Cook. Introduction copyright © 2007 by Linda Fairstein. All rights reserved. Printed in the United States of America. No part of this book may be used or reproduced in any manner whatsoever without written permission except in the case of brief quotations embodied in critical articles and reviews. For information address HarperCollins Publishers, 10 East 53rd Street, New York, NY 10022.

HarperCollins books may be purchased for educational, business, or sales promotional use. For information please write: Special Markets Department, HarperCollins Publishers, 10 East 53rd Street, New York, NY 10022.

FIRST EDITION

Designed by Lovedog Studio

Library of Congress Cataloging-in-Publication Data is available upon request.

ISBN: 978-0-06-081553-0
ISBN-10: 0-06-081553-1

07 08 09 10 11 BVG/RRD 10 9 8 7 6 5 4 3 2 1

Contents

Otto Penzler and Thomas H. Cook | *Preface*   vii

Linda Fairstein | *Introduction*   xiii

Tom Junod | THE LOVED ONES   1

Neil Swidey | THE INSIDE JOB   33

Steve Fennessy | THE TALENTED DR. KRIST   53

Sean Flynn | THE CASE OF THE KILLER PRIEST   79

Matthew Teague | DOUBLE BLIND   109

C. J. Chivers | THE SCHOOL   131

Pamela Colloff | A KISS BEFORE DYING   187

Steve Fishman | THE DEVIL IN DAVID BERKOWITZ   209

Allison Hoover Bartlett | The Man Who Loves
    Books Too Much   231

Ariel Levy | Dirty Old Women   249

Dan P. Lee | Who Killed Ellen Andros?   261

David Bernstein | Fatal Connection   281

Mark Fass | Last Seen on September 10th   295

Brian Boucher | My Roommate, the Diamond
    Thief   311

Douglas Preston | The Monster of Florence   323

Preface

THE COMMON THREAD OF CRIME is crisis, which has the striking power to generate suspense in its development and poignancy in its outcome. How, the heart asks, did this crisis come about, by what means will it be resolved, and at what human cost?

The nature of human crisis is staggeringly diverse, as is the human reaction to it. In Tom Junod's "The Loved Ones," crisis comes not from the agency of man, but through the murderous intervention of nature into his otherwise routine affairs. Churning across an overheated sea, the massive storm closes in upon New Orleans, then hits it dead-on. Here is crisis on an epic scale, a natural catastrophe to which, on a small scale, individual human beings must respond. How the owners of a long-respected nursing home did, in fact, respond, whether dutifully or criminally, is now the subject of a much-publicized investigation. Thirty-four people inside that home were drowned by the steadily rising waters that finally engulfed them. But could they have been saved from this crisis? And if not, then why are any but a murderess named Katrina being charged with their deaths? Is this reaction to crisis, the human need to find human fault though only nature is to blame, not itself a crime, or at least a grave injustice?

Political crises, like the massive ones of nature, also seem beyond the scope of man. What single human being could have stopped the rise of Hitler or Stalin or Mao, and in doing that, prevented the slaughter of untold millions? The complex forces that created the lethal mix of religion, ethnicity, and regionalism that, in turn, drove a select group of Chechen terrorists to seize a school in Beslan were, in their way, no less overwhelming than Katrina's driving winds and rushing waters. But the crisis that created the invasion of a school now created the subsequent crisis of what to do about it, and it was here that the crisis was compounded. C. J. Chivers's "The School" presents the nature and cruel depth of that heartbreaking resolution in minute-by-minute detail, from the initial arrival of the terrorists, through the agonizing hours of the school's capture, and the final choice—or was there one?—to slaughter a world of innocents in a series of explosions.

It is not just the overweening forces of nature and politics that create human crisis, however. We small creatures may do so, too. We can do it to ourselves, as a none-too-wily embezzler does in Neil Swidey's "The Inside Job," a tale, by terms comic and horrifying, in which greed and delusion seem to have created a crisis—perhaps a meltdown—of intelligence.

But if delusion is our enemy, it equally may be said that trust is no friend of clear-thinking, as Brian Boucher's "My Roommate, the Diamond Thief," so amusingly illustrates. In this case, we are warned to distrust the smiling applicant for that spare bedroom down the hall, since, to do otherwise, may create a rather odd crisis of cohabitation to which, after much dithering, we must eventually respond.

In other rooms, to play off Truman Capote's celebrated title, there are other crises. The crisis of older women who seek men in boys, of a priest more demonic than saintly, of a spy who came in from the cold, though not before the application of quite considerable heat. In these stories, human beings work in a double-blind of awareness. They know, but somehow don't know, what they are doing. Does a woman not know when her lover is a little boy? Of course. Does a spy not know the nature of his duplicity? Without doubt. Does the Son of Sam not know that his own insights can't be trusted? Yes, they know, but at the same time, as is so well noted in Ariel Levy's "Dirty Old Women," Matthew Teague's "Double Blind," and Steve Fishman's "The Devil in David Berkowitz," they don't *exactly* know, because the crises either inside or around them create a mental blur, so that all is seen through a glass darkly, particularly themselves.

But can responding to one crisis alleviate a preexisting one? So it seems to have done in Mark Fass's "Last Seen on September 10th," when, in the wake of that cataclysmic attack, a young woman doctor disappears. Her family strongly believes her to have been killed when the Towers fell, while authorities are no less convinced that she was not. Did she use a great national crisis to resolve the smaller one within her, choose to leave a life she hated through a covering cloud of dust?

In these and other stories of true crime, the authors of this year's edition of *The Best American Crime Reporting* present man consumed by crises both within and without, crises of circumstance and crises of conscience, crises of action and reaction. These are stories as diverse as life on earth, both tragic and comic, but always, deeply, and at times profoundly, human.

Several elements of the 2007 edition of *BACR* are different from previous editions, not the least of which is the title. It was reported to us on numerous occasions that readers were confused about whether the contents were fiction or nonfiction when the series was titled *Best American Crime Writing,* as it was for its first five years. The new title, we would like to think, should eliminate any doubts.

The second change is that this year's Guest Editor, the former

Assistant District Attorney in New York City and current best-selling mystery writer, Linda Fairstein, played a greater role in selecting the final fifteen stories from the finalists. She was, as expected, utterly professional and dedicated to making the collection the best it could possibly be, reading and evaluating every story while on a publicity tour for her most recent novel. How she found the time to do all that, as well as to write her fascinating and informative introduction, only she can say.

While on the subject of Guest Editors, it seems appropriate to express our profound gratitude to the previous authors who filled that role so admirably, helping to establish this series as the most prestigious of its kind: Nicholas Pileggi (2002), John Berendt (2003), Joseph Wambaugh (2004), James Ellroy (2005), and Mark Bowden (2006).

In terms of the nature and scope of this collection, we defined the subject matter as any factual story involving crime or the threat of a crime that was written by an American or Canadian and first published in the calendar year 2006. Although we examine an enormous number of publications, inevitably the preeminent ones attracted many of the best pieces. All national and large regional magazines were searched for appropriate material, as were nearly two hundred so-called little magazines, reviews, and journals.

WE WELCOME SUBMISSIONS for *The Best American Crime Reporting 2008* by any writer, editor, publisher, agent, or other interested party. Please send the publication or a tear sheet with the name of the publication, the date on which it appeared, and contact information for the author or representative. If first publication was in electronic format, a hard copy must be submitted. All submissions must be received no later than December 31, 2007; anything received after that date will not be read. This is neither arrogant nor capricious. The timely nature of the book forces very tight deadlines that cannot be met if we receive material later than that date.

The sooner we receive articles, the more favorable will be the light in which they are read.

Please send submissions to Otto Penzler, The Mysterious Bookshop, 58 Warren Street, New York, NY 10007. Inquiries may be sent to me at *ottopenzler@mysteriousbookshop.com*. Regretfully, materials cannot be returned. If you do not believe the U.S. Postal Service will actually deliver mail and prefer to have verification that it was received, please enclose a self-addressed stamped postcard.

Thank you.
Otto Penzler and
Thomas H. Cook
New York, March 2007

Introduction

MIDWAY THROUGH my thirty-year prosecutorial career in the great office of the New York County District Attorney, a forensic pathologist called to tell me about a radical scientific technique that might change the nature of criminal investigations. It was the fall of 1986, and the homicide I was working on had all the necessary elements to thrust it into the headlines from the moment the victim's body was found in Central Park, and to keep it there long after the verdict, eighteen months later. The new phrase that described this phenomenon was "high profile" case. These matters were most likely to get bold ink if they involved sex, drugs, booze, an unnatural death, and the hint of something even edgier—a frisson—running as an undercurrent beneath the known facts. My case had it all.

It had something else new, too. The call from the medical examiner invited me to be one of the first prosecutors in the country to study the potential of DNA. Now my three favorite letters of the alphabet, at the time the process had no place in the criminal justice system. There was one laboratory in the country able to do the analysis—the FBI in Quantico. We had to provide the biologists with fluid samples larger in size than a quarter—unlike the advanced methodology of today which amplifies tiny amounts of substance like a Xerox machine—and along with the body fluids we had to send newspaper stories about the crime. Requests for analysis came to the FBI from cities all over America, and the supervisors chose their cases from among the dozens submitted by jurisdictions nationwide by the volume of press coverage the case generated. They wanted to be certain that the power of this science to solve murders and exonerate the wrongly accused would also land on the front pages to put this science on the map.

We had enough headlines to fill a steamer trunk. Our two legendary tabloids—the *New York Post* and the *Daily News*—had dedicated an entire "wall of shame" in the press room of the criminal courthouse to the sex crimes unit I had led since 1976. The facts of a case weren't always important to their stories. The veteran reporter who had the *Post* crime beat for almost half a century often created entire paragraphs composed of fabricated quotes from me or my colleagues when we followed DA Robert Morgenthau's policy of not speaking to the press about pending matters, not trying our cases on the courtroom steps. "Why does it bother you?" the reporter asked when I complained about one of his stories. "At least, when I put words in your mouth, I make them tasteful."

Even the *New York Times* made a rare foray into A1 coverage of homicide with this case. It was in part because of the crime scene itself—in Central Park, on a quiet lawn off the roadway, directly behind the Metropolitan Museum of Art. The great Murray Kempton mocked the defendant's bad luck to sustain such relentless coverage: "That should teach him—you never murder anyone in a landmark location." Both the victim and her killer were teenagers from "good" families. There were private schools involved, many kids from privileged backgrounds who were partying with the victim and defendant in the hours before the homicide. Underage drinking and the casual sex of upscale teens gave the mainstream media larger social issues to explore. Both kids were physically attractive—don't ask me why that should matter in a murder case, but I can assure you it guarantees better placement in the papers and an endless array of photographs of the deceased, the killer, and everyone who knew them.

So the New York City lab forwarded the body fluids—blood and saliva—that we hoped to link to the clothing that smothered the victim after she was beaten and choked by this young man—a friend of hers—whom she had accompanied into the park after a night bouncing with acquaintances. And I packaged dozens of pages of feature stories—many of them wildly inaccurate—and sent them off to Quantico, too.

The FBI accepted our case. We had to wait six months for a preliminary DNA result—that was rushing the techs at that time—while today I would be begging the forensic team to get me an answer—match or no match—within twenty-four hours. Throughout that long period, the detectives and I continued to build our case the traditional way, interviewing scores of witnesses and canvassing Central Park on random mornings, looking for joggers and bicyclists and dogwalkers who might have seen a fragment of this deadly encounter. I took countless tutorials to learn the complicated science of genetic fingerprinting, expecting to have to make it clear to the jurors who would be chosen to evaluate the evidence.

When the date came to hold the pretrial evidentiary hearing on the admissibility of the scientific results, the court's ruling reflected attitudes across America in those years. This new technique seemed too confusing, not reliable enough to present to a jury. Salivary amylase mixed with blood proved the victim's jacket had covered her bleeding mouth at the time of her death, but the jury would never learn that fact. The judge didn't think this DNA stuff would fly, so he declared the lab's findings inadmissible. It would not be until 1989 that any court in this country accepted the validity of this dazzling forensic technique.

Meanwhile, the media coverage remained intense. The defendant— a drug-addicted dropout with a history of burglarizing Park Avenue apartments to support his habit—was photographed for the cover of a national glossy magazine, like a male model, in a navy blazer and rep tie. He was out on bail, so photographers staked out his apartment and snapped him as he and a string of girlfriends partied on, right up through the time of the trial. Other press hounds hung out in SoHo, near the apartment in which Jennifer had lived with her family, rifling through morning garbage in hopes of finding papers or effects that once belonged to the vibrant eighteen-year-old who'd been killed.

No tidbit was too insignificant for a story. There were items when the killer was accompanied to a court appearance by his old family friend, the Archbishop of New York; pieces about curious crowds lining up every night to get into the Second Avenue bar at which the doomed young woman had met up with her executioner; and features about the latest designer drug alleged to have been ingested by the defendant—the first time I'd heard of Ecstasy—washed down by tequila shots and beer chasers. There were endless headlines incorporating the phrase "rough sex"— words never uttered by the perp, but always associated with the crime because of tabloid accounts that had adopted the expression as a mantra for the case; and there were frequent references to a "sex diary" that did not in fact exist. The defense attorney referred to it that way, and so the reporters did, too—although the judge finally examined the little date book the victim kept by the telephone in her mother's kitchen and declared there was nothing about sex in it. Still, papers sold whenever a story about the "sex diary" ran.

There was a dreadful cost to this endless publicity, characterized by a reckless disregard for the truth. It saturated the jury pool of usually savvy New Yorkers before we got a dozen of them anywhere near the box. Lawyers on both sides of a murder case can usually select their twelve jurors, four alternates, from a pool of fifty intelligent citizens. In this instance, we went through 483 prospective jurors, most of whom had to be excused because they claimed to have formed opinions about the defendant's guilt—or innocence—

based on more than a year of news stories. Many parroted the "rough sex" defense while others seemed disturbed by the young victim's nonexistent "sex diary." Some were titillated by the stories, and a few admitted plans to draft and sell screenplays of their experience, egged on by the months of press attention.

In March of 1988, as the jury neared a deadlock after deliberating for nine days, the defendant, Robert Chambers, pleaded guilty to the crime of manslaughter, for causing the death of his friend Jennifer Levin. The day of his arrest, one of the headline writers had tagged him "The Preppy Murderer"—and although there was nothing in his pedigree or his drug-addicted lifestyle that matched the label, it is what the press calls him to this day. Chambers served his fifteen-year sentence, was released from state prison on Valentine's Day (how the tabloids loved that irony), was rearrested for possession of heroin and cocaine, which earned him another stint behind bars, and still remains a surefire subject for headlines, interviews, and more photographs. From the looks of it, the hard time and heavy drugs seem to have taken their toll.

In the twenty years that have elapsed since the conclusion of that case, DNA has indeed revolutionized the criminal justice system, as its early supporters predicted it would. It's impossible to open a newspaper or magazine without a story that trumpets its involvement in solving cold cases, freeing someone from death row, or identifying remains of humans pulverized in disasters—natural ones or those of homicidal origin. Brilliant investigative journalists have explored its ability to link criminals to their deeds in a way the best detectives have been unable to do, as well as to use it to exonerate men long imprisoned for crimes they didn't commit.

Before I stepped away from my prosecutorial role in 2002, I worked on the haunting case about which Mark Fass wrote that appears in these pages. I know DNA has the power to resolve the story of the missing physician, and I hope to read that piece before too long.

Terrorism on our own soil and abroad continues to impact our lives in ways most of us never imagined a decade ago. The idea of airplanes being used in concert as lethal weapons was unthinkable to most of us, just like the imprisonment of more than a thousand people—so many of them children—in a small school in Beslan.

Killer storm and killer priest, David Berkowitz reborn and Son of Sam redux in the peaceful hills of Tuscany, con jobs and jewel thieves—age-old themes with very modern twists.

When I try to draw from my prosecutorial experience to write crime fiction, I frequently find myself tempering many of the details. Truth *is* so much stranger, so much more bizarre than fiction, and frequently so much more riveting—as these writers prove in each of the entries in this book.

I love great crime stories, and I like them even more when they are written with style and dignity, insight and élan . . . and oh, yes, when they are based on the facts.

—Linda Fairstein

The Best American CRIME REPORTING

2007

Tom Junod

THE LOVED ONES

FROM *Esquire*

IT WAS THE RIGHT DECISION. Of course it was. Mamaw was killing herself taking care of Papaw. Papaw was killing himself taking care of Mamaw. You were killing yourself taking care of them both. They were going to burn the house down if they kept living in it. They were going to kill themselves or someone else if they kept driving. They couldn't see. They couldn't hear. They couldn't always remember your name. They were speaking gibberish. They were staring out into space. They fell asleep in the middle of conversations. They either weren't taking their pills or they were taking too many. They were found wandering around. They were falling. They were in wheelchairs. They were immobilized. They were sick. They were old. It was—and these were the words you heard yourself saying, the words you heard everybody saying, everybody except them—time.

It couldn't have been an easy decision, no. That it was a decision, and that you had to make it, was in itself a terrible burden. That you were the one called upon to do the final arithmetic seemed cosmically unfair. Your life and theirs, in a ledger. Well, not just your life—your spouse's, your kids'. You had to think of them, too. Did money play a part? Sure it did. But more important was the question of quality of life. Theirs. Yours. You were being *eaten alive* . . . and so in the end you did what you thought best. You made the Decision.

MR. COBB, how are you doing?" I asked James Cobb, a lawyer in New Orleans, Louisiana.

"It depends on what you mean," Mr. Cobb answered. "If you mean how am I doing after losing my house and every fucking thing in it, and after being forced to live in a two-bedroom shithole with my wife and two kids and being told how *lucky* I am to get it, and after being *fucked*—and I mean absolutely fucked—by my insurance company and by the United States government (and by the way, just so you know, if anybody from New Orleans, Louisiana, tells you that they're not getting fucked by their insurance company and by the United States government, they're fucking *lying,* all right?) . . . if you mean, how am I doing after all that is factored in: Well, I guess the answer is that I'm doing fine. Now, how can I help you?"

Jim Cobb and I had never spoken before. These were the first words he spoke after my initial greeting. I was calling him because he represented—and represents—Sal and Mabel Mangano, the couple who operated St. Rita's nursing home in St. Bernard Parish, just southeast of New Orleans. They had not evacuated their residents when Hurricane Katrina was making its way to Louisiana—they had not evacuated in the face of what was said to be a mandatory evacuation order—and when the levees failed and St. Bernard was inundated with ten feet of water, thirty-five helpless people died. No: drowned. No: drowned screaming for someone to save them, at least according to the initial press accounts. No: "drowned like rats," in the words of a prosecutor in the office of Louisiana attorney general Charles Foti, who was charging the

Manganos with nearly three dozen counts of negligent homicide. Now they were notorious—icons of abandonment whose mug shots after their arrest personified more than just the prevailing stereotype of unscrupulous nursing-home owners. An entire American city had been left to die, and sixty-five-year-old Sal and sixty-two-year-old Mabel Mangano had somehow become the public faces of a national disgrace.

I was calling Jim Cobb to talk to him about the decision the Manganos had made but also about something else, something at once more universal and more personal: the Decision. My own parents are elderly. I have not made the Decision, but there is not a day when I don't think about it and dread it, and in this I am not so different from many of my friends and millions of people from my generation. The horror of St. Rita's was a nightmarish realization of my dread, a brutal rejoinder to the hopeful voice that inoculates children from the emotional consequences of institutionalizing their parents: *It's for the best.* This was not for the best, nor could it ever be rationalized as such. This was tragic theater catching up with a social and moral issue that had already caught up with America, and in the aftermath of Katrina, I was haunted by reports that the St. Rita's staff had tied residents to their beds and left them to face the rising waters alone. I was transfixed by Jefferson Parish president Aaron Broussard breaking into tears when he said that the mother of one of his employees had telephoned for help from St. Rita's for five days and had died when no help came. I was even fascinated by the multiple rage-gasms of CNN's Nancy Grace, who brought herself off by urging the government to redeem itself by bringing Sal and Mabel Mangano to justice. And when I later found out that little of what I had seen or heard about St. Rita's was actually, you know, *true,* I began to wonder whether the Manganos, who had made the wrong decision, were paying the psychic price for all the millions who had either made or were making the Decision and had to be assured that it was right.

I offered some of this to Jim Cobb. He responded helpfully,

translating it into the ungoverned language of his poor dying city. "Yeah," he said, "people need to look in the mirror. I've done a lot of nursing-home work. When a nursing home gets sued, it's because a resident died. And then the kids become avenging angels for Mamaw and Papaw. Well, where were you when Mamaw and Papaw were shitting all over themselves and we were cleaning up? You weren't avenging angels *then*. You want to talk about Sal and Mabel? Let's talk about Sal and Mabel. They cared as much as you did. They were wiping Mamaw and Papaw's *ass* while you were driving to Destin."

TAKE CARE OF THE OLD PEOPLE. It's what people are supposed to do in that part of the world. It's what they learn to do when the storms come. And this time, the storm that was coming was supposed to be major, was supposed to be the one that could bring on the deluge that everyone feared. So Steve Gallodoro and his brother and his sister decided to evacuate their father, Tufanio. They decided to put him in a car and get him the hell out of St. Bernard Parish, which is low-lying and vulnerable to storms. It was Cheryl this time: She was the one who decided to take it on, since Steve himself was a fireman in St. Bernard and had to be around in the event of an emergency. "They were headed to Tennessee," Steve Gallodoro says. "Sixteen hours later, they were in Jackson, Mississippi, and my dad could physically go no farther. He could no longer sit up in the car. They were rescued by a man who saw them at a gas station and said, You look like you need help, we have a big house, you can stay. And so they stayed with him. We refer to him as an angel."

That was 2004. That was Hurricane Ivan, and though it was indeed major, it spent most of its force in the Florida Panhandle and brought damage, but not deluge, to Louisiana. It was, however, decisive in its way: It brought the Gallodoros to the Decision. "My father was eighty-two years old," Steve Gallodoro says. "He had a couple of strokes, he was paralyzed on the left side, he was confined to a wheelchair. We were physically unable to care for him any-more. We tried the sitters, the aides, but it was too much." Fortunately there were four nursing homes in St. Bernard Parish, and one, St. Rita's was just six or seven minutes away from where Tufanio Gallodoro's three children lived. It had been in business for twenty years and was a family operation, run by Sal and Mabel Mangano, whose own home was on the twenty-acre property, next door to the homes of their daughter Tammy and their son, Sal Jr., known as "Little Sal," and his wife, TJ. The Manganos, all of them, were in St. Rita's not just every day but night and day. Sal was known for eating breakfast with the St. Rita's residents and Little Sal for being in the building as late as midnight, fixing what needed to be fixed. One of the things Little Sal would say to families shop-ping for nursing homes—and says even now, as a piece of advice—was this: "Find one that's family run, because if something goes wrong, you know who to point your finger at."

Tufanio Gallodoro became a resident of St. Rita's almost a year before the next storm season. According to Steve Gallodoro, there was still some "emotional upset" in his family about putting Tufanio in a nursing home, but that was eased by the proximity of the place and by its policy of keeping its doors open to family members long after most other nursing homes locked up. "He was visited every day," Steve Gallodoro says. "We would come by and shave him. We would wash his hair. We would give him a haircut. We would feed him." Besides, Tufanio's nickname was TJ, just like Little Sal's wife. He liked TJ, who, during the birthday party the Manganos threw each month for their residents, would dance with the men and sometimes dance on the tables. TJ liked Tufanio, too, and that's the way it was, Little Sal says: "I used to tell families who were leaving a loved one there, 'You're not the only ones who have the right to love them. We have the right to love them, too.' "

"HEY, YOU UGLY BITCH!" Jim Cobb shouts through the open window of his big green BMW. He's driving down one of the alleylike streets in the business district of New Orleans, on his way to what's left of his home, and he's spotted a former client on the sidewalk, a tall black guy who's wearing a sheer black jersey and a black skullcap, white iPod plugs in his ears. He's got that New Orleans thing about him, the spindly hard glamour, the high cheekbones, the Asiatic cast to his eyes.

"Hey, bitch, I saw you on CNN defending those people," the client says. "You gon' to to *hell* for that shit."

"Fuck you, bitch," Cobb cackles, and closes the window before heading out to where his city is no more.

You know, you always hear what America is going to lose if it loses New Orleans, and it's always in terms of the jazz or the French Quarter or the red beans and rice or whatever. It's never in terms of *this*—its prickly racial proximities; its ongoing realization of its mulatto history; its men calling one another bitch as a matter of course; its citizenry still drinking, still cursing, still talking without undue deliberation of consequence. It's never in terms of the human artifacts of all those vestigial tendencies, like Jim Cobb. Cobb is fifty-three now. He's lived in New Orleans all his life, and with his trimmed gray beard, his textured face, and his wrinkle-centered, red-rimmed hound-dog eyes, he looks like one of those dissolute Confederate generals of legend who kept a flask on his hip but still managed to lead those boys up the hill. He loves his causes, and now that he's convinced that the cause he *really* represents by representing Sal and Mabel Mangano—the cause of his beloved New Orleans itself—is a lost one, well, the man will say *anything*.

"Did you see Bertucci's testimony?" he's saying as he's driving. "Was it good for my case? *Fuuuuuuuck*. It was awesome for my case. It was so good, I'm considering jerking off while reading it." For one of the civil lawsuits against the Manganos, Cobb has just taken the deposition of Dr. Bryan Bertucci, the elected coroner of

St. Bernard Parish and the man Cobb regards as the state's star witness in its case against the Manganos. It was Bertucci, you see, who offered St. Rita's two school buses for use in an evacuation, and Bertucci who told the world of the nursing home's disastrous reply: No. "The state is trying to prove that Sal and Mabel were negligent," Cobb says. "That means willful, wanton, reckless disregard. So I ask him, 'Have you ever witnessed them treat their patients in a careless manner?' 'No.' 'In a negligent manner?' 'No.' 'In a reckless manner?' 'No.' I mean, I'm practically reading from the *statute,* man. But wait, it gets better. He says, 'No, as a matter of fact, in my opinion they ran the best nursing home in the parish.' All right? This is *their* freaking witness."

At the same time Cobb's saying all this, however, he's on the cell phone with one of his colleagues, talking about a doctor from his neighborhood whose house burned to the ground the night before. The neighborhood is Lakeview, and every house in it is striped by a piss-colored high-water stain that runs as high as the top of the front door. They're all still standing, though, except for the doctor's, which is now knee-high and smoldering. Still on his cell, Cobb parks along the curb and then gets out of his car and climbs on the blackened ruin, saying, "This lucky mother*fucker*—his house burned down. What? He's upset about it? Well, he's a doctor. He's too stupid to know that it's good. Are you telling him he should be breaking out the fucking champagne? His homeowner's goes into effect! He gets full value for his house! The only thing I get is flood insurance. I have to go back! He's free! Tell him congratulations. No, tell him I want to know the dago he hired to do this. I want to get some of that Italian lightning for *my* house."

And then he goes to his house, which, like all the other houses in Lakeview, is empty and dead. Lakeview is dead. The Ninth Ward of New Orleans is dead, too—famously dead, savagely and spectacularly dead, *vehemently* dead, as dead as Nagasaki in 1945. But Lakeview is different. It's gangrenously dead. It's a museum of itself, a museum that stretches for miles, with the only visible life-forms either grotesque, as in a grown man riding a Big Wheel alone down an uninhabited street, or predatory, as in the looters still plying their trade, with boxes yet. Or simple, as in mold. There's a lot of mold in Lakeview, indeed a lot of mold in Jim Cobb's house, scavenging black mold with the characteristics of fire, stoked in the foul remnants of flood. Floodwater still fills his pool, still fills his crawfish pots and his turkey fryer, and he's uncharacteristically quiet while he's in his house, until he goes outside and starts walking toward the lake, where the vista opens to the wartime view: the black helicopters hovering static over what passes for a levee, the X's spray-painted hastily on the doors of the houses, the occasional 1 or 2 mixed in with the zeros, noting how many bodies were found inside.

"You know who died in these houses?" Cobb says. "Old people. The storm wasn't a black thing or a white thing; it was an old thing. Sixty-five percent of those who died were over sixty-five. Forty percent were over seventy-five. It was a complete fucking catastrophe for old people. And what does the attorney general do about it? Who are the people he arrests? Two senior citizens, Sal and Mabel Mangano. He arrests *them* for neglect while Michael Brown and Ray Nagin and Kathleen Blanco and Michael Chertoff and George W. Bush get a pass? No fucking way, man. They'll have to kill me first."

THEY EACH HAD FAVORITES, the Manganos did. Oh, sure, they treated everybody well: Mabel used to walk around with fifteen or twenty bucks' worth of change in her pocket, and it was for everybody. If a resident wanted a Coke, Mabel bought him a Coke. She'd cut his hair, too, even if the resident's family didn't give him any money. More than anyone else, the ones she doted on were the ones who never saw their families.

Still, her favorite was Janie. Definitely. Janie was a little slow, and Mabel loved her. Is it all right to say that? Because she did. Before

Sal and Mabel bought the Hummer, they had a Lincoln, and as Little Sal says, "On some days I'd drive up to the nursing home and there they'd be, Janie driving my mom's Lincoln up and down the driveway, Mom sitting shotgun." Janie had never driven a car in her life—no one had ever thought to let her—and sometimes Mabel would tell her that one day they'd get in the Lincoln and she'd let Janie drive all the way to New York City. Of course, it wasn't going to happen. But it was Janie's dream.

You have to do that when you run a nursing home. You have to keep dreams alive. You have to give the residents something more to look forward to than the relief of death. The Manganos weren't sophisticated people; they weren't particularly educated people; but *that* they knew how to do. It's why they got into the business. Mabel's grandmother, Rita Serpas, was in a nursing home in St. Bernard Parish back in the old days. She was getting forgetful; she'd started going to the highway with dollar bills squeezed between her thumb and forefinger and hitching rides to Canal Street. The nursing home was the kind that gave nursing homes a bad name: three or four beds to a room and the owners free to do as they pleased, since the industry was less regulated back then. Mabel used to visit her grandmother and thought she—and her family—could do better. She and Sal had twenty acres of land in St. Bernard, and when a new highway came next to it, Mabel told Sal that she wanted to build a nursing home. He never thought that much about it, never thought much beyond "Let's do it." They'd run some businesses before—a small trucking business, a feed store— and Sal was always looking for ways to better himself. Mabel did all the paperwork, without a lawyer, and Sal, a mechanic, oversaw the construction of the sixty-room building. St. Rita's opened on September 23, 1985, with a full staff and one resident, because that was the rule: Before you could open for one resident, you had to be fully staffed. In a week, Sal and Mabel had seven or eight residents, and in a year they had enough to have a parade.

The parade was held the Sunday before Carnival, and it was a big deal, not only for the nursing home but also for the neighborhood. The Manganos wanted to make sure everyone in St. Bernard Parish knew about St. Rita's, so they helped the residents get dressed up in costumes and tuxedos, loaded them with beads, and put them on seven floats, along with family members. The residents who were in wheelchairs went on a flatbed trailer, their chairs tied down by Sal himself, and there was a double amputee they named Carnival queen. After several years, the parade got *too* big, and so the one big event allowed by the Manganos' insurance policy became the feast of St. Joseph. Every March 19, the Manganos fed up to eight hundred people. They baked and gave away a few thousand cookies, made twelve or fifteen casseroles, and stuffed three hundred artichokes. They invited the parish council to eat with them, and the residents—well, the residents they dressed up as saints.

It was fun. They *had* fun, Sal and Mabel. They wanted people other than their residents to want to be there, and people came. People even came during hurricanes and waited out the storm with them. Not just their family—their whole *clan:* grandchildren, nephews, staff members who were working, staff members who weren't working, a few of their neighbors, and then just some people who didn't want to be alone for the storm. Hell, in addition to their residents, they'd have more than thirty people staying with them during big storms, and in the words of Little Sal, "Once you stayed with us the first time, you wouldn't even have to call the next year to feel welcome." Evacuate? They had an evacuation plan, sure; they were required by law to have one. But they never evacuated. Twenty years, hurricanes came buzz-sawing in off the Gulf, and Sal and Mabel Mangano stayed put. Why would they move? People came to *them.* They had faith in the levees, faith in their building, but, more than that, faith in themselves. They survived. Their clan survived. Their residents survived. And then, Little Sal says, after the storms would pass, "There was always an abundance. We'd have fried shrimp and softshell crabs and oysters and redfish and everything from people's refrigerators. People from the neighborhood would bring their food to us before it went bad. We had big barbecue grills going; it was an *event.* "

WHO'S GOING TO TAKE CARE of old people? More to the point, what should you expect from the people who *do* take care of old people when their families can't or won't do it anymore? Even more to the point, what should you expect from the people who take money to take care of old people because *you* can't or won't do it anymore? Do you expect them to love your mother or father as much as you do? Do you expect them to love your mother or father *more* than you do? Do you expect their love to be absolute? And do you expect their love to be absolute because you found out that yours wasn't—because you made the Decision? Or do you expect their love to be absolute because they're getting paid for it, and their obligations are legal and contractual, whereas yours were strictly moral? Or, in Cobb's translation: "What is it we can expect from caregivers who are taking care of your parents for ninety-five bucks a day? That's the Medicaid rate, I believe. Ninety-five bucks a day, and for that a lot of people think nursing homes should be the Ritz-Carlton Naples."

These are the issues Charlie Foti has to hash out as attorney general of the state of Louisiana. Well, not really. He really has to decide how to enforce the law, which means that he has to decide whether, say, the prosecution of Sal and Mabel Mangano for thirty-four counts of negligent homicide is in the state's interest. (The thirty-fifth body was found after the Manganos were arrested.) But Charlie Foti is interested in old people. They mean a lot to him, personally and politically. They're his *constituency,* politically. When he was sheriff of Orleans Parish, he had a big dinner every Thanksgiving for old people who were too poor or too alone to have one for themselves. He didn't forget them, and when he ran for AG in 2003, *they* didn't forget him, helping make him the state's top lawyer. And personally—personally he just likes them. For many years, he took care of his aged father. His father died in 2004 at the age of ninety-three, but when the phone rang for the first year Foti was in office, it was as likely as not the old man, calling for reasons any son with an old father knows all about. And Foti always took the call, no matter how busy he was. It's not easy watching your parents get old, but from Charlie Foti's point of view, it's not half as difficult as watching them die.

And so, according to his spokeswoman, the attorney general has made "elderly issues his first priority" since he entered office. In fact, he and Fred Duhy, the lawyer in charge of his Medicaid-fraud unit, were just about to launch a major public-relations campaign about what Duhy calls the "plight" of the elderly before Katrina came along and provided all the awareness, and all the plight, they would ever need. "When you have elderly people and infirm people in your care, you have a greater standard of care, because you're talking about people who can't take care of themselves," Duhy says in his office one afternoon before he goes to see his boss. "We deal with cases every day where people in nursing homes threaten to withhold food and water from people who can't reach for it. We just arrested someone who flung food at someone's face." Is Duhy saying that the Manganos ran that kind of nursing home? No, he's not. What he's saying is that the case against them is similarly straightforward. He is saying that they knew—that they had to know—the extent of the storm coming their way. He is saying that they had an evacuation plan and did not follow it. He is alleging that Louisiana's governor issued a mandatory evacuation order on the Sunday afternoon before the storm hit in the early hours of Monday morning, and they ignored it. He is saying that the other three nursing homes in St. Bernard Parish all evacuated, and they lost one patient among them. "Here, read this," he says, and opens his copy of the Louisiana criminal code to the page on criminal negligence, which, in the language of the statute, "exists when, although neither specific nor general criminal intent is present, there is such disregard of the interest of others that the offender's conduct amounts to a gross deviation below the standard of care expected to be maintained by a reasonably careful man under like circumstances."

"When this results in a death," Duhy says, "you have negligent homicide. It's not a big mystery."

Then he goes into the conference room, where, taking a seat at the end of a long table, behind unkempt stacks of paper, is Charlie Foti. This is the other thing you have to love about this part of the world: People still have faces, and everybody seems to have the right one. Charlie Foti *looks* like the guy who ran the jail in New Orleans for thirty years. He's wearing a rumpled white shirt and a loosened tie, and he looks damp, man. He doesn't just sit down; he slumps in his chair, so that his eyes are about table level, and then he doesn't *move*. He doesn't blink, doesn't look at anyone asking him questions. What he does is belch, softly and without excuse, and then set about lovingly chewing an unlit cigar into cud. When he starts talking, it's with the intention of talking without interruption. He says, "Do you expect these nursing-home people to have the responsibility to protect their patients? . . . You might not ask for the responsibility, but you got it. . . . You just gotta do what you gotta do. . . . My poor brother evacuated my father when he was ninety-two. . . . St. Bernard Parish evacuated prisoners. . . . We evacuate criminals but not people who can't move? . . . If I make that decision and I die, woe is me. . . . If I make that decision for someone who can't walk . . ."

He is as patient and oblivious—and as seemingly drowsy—as a snapping turtle, and he just keeps sinking deeper into his chair until he is asked this: The fact that a lot of the most lurid details reported in the media didn't turn out to be true—how does that affect your case? That's when his head turns, quickly, and he snaps, "What didn't *happen?* They died in their beds. That will be horrendous enough." And he's right, of course. Sal and Mabel Mangano may not be guilty of the crimes conjured up by the media and the public's imagination. Negligent homicide may be notoriously difficult to prove. Charlie Foti for all we know may have, as Jim Cobb says, "the legal acumen of an unlit charcoal briquette—and that's being too hard on charcoal briquettes." But on his side of the ledger he has thirty-five helpless people, horribly and inexcusably dead. Cobb has only Sal and Mabel, and they are already guilty of staying alive.

TAKE CARE OF THE OLD PEOPLE.

Jimmy Martinez came to St. Rita's to wait out Katrina with his wife, Peggy, who had Alzheimer's. Gene Alonzo came to wait out the storm with his brother Carlos, who was severely disabled from a boating accident. Nine families came before the storm and got their loved ones out of there. For Steve Gallodoro, however, there were no easy choices. He couldn't evacuate Tufanio because the last time anybody tried that, his father almost died. He couldn't stay with Tufanio because he was a fireman and had to work during big storms. So on Saturday he went to talk to the people who were taking care of his father. He went to St. Rita's, and he says, "The Manganos assured me they'd contracted with bus services, they had staff coming in, they had two facilities to transport the residents to if the call for evacuation was made. They said, We are the professionals, leave him with us, he's better off. My sister had some emotional struggles about leaving him, but I told her the Manganos had a plan in place, let's leave him with them.

"My family left the parish early Sunday morning," he says. "I was at the firehouse. I cleared up things that needed to be done, got in my unit, and went to St. Rita's. I walked up to Sal Mangano and asked what he needed. I said, However many men you need for the evacuation, I'll give them to you. He told me they were not evacuating. They decided they were going to stay. I left and ran into someone from the parish. I informed him of what St. Rita's had told me, and he said, We'll go back to the government center and have the coroner call them. So Dr. Bertucci called and advised them that they should leave and offered buses and manpower. The Manganos refused.

"Then we were in the middle of the storm. The next morning the water started coming up, and I couldn't get back to St. Rita's. I had no contact with the eastern end of the parish, but I heard that it was dry. That was inaccurate. But I thought that if something had happened, I would have gotten some word. So we got into boats on Monday and started rescuing. As soon as we left the complex, we could not travel any great distance without filling the boat with survivors. People were on rooftops, and to get to St. Rita's I would have had to pass people by. I didn't do that, and so I didn't get to St. Rita's until the next morning."

You know what came next. You know what Steve Gallodoro saw when he got into a boat on Tuesday morning and went to St. Rita's. And, given what you know: Does it matter what the Manganos have to say? Does it matter that they say they told everyone who asked—Steve Gallodoro included—that they were staying put for the storm? Does it matter that they say no government official called to inform them of a mandatory evacuation order? Does it matter that Dr. Bryan Bertucci, the one government official who did call with an offer of two school buses, has admitted in his deposition that he never pushed the issue: "No, I didn't say, 'You got to leave,' " Bertucci says. "That's not my job. But I was suggesting, obviously, I thought they should leave, or I wouldn't have offered them the buses."

It matters to them, of course. It matters to the Manganos because they have been charged with legal responsibility for the death of Tufanio Gallodoro and nearly three dozen others. To Steve Gallodoro, though, there is nothing they can say that changes anything, because there is nothing they can say that changes these facts: Tufanio Gallodoro couldn't swim. Tufanio Gallodoro was deathly afraid of the water. Tufanio Gallodoro drowned. For his son, the horror of St. Rita's will always be a moral horror, and he will never stop holding the Manganos morally responsible.

———

"SO YOU MET WITH Charlie Foti," Jim Cobb says. "Did Charlie tell you that the first witness I'm going to call is Charlie Foti?"

Well, yes, he did. His employees did, anyway. Fred Duhy did. It's one of Cobb's more entertaining characteristics—making you privy to secrets he has told everyone under the sun. Back in the spring, when it became clear that the attorney general was going to move forward with the prosecution of the Manganos—that he wasn't, in Cobb's words, going to "stand down"—Cobb went to Baton Rouge for a meeting with Duhy and, for as long as Cobb succeeded in holding his attention, Charlie Foti. "He kept going in and out of the meeting," Cobb says. "You've heard of ADHD? Well, he's ADHDDDDDDDDDDDDDDDDD." Cobb's intention was to get Foti to stand down by citing all the officials who to his mind had more legal responsibility than Sal and Mabel Mangano for the thirty-five deaths at St. Rita's. According to Cobb, the meeting went like this: "Duhy leaned over and said, Is that some sort of veiled threat against the attorney general? I said, I don't think there's anything *veiled* about it." According to Duhy: "He told us point-blank that he intended to call the governor or whoever. I don't think there's anything to it. And I don't appreciate this 'stand down' business. I don't appreciate someone telling me how to do my job. I'm going to do my job the way I see fit, and I'm not going to be bullied."

Cobb has said he doesn't want to go to trial. Normally sparing with biblical references, he has even gone so far as to say, "Father, take this cup." At the same time, he has pursued a course of such single-minded provocation with Charlie Foti that you wonder if his intention is to make it impossible for Foti to let the prosecution go away so that he can put Foti on the stand.

Why Foti? Simple. Because Cobb wants a chance to ask him, *Why the Manganos?,* when on April 1, 2005 ("April Fool's Day," Cobb says), Louisiana governor Kathleen Blanco approved an emergency-evacuation plan that gave legal responsibility for the evacuation of nursing homes to Louisiana transportation secretary Johnny Bradberry.

And because in December 2005, Secretary Bradberry told Senate investigators that "we put no plans in place to do any of this."

And because, according to *The New York Times,* the state "even turned down an offer for patient-evacuation assistance from the federal government," in much the same way the Manganos were said to have turned down an offer of assistance from the St. Bernard Parish coroner.

And because St. Rita's wasn't the only nursing home in the area that didn't evacuate for Katrina. Indeed, only twenty-one of fifty-seven nursing homes did.

And because the thirty-five people who died at St. Rita's weren't the only people who died in unevacuated nursing homes and hospitals when the levees failed—more than two hundred did.

And because the storm itself left St. Rita's unscathed. It was the failure of *the levees* that sent the ten feet of water that swallowed up the one-story structure in less than an hour.

And because even the commander of the Army Corps of Engineers has admitted that blame for the failure of the levees lies with the Corps itself.

And because the same thing that killed thirty-five people at St. Rita's killed *more than fifteen hundred* people in the New Orleans area. "And guess what?" Cobb says. "It wasn't Sal and Mabel. It was a flood caused by the negligence of the Army Corps of Engineers and the levee boards. And so if Foti is going to charge someone, why not charge the motherfuckers who killed fifteen hundred people? Why charge Sal and Mabel? Why isn't he doing his *job?* Which is what I intend to ask him if he persists in fucking around with me and the Manganos. I don't want to, but I will. We're looking to try the ultimate responsibility for Katrina. Everybody talks about re-sponsibility. The fact is, nobody wants it. That's what this whole prosecution is about. The state doesn't want to be responsible for its part in the whole fucking catastrophe. The attorney general thinks the case is about responsibility, too? Fine, let's go. You take Kathleen Blanco and the Army Corps of Engineers. I'll take Sal and Mabel. Let's get it on."

"SAL WAS MAKING the rice for the red beans when the water came," Mabel says. "The beans was all ready. We figured the power would go out, so we made the beans the day before."

Yes, that's Sal and Mabel Mangano sitting in a conference room in Jim Cobb's office. Last seen as Sal and Mabel *M-a-n-g-a-n-o,* when Nancy Grace asked a guest to spell their surname so that all of America could identify them and hunt them down. Last seen as the most villified man and woman in the country, after Charles Foti announced their arrest to the national media. Sal and Mabel. They've been married forty-six years, after meeting at a dance in New Orleans. Now they live in a FEMA trailer like everyone else. They're sitting next to each other at the long table, occasionally holding hands. Mabel's got the soft voice, the blue blouse, the big hair, the cantilevered eyebrows, the handbag either on the table or in her lap, the tissues squeezed in her free hand. Sal's the blunt instrument. He's a squat man, a mechanic with thick fingers, his hair combed straight back off his forehead. In back of them, hovering around them, pacing, standing, always standing, never sitting down, is Sal Mangano Jr., Little Sal, an amalgam of both his parents, compact and muscled in a short-sleeved shirt, like his father, but with the same polished face as his mother, with the same perpetually amazed and amazing eyebrows, combined with black hair combed straight back from a widow's peak and a black Sharpie's mustache. He's forty-three. He does most of the talking while chewing the *shit* out of a black coffee straw, but when his father, out of nowhere, says, "Take that stick out of your mouth," he does as he's told without saying a word.

———————

AND SO: SAL WAS MAKING the rice for the red beans when the water came. It was ten-thirty in the morning on Monday, August 29. Katrina had hit in the wee hours, and the lights had gone out, but the generators had kicked in, and they had power for everything except the air conditioners. They had prepared in their usual way. They had water, they had diapers, they had generators, they had medicine, they had ice, they had the red beans already done. And, at ten-thirty in the morning, they told themselves they had made it; they told themselves they had survived the storm, just as they had for the last twenty years. Their clan was with them—the workers, the non-workers, the children, the children's children: thirty-one people in all. And the residents: sixty-two of them. All that was left was to go outside and check the wind damage sustained by the one-story building that was long and low and straight as a piece of pipe.

Then the nursing home started filling up with water. *Woe-tah:* That's how the Manganos pronounce it. There has been some talk of a wall of water coming down the road with a rumble, but the Manganos just remember the water's incessant *rise.* "Even when it's two feet deep, you hope it's going to stop," Mabel says. "But it didn't. It just kept coming in." Or, as Little Sal puts it, "When I jumped outside onto the patio, the water was about two or three feet deep. My house is 150 feet away from the nursing home. My fence is five feet tall. By the time I got to my fence, I was able to swim over it." He was with his wife, TJ, and his son Tanner and Emmett Unbehagen, the husband of one of the nurses. They were trying to get to their boats, which had been parked on the lawn. Little Sal's boat was caught in an oak tree, and they rode the current of water coursing through his living room to get it, spark plugs and keys in Little Sal's mouth. Emmett's boat was chained to a trailer, and by the time they got to it, the chain was pulling it under the water. Tanner took a gun and shot the chain. Then they started the boats and went back to St. Rita's and all its drowning saints.

People were already hanging from the gutters when they got there. Well, Big Sal was on the roof, trying to keep the doors open. But Mabel was hanging from the gutters, holding on to Janie. Or Janie was holding on to her. When the home first began flooding, Mabel hooked Janie with one arm and held a resident floating on a mattress with the other. She was standing on a platform that was filled with flowers the residents grew. Then Janie, panicking as the water rose, began grabbing at Mabel with her legs, and Mabel was pulled under the water. She figured then that if she stayed inside, she was a goner, so she made her way outside with her human cargo. There had been life jackets stored away in a shed, and Tanner had gotten them when the flood first started. Mabel had one on, and so did some of the children. Very few of the workers could swim, and they were holding on to anything they could, anything that would float. The residents, the lucky ones, were on mattresses.

"You know, you hear that we tied people to mattresses," Little Sal says. "Actually, that wouldn't have been such a bad idea, because mattresses in nursing homes are in waterproof liners. They float." Indeed, according to the Manganos, that was the margin of life and death at St. Rita's. The residents who made it onto mattresses rose with the flood. The immobilized residents—the ones who couldn't get off their chairs or out of their wheelchairs—were gone, says Little Sal, "before we got the boats in the water."

The building started falling apart from the inside out. Walls were popping out, TJ says, "like dominoes." And yet, Mabel says, there was no screaming. No: "It was so quiet, it was almost eerie." Residents and nurses and staffers were praying in the dark. The only screaming, Little Sal says, was the back-and-forth hollering of the people forming a chain of rescue. Mabel's brother Tony Buffone was in the hallway, pulling residents out of the rooms. Little Sal was taking them from Tony and bringing them to Tanner, who was putting them in the boats. Emmett and TJ were driving the boats, and Tammy's son Johnny was pulling people from the boats to the roof, along with a worker named Wayne King. Big Sal was at the door. The wind, which had been calm when the flood first started, kicked in again, and whitecaps topped the water.

One end of the building became blocked with floating furniture and debris, and when they tried to get in through the patio door, water had sealed it shut. So Tanner found his gun again and shot out the glass. Water by this time had climbed above the doorjambs, and Uncle Tony had to dive into the rooms to find residents and take them back under the water to get them out. "Uncle Tony was hollering into the rooms," Little Sal says. "And I'd say, 'No, Uncle Tony, that one, he can't holler back. Go in.' We kept going down them hallways till Uncle Tony didn't bring anyone else out." They kept making their way down the hallways until water sealed the building like a tomb.

There was a place for the living, and it was the roof. More than fifty people, half of them elderly and incapacitated, were marooned there, until Little Sal and the rest of them started loading them in the two boats and taking them away. They went first to Tammy's house, which was on the property, about three hundred feet from St. Rita's. Then they went a little more than half a mile to the Beauregard Middle School. It was an old courthouse, three stories high, and Little Sal and Tanner began carrying the residents up the stairs, until they couldn't anymore, until they ran out of strength and started constructing beds out of desks and filing cabinets to keep the residents out of the water on the first floor. Sal Sr. and Emmett found some help and went back to the nursing home, where they cut a hole in the roof and found several people clinging to a floating ice machine, including the head of nursing and a nurse named Thelma Lee. Thelma was diabetic and had almost slipped into the water when her blood sugar dropped. The head of nursing had grabbed her by the hair, had held her by the shoulders, and then when a Tupperware container of bread came floating by, had fed her until Thelma regained enough strength to hang on.

They had been floating for six hours, and the five of them—three staffers and two residents—were the last people rescued from the building on Monday. Dark came, and it was black dark. While the Manganos stayed on Tammy's second floor and the residents and staff members stayed at Beauregard, the dead began their extended occupancy of St. Rita's. And in the morning Little Sal got in his boat with Tanner and his nephew and went back to see if there was anybody left *but* the dead. "And my nephew heard someone hollering, 'Little Sal, Little Sal, don't leave me.' It was Miss Janis. She was in her room when the water came. A dresser fell down, the door came open, she fell onto the door, and the dresser floated. The only person she was looking for was me, she didn't care about the moon and the sun, but that's the way it was all the time. She said, 'I knew you wouldn't leave me, Little Sal.' "

And that's it. That's the Manganos' story. Is there anything left to say? Well, yes, there is, and Little Sal is going to say it, because he's heard other accounts of the rescue, and they give credit to everyone except the Mangano family and the other workers at St. Rita's. The story that has been accepted in the press is the story of local people coming upon the nursing home in an impromptu flotilla and saving old people while the Manganos saved themselves. "They're saying what happened in my *yard*," Little Sal says, bouncing on the balls of his feet behind his parents. "How can they tell me what happened in my yard? I hear how we left, I hear how all those people came and saved people from that building. Well, it happened too fast for that. Okay, some boys came later on in the day to help us. But nobody saved anybody from that building but us. And if anybody tells you different, they *lying*. I hear about the bad choices we made. I think we made some pretty good choices, once the water came. We saved fifty-eight people with six people in two boats. If ever there's a flood, I'm the man you want next to you, because I'm going to save your life. I don't give a shit whether I like you or not."

———

IT WASN'T UNTIL TUESDAY that I was able to get clear to go to the nursing home," Steve Gallodoro says. "I was with a friend from the parish council and some other guys. We saw no one around the facility, no movement whatsoever. I thought at the time that they must have at the last minute evacuated, but as we got closer to the front of the building, I saw the Hummer the Manganos owned and knew they hadn't evacuated.

"I swam into the water," Steve Gallodoro says. "I couldn't open the glass door, so I had them bring me to the patio area. I climbed up on the patio; it had three feet of water, one of them glass doors was broken, and as I was walking to the door, I came across a body. I moved the body around to see sort of who it was, and it was an elderly female. I walked into a doorway, and as soon as I stepped in the doorway, there was another body floating. It was another female. I was in the TV room of the lobby in the north wing, and I came across another body about ten feet later, another elderly female. There was four feet of water or so, beds floating, furniture floating. It would have been impossible for me to walk any farther down the hallways. I hollered, 'Fire Department, is anybody here, does anybody need help?' and it just echoed."

THE DAY AFTER THE FLOOD, you could still take the roads through St. Bernard Parish, if you had an airboat. You could follow the asphalt, which was visible through the water. There were even stop signs, poking up through the surface at street corners. It was the same world, except that it was entirely underwater. Todd Baker, a biologist from Louisiana's Department of Wildlife & Fisheries, had been pressed into rescue operations, along with a few of his colleagues and a state trooper. The state trooper wanted to check out St. Rita's and knew how to get there. They took the airboat along the roads where the Manganos had held their parades.

"We get to St. Rita's," Baker says, "and I'll never forget it. There's a guy in a flatboat. He says, 'Don't go in there unless you want to see thirty dead bodies.' He says, 'I pulled out everyone I could.' He says, 'I took them over to the school.' Then he says, 'Thank God you showed up.' We were apparently the first search-and-rescue people he'd seen.

"The school was the most depressing stuff I've ever seen. People were hanging out of the windows because of the heat. All ages. When we pulled up to the back side, there was a guy cooking hamburgers, because people were emptying their food. And then we walked through the door and that's when it hit us—the smell. There were nursing-home patients lying everywhere. In the back they'd stacked filing cabinets or desks, and the people on them were pretty bad; one was a double amputee. Half of them looked like they were dead or about to die.

"What he said about the thirty dead bodies didn't register until we hit the school, and we thought, Oh, God, these are those who *survived,*" Todd Baker says. "It's disgusting is what it was."

"People say we left people in that building," Sal Mangano says. "If anyone was still alive, we're taking them. But we had no place for the dead."

And so they helped with the living—on Tuesday, Emmett in his flatboat and Little Sal and the entire St. Rita's staff helped Baker and the others from Wildlife & Fisheries move the survivors to triage—and then, when they saw a dump truck making its way through the water, past Tammy's house, the Manganos did what everyone else did: They got on. They got out. They evacuated St. Bernard Parish. There were eleven of them, and the dump truck took them to the jail, and then they went to a shelter set up at a warehouse, and then they got on a bus and went to Algiers, and then they went to the New Orleans airport, and then they went to another shelter, in Terrell, Texas, and then Sal paid a bus driver $200 to take them all to a town near Shreveport, where they got a hotel

room and went to a Wal-Mart and changed their clothes for the
first time since the flood.

The *bodies,* though: The bodies stayed behind in the nursing
home. They hadn't been evacuated, and now they couldn't evacuate
and nobody would evacuate them. TJ Mangano says that she would
never have left if she hadn't been assured by the police that a recovery team was on its way, but no recovery team came. Steve
Gallodoro says that he tried to initiate a recovery effort of his own
but was told that the parish had no body bags and that even if he
did start pulling bodies out of the water, "nobody would accept
them." And so the bodies stayed. They stayed as the flood receded
and the sun came out and the days got hot and the story of what
had happened at St. Rita's started leaking out in the press, and a
nation that had decided to put its elderly where they could not be
seen now had its conscience inflamed by the grotesque spectacle of
their abandonment. They stayed as the state of Louisiana and the
federal government came to a stalemate over the recovery of the
dead and, in the words of Robert Jensen, CEO of Kenyon
International, the company that finally *did* the recovery for the
state, "it became a job that everybody waited for someone else to
do." They stayed until the federal mortuary team that attempted to
do the job couldn't do the job because the job was so terrible. They
stayed in the building for eleven days, until at last, on September 9,
Kenyon came with its hazmat suits and took the bodies out in a
hideous parade witnessed by Fred Duhy and other representatives
of the attorney general. And though it was not just government
that collapsed during Katrina, but rather the very *idea* of government as an entity that took care of its people and its dead, it isn't
government that Duhy is angry at when he says that "by the time
that last body came out, I was ready to spit nails."

It is Sal and Mabel.

IN 1992, TOM RODRIGUE went to visit his mother, Eva, in New Orleans. She lived alone, and he was used to knocking on a locked door. This time, though, he pushed on the door and the door swung open. His mother was gone. He went looking for her in his car and couldn't find her; he came back to the house and the phone rang. It was a nun from Charity Hospital, saying that his mother had been found wandering a vacant lot with a wad of cash. She went to St. Rita's and was there for a very long time. Miss Eva, the Manganos called her, and, as Rodrigue says, "she was kind of the mascot for the place." On the weekend of Katrina, Rodrigue called the nursing home several times, telling whoever picked up the phone what was coming in the Gulf. You see, Rodrigue was an emergency-operations manager for Jefferson Parish. He knew damned well what was coming, but he could never get the Manganos on the phone, and when he called his counterpart in St. Bernard Parish, he was told that the coroner had called St. Rita's and offered buses. "What else can I do?" his counterpart said.

On September 4, the president of Jefferson Parish, Aaron Broussard, went on *Meet the Press* and, with tears in his eyes, told this story about Rodrigue's experience: "The guy who runs this building I'm in, Emergency Management, he's responsible for everything," Aaron Broussard says. "His mother was trapped in St. Bernard nursing home, and every day she called him and said, 'Are you coming, son? Is somebody coming?' And he said, 'Yeah, Mama, somebody's coming to get you. Somebody's coming to get you on Tuesday. Somebody's coming to get you on Wednesday. Somebody's coming to get you on Thursday. Somebody's coming to get you on Friday.' And she drowned Friday night. She drowned Friday night."

This was, of course, untrue, and lavishly so. Miss Eva died on Monday, August 29, in the initial flooding. She never made it to the roof, much less had access to a telephone. Nevertheless, when Broussard went back on *Meet the Press* three weeks later and was asked to explain, this is what he told Tim Russert: "Listen, sir, somebody wants to nitpick a man's tragic loss of a mother because she was abandoned in a nursing home? Are you kidding? What kind of sick mind, what kind of black-hearted people want to nit-pick a man's mother's death?"

Certainly, Miss Eva's death was horrible enough. What happened at St. Rita's was horrible enough. But St. Rita's became *something else* in the weeks following Hurricane Katrina. The story alchemized ac-cording to the laws of political expedience and media opportunism, and Sal and Mabel Mangano went from caregivers to fuckups to criminals to monsters. On September 8—the day before the recov-ery of the St. Rita's dead—Charlie Foti announced that Sal and Mabel were wanted for questioning. At this time, they were on a bus on their way to Lafayette, and when they heard they were wanted by the attorney general, they started looking for Jim Cobb, who with his family had been displaced to a hotel in Houston. On September 12, Nancy Grace was on CNN, quivering as she contemplated what they would be charged with: "I'm thinking negligent homicide. Especially if some jury in a parish down in Louisiana gets wind that these two owners row, row, rowed away, leaving all the elderlies to die in their wheelchairs. Oh, *yes.*"

A day later, Cobb met with the Manganos and listened to their story. He called Fred Duhy and told him he would break the cardi-nal rule of defense attorneys: He would bring his clients in for a meeting with the prosecutor. "I told Duhy, 'I've talked to them, and I think you need to do that, too.' Duhy says, Deal. I go to a meeting with Sal and Mabel. I tell them, 'If you tell them what you told me, they can't arrest you.' She's all upbeat. On the fourteenth I get the call. It's Duhy. 'Jim, bad news. The meeting's off. I have an arrest warrant for your clients.' I ask him, 'What's the charge?' He says, 'Thirty-four counts of negligent homicide.' Thanks, Fred. Thanks for not piling on. Now I have to go back and tell Sal and Mabel. She falls into my arms, sobbing like a baby."

It's been war ever since, with Foti and Duhy attempting to fun-nel the faults of the state into the vessel of the individual, and Cobb

attempting to funnel the faults of the individual into the vessel—
capacious, in this case—of the state. And when Cobb is told that
Foti and Duhy have claimed that the prosecution of the Manganos
actually *saved lives,* because when Hurricane Rita hit a few weeks
after Katrina, you can bet that every single nursing home in
Louisiana and Texas knew to evacuate, here is what he has to say:
"Have you ever heard of that nursing home in Bellaire? It's in a
high-class neighborhood in Houston. The nursing home evacuated, the bus caught fire, and they fried twenty-three seniors on the
interstate. I was in Houston when the Manganos called, so I went
to the nursing home. It was *dry.* They shouldn't have evacuated.
They made a *terrible mistake.* Is Charlie Foti taking credit for that?
Congratulations, General. We drown ours, you fry yours."

So why didn't they evacuate? That's the big question, isn't it?
Fred Duhy says that governor Kathleen Blanco issued a mandatory
evacuation order for St. Bernard Parish at 1:30 P.M., Sunday, August
29, 2005. He says that the Manganos ignored it for one reason, and
for one reason only: money. "There's the contract with EMS. That's
the initial expense. Then there's the cost of transportation itself.
That's the second expense. Then when the new facility takes the
residents in, the Manganos lose all that Medicaid would've paid. It's
a very expensive proposition. . . ."

In fact, there is no record of a mandatory evacuation order being
issued for St. Bernard Parish, either by the governor or the parish
council. There is certainly no record of anyone calling St. Rita's and
telling the Manganos that a mandatory order was in effect. The
government's effort to evacuate St. Rita's nursing home amounted
to this: Dr. Bertucci. Two school buses. And that's it.

And yet, as Charlie Foti says, "you don't need the government to
tell you that a major storm was on the way." If the Manganos had
evacuated, they would have saved lives.

So why didn't they? They say—well, they say a few things. They say that a resident died on Sunday morning, and they couldn't get an ambulance to take the body without Dr. Bertucci's intervention, so how in the world could they have gotten an ambulance service to evacuate their most at-risk patients on Sunday afternoon as Katrina bore down on them? They say they were afraid they would have lost at least five patients if they had put them on school buses. They say they never thought the levees would break. And they say they didn't leave because they had never left, that they stayed because they had always stayed. . . .

But maybe none of these explanations are sufficient, psychologically. Maybe the only psychological explanation that makes any sense is the unexpected offshoot of the Manganos' twenty years of running an institution and seeing people institutionalized: love. Maybe they stayed because they believed they loved their residents as much as anyone did, even their families. Maybe they stayed because they believed they knew their residents better than anyone did and knew what was best for them. Maybe they stayed because they weren't going to let the government decide the fates of their residents, their favorites, their saints. Maybe they stayed because they believed that to evacuate was to abandon people who had already been abandoned. "We stayed for these people," TJ Mangano says. "We wasn't about to leave them. If one of them wasn't going, we weren't going."

Indeed, even when Little Sal is talking about the thirty-five who died, he never simply says, "He died," or "She drowned." He says, "I didn't save him," or "I didn't rescue him." He says this not as an apology but rather as a reminder of his own role in who lived and who died—his power. The Manganos were not irresponsible; they were, if anything, too responsible, for they had only done what the families of the residents asked them to do.

Until, of course, they didn't die. That's where the contract between them and the families of the dead broke down—in the unforgivable fact of their survival.

And so there they are, in the conference room, Sal and Mabel, the Manganos. Mabel is squeezing a tissue, her face is shiny and wet, and there's a sense that she's not the person she was when she first sat down—that she's slipping away behind some scrim of personal devastation. Sal is holding her hand. Little Sal is pacing.

"I loved them, I loved these people," Mabel says. "I miss them, my heart aches."

"We loved them," Big Sal says. "We loved what we done. Sure, we done it for money, it was our livelihood. But we never even had a budget. . . ."

"Whether or not we saved your family or lost your family, we are sorry for the water that came in," Little Sal says. "But not for the decision to stay."

You know what's the worst thing for them? That they can't do it anymore. That they can't . . . care. They were really good at caring. They had it inside them. And so their dream, if they escape the criminal charges, if they have a dime left after the thirty-one lawsuits and Jim Cobb's legal bill, is to rebuild. Right there. On the property. St. Rita's. There are staff members who have told them they want to come back. There are people in St. Bernard who have said they are waiting for the day when they can live with Sal and Mabel. . . .

And that's the thing for Steve Gallodoro. That's one prospect he does not want to contemplate. "I don't need to see them go to jail. The only thing I want to see is that they are never given an opportunity to hold a license that would enable them to care for any elderly, handicapped, disabled, because they have shown they are not responsible, and I need to know they can never be responsible for the lives of other people again."

But it's not his decision anymore. It's yours. Would you ever put your loved ones in a nursing home run by Sal and Mabel Mangano? Would you ever put your loved ones in a nursing home at all? Would you make the Decision?

I would. But every day I pray that I won't have to.

TOM JUNOD *lives in Marietta, Georgia, with his wife, his daughter, and his pit bull. He's a writer for* Esquire, *and has been so for ten years. He'd like to report that despite the ambivalence toward institutional care he displays in "The Loved Ones," his mother entered an assisted living facility last fall after the death of his father, and is feeling better than she's felt in years, despite her ongoing complaints about the food.*

Coda

Members of the press engaged in an orgy of self-congratulation in the sad wake of Hurricane Katrina. "We've gotten our mojo back"—I mean, you actually *read* that. You actually read the bloviators bloviating upon their own recovered potency, as if years of humiliation at the hands of the Bush administration could be redressed by the fact that Anderson Cooper did a lot of his reporting with tears in his eyes. Meanwhile, a lot of the original reporting out of New Orleans—the reporting that helped fix the catastrophe in the minds of the public—remains startlingly sensationalist and inaccurate, perhaps none more so than the reporting that led to the indictment of Sal and Mabel Mangano on charges of criminal neglect and negligent homicide. And here's the thing: no one went back and tried to fix it, which makes it a pretty good metaphor for New Orleans itself. An American city still dies a little bit, day by day; and yet, with the trial of the Manganos in the offing, they remain the only people charged with the crime of neglecting their responsibilities, in part because of all those telegenic tears.

NEIL SWIDEY

THE INSIDE JOB

FROM THE *Boston Globe Magazine*

JUST AFTER 4 O'CLOCK, when John Ferreira was looking the other way, a prankster pushed him into his pool. It's a gorgeous pool, rimmed by smooth boulders and an elaborate waterfall, and surrounded by golf-course-quality turf, all set against the backdrop of 120 acres of his private forest. Still, it's no fun being tossed into the water fully clothed.

But Ferreira emerged a few seconds later, flashing a big grin. Standing on the patio, a puddle forming around his feet, he pulled off his yellow T-shirt and wrung it dry, as 500 of his employees and their families looked on, smiling.

Outside of his circle, few people know the 47-year-old Ferreira, who grew up poor on a dairy farm in southeastern Massachusetts and never went to college. But he's a notable figure in New England's construction and landscaping world, as well as in every corner of Rehoboth, his tiny farming hometown that has turned into a bedroom community dotted with trophy homes, many of them built by Ferreira. He's the definition of a big fish in a small pond. Yet even after his net worth swelled into the millions, even after he was elected chairman of the Rehoboth Board of Selectmen, he never departed from his daily uniform of a T-shirt, jeans, and work boots.

An hour after his unplanned swim, Ferreira, with sunglasses in his dark hair, walked several acres to get to the far end of his lawn. There, an inflatable kiddie land that would rival any small amusement park's had been erected for the day. There was a "Bungee Run," a mechanical bull, and a gladiator pit, which Ferreira stepped into and began jousting with the police chief from a neighboring town. After about 10 minutes, with the police chief sufficiently vanquished, Ferreira stepped out of the pit. He walked by his oversize garage where he stores his helicopter, and then he headed for the patio behind his white, crushed-marble house, to watch the party's second musical act, a raucous R&B band.

Through the evening, right up until the dazzling 22-minute fireworks show, Ferreira shook hands, slapped backs, and made sure his guests were having a good time and that their cups never ran dry.

The party on this muggy July day was Ferreira's 2006 summer bash. When he and his wife began the annual tradition of opening their home to his employees and their families 18 years ago, he had a much smaller home and a lot fewer employees. This year, 989 people had accepted his invitation, and there were security checkpoints, guest lists, and bracelets handed out so the crashers couldn't slip in like last year.

Ferreira is popular with his people. He's a hard worker who demands the same of his employees, but he's always run his operation like a small family business and always enjoyed sharing the spoils. Yet, after a decade of his business's runaway growth, finances had become strained over the preceding year. Ferreira couldn't understand why, even as his sales volume grew, his profits fell. As he pushed his managers to find ways to pump up the bottom line, he came to the conclusion that his enterprise had simply gotten too big. So he began to reverse course. At Christmas, he cut way back on his usually generous employee bonuses. In January, he began downsizing his front-office staff. In February, he closed two of his landscape supply stores.

But by the time his party rolled around in July, Ferreira and every one of his remaining employees could explain the mystery behind his company's cash-flow problems with a single word: *Angela*.

FERREIRA HAD MADE up his mind.

It was March of 1999, and every time he needed a figure calculated or a report run, Angela Platt, the woman the temp agency had sent over to help out in accounting, was there with it. In her mid-30s at the time, she was tall, quiet, and big-boned. Besides her mouth full of protruding teeth, she had the ordinary, familiar look of a diner waitress who calls everyone "Hon."

Ferreira has a preference for chopped sentences and quick movements, and is more of a talker than a listener. During this period of aggressive growth for his various construction, real estate, and landscape supply companies, he was particularly hard to keep up with. But Angela always did. He knew little about her, other than that she had recently moved from Oregon, was married with two kids, and had no college degree.

"Why isn't everybody like Angela?" Ferreira would ask the other women on his business staff. "She never leaves her office. She doesn't hang out at the copy machine and talk. She just works all day long."

He paid the temp agency a fee so he could make Angela his permanent employee.

Ferreira had reason to trust his gut. It had taken him far. His company, Ferreira Construction, had ridden the building boom of the 1980s, but he downsized and regrouped before everything went bust. When his competitors went into bankruptcy, he went shopping, snatching up land and equipment at auction for pennies on the dollar. In 1991, he bought a foreclosed 14-acre swath of prime space on Route 6, not far from I-195, but didn't know what to do with it. So he put up a trailer and started a cash-and-carry business, selling stone to small-time contractors. He named it J&J Materials, after his young kids, John and Jennelle.

By the time they were in high school, the business had grown to four locations and was grossing more than $13 million a year. In 1997, he paid $285,000 for a troubled company called Nantucket Pavers. It grew into a multimillion-dollar business, supplying manufactured bluestone patio blocks to Home Depot stores from Maine to Maryland. He enjoyed his millions, buying a Dodge Viper as well as the helicopter he once used to chase down a carjacker in town. He took yearly trips to the Azores, the Portuguese archipelago where his grandparents were born. Still, he was determined to appreciate his money as much as when he bought his first John Deere backhoe in 1979, and spent every Sunday waxing it. When his son got old enough to drive, he helped him buy a pickup truck, but insisted that the kid make a monthly payment. As for his own ride, Ferreira would take over the pickups that his salesmen turned in after they had racked up too many miles.

"You have to have respect for money," he said, "and where it comes from."

Ferreira keeps no computer on his desk, but he knows his way around financial reports and insists on stamping his checks and reviewing weekly cash reports himself. He grew his companies in an ad hoc way, often buying small businesses and either selling them off and keeping the land or integrating them into his larger operation. (Full disclosure: Ferreira sold one such small business to my brother-in-law.) The result was a phalanx of nearly a dozen companies, eight or so of them active, each with its own financials, in an enterprise that grosses $25 million a year. Within a year of working for him, Angela had advanced to the point where she was controlling the books for four of his companies.

THE EMBEZZLER'S DILEMMA: You want the money you steal to change your life, but, unless you plan to run off to the Cayman Islands, you can't let anyone around you know your life has changed.

On June 15, 2000, the dutiful bookkeeper cut her first check made out to herself in her maiden name, Angela Buckborough, for $2,694.83. A modest start. That year, she stole just shy of $30,000, according to an audit Ferreira later commissioned. In 2001, she took around $55,000. She grew emboldened in 2002, swiping nearly $360,000. Yet throughout this period she was careful never to take more than $10,000 at any time, and around the office, she was the same old Angela.

She still wore nondescript, discount-rack outfits. Her home was a dumpy, cluttered split-level in Cumberland, Rhode Island. Her only public extravagance came once a year, when she and her husband, Kevin Platt, would go all out in decorating their house for Halloween.

Kevin is a short guy with a big gut, a scruffy, red-gray beard, and, as everyone said, "more gold chains around his neck than Mr. T." One acquaintance described him as "kind of rednecky." He did not work, leaving him ample time when October rolled around to turn his front lawn into a mini Spooky World. (In fact, when Spooky World went out of business and auctioned off its ghoulish attractions in 2004, Kevin was a big buyer.) He had animatronic ghouls, a skeleton in the driver's seat of a customized Buick hearse, and a 20-foot monster called "The Slayer." The display inevitably drew the attention of the local papers and TV stations, and then so many drive-bys that he and Angela had to hire a nightly police detail.

Angela's co-workers took notice. Some carpooled to check out the scene, among them Cheryl Santos, Ferreira's sister and credit manager. Everyone around the office called Santos "Punkie," the name she had gotten as a toddler with a round face like a pumpkin. With short, frosted hair and glasses, Punkie is friendly and guileless, but indispensable around Ferreira's office. She liked Angela, but after seeing the overblown Halloween display, she had to ask, "How can you afford all that?" Angela explained that Kevin had built some of the attractions, and persuaded people to loan him the rest.

There were other things that made Punkie curious. Angela once remarked that she had property in Vermont. Punkie knew Angela made just over $40,000 a year, and her husband didn't have a job. But again, Angela had a ready answer. She said her in-laws had given them a spit of land with a junky trailer. Punkie could accept that, but she never understood a much smaller matter. "She bought lunch *every* single day—and not just a sub or something. She'd get takeout from Applebees, from Chili's. I mean, jeepers crow, that adds up!"

NOT LONG AFTER Sandy Brown opened Stonebridge Stables in the spring of 2003, Angela brought in her redheaded 10-year-old daughter and signed her up for riding lessons. The bubbly Brown was not yet 30 and was excited to make a go of her new business in a leased horse barn in Lincoln, Rhode Island. The more she got to know Angela's family, the more she liked them, even if Kevin's look struck her as "truck driver/Hell's Angel." (Brown saw less of their teenage son, who was from Kevin's first marriage.)

At the start of 2004, Angela told Brown she wanted to buy her daughter a horse. For $7,500, Brown found her a quarter horse/Thoroughbred cross. A few months later, Angela overheard Brown talking about how she was looking for an investor to go in with her on a horse purchase. "People do that?" Angela asked. "I want to do that." Angela had money to burn. In 2004, her take from Ferreira's kitty galloped to nearly $2 million.

She quickly took to the life of show-horse impresario, paying for Brown to fly across the country, eventually finding and buying Angela eight more horses, with escalating price tags—one horse alone was $85,000. Every time a stall opened up in Brown's barn, Angela claimed it. The show-horse world can be a rarified scene, and Brown sensed that Angela liked being a somebody in it. Before she dispatched Brown for one shopping trip, she told her, "Get the biggest, nicest jumper these people have ever seen."

Brown felt grateful for the gift of her well-heeled customer. Angela was so giving, showering her with Christmas and birthday gifts like all-expense-paid trips to Las Vegas and the Kentucky Derby. Brown's husband warned her, "Don't base your entire business on them," but Brown chalked that up to his over-cautiousness. "You feel you're going to ride this until it ends."

In September of 2004, John Ferreira had a scare.

The certified public accountant he had hired six months earlier to be his controller just disappeared. Eventually, Ferreira learned the man had been facing domestic violence charges, and in due course had been convicted and sent to prison. Ferreira was nervous. What else didn't he know about this guy who had been in charge of his company finances? He decided to bring in a forensic audit team to pore over his books.

Meanwhile, Angela was feeling pressure from elsewhere. There was at least one person in Ferreira's operation who didn't see her as sweet and competent. Mike Albernaz is a beefy, middle-aged guy with a salt-and-pepper goatee and a Rodney Dangerfield laugh. The general manager of the Nantucket Pavers plant, he often found the inventory and profit-and-loss reports that Angela gave him didn't make sense. Nantucket was in the black, but just not by what Albernaz thought it should be. "Jesus, I know we're doing well," he said, "and it's not showing." When he would point out errors to Angela, she would respond dismissively, saying she would look into it, but then never get back to him.

Albernaz took his concerns to Ferreira, but the boss was more worried about his companies that weren't making money. Albernaz thought maybe Angela was just following Ferreira's orders, transferring funds from one of his healthy companies to one that was struggling. As much as he didn't like Angela, Albernaz never took her for a mastermind.

Neither did Ferreira. When the forensic auditors showed up, they said their protocol was to go directly to the banks to get all company statements. Ferreira thought that was a waste of time. He designated one of his most trustworthy employees as the point person to work with the auditors. "Angela will give you anything you need," he told them. "She's got it all under control."

KEVIN AND ANGELA married in 1993, a few years after the death of his first wife. Their time living in Oregon was rocky. Kevin would later relate how he came home one night in 1998 and found that Angela, who he said had a drinking problem, had left with the kids. Ignoring the restraining order Angela had filed against him, he followed her to Cumberland, Rhode Island, where she had spent much of her life. "If you hate me that much," he told her, "I just want to see it in your face." They reconciled, and she stopped drinking. Angela went to work for Ferreira. Kevin had no job, except for sifting through other people's garbage on the night before the town's weekly trash pickup and selling his finds at flea markets or on eBay. He even coined a name for himself: the garbage-o-later.

His supplemental income became less necessary as the family's economic outlook improved. As Kevin spotted some vintage hot rod or antique gun that he wanted while he trolled eBay, he'd ask Angela, "What do you think?" Angela, who always managed the family finances, would usually reply, "Yeah, go get it."

If he wondered where she was getting all the money, he never pressed the issue.

That changed one day in December 2004, according to accounts they both would give later. Standing in their bedroom, crying, Angela told Kevin she'd been embezzling from Ferreira.

"How much?" he asked.

"I don't know."

"Well, it needs to stop right now."

It didn't. And that didn't seem to trouble either of them.

In June of 2005, Angela and Kevin threw an open-house party to celebrate the near completion of the Vermont log cabin they had broken ground on the year before. West Haven, a Vermont village near the New York border, consists mostly of working farms set against the Green Mountains, with modest, tired farmhouses sitting near the road. Angela and Kevin's home sat in the center of a 50-acre meadow, with a winding driveway leading past a custom swimming pool. It was less cabin than showpiece. Inside, there was an African hardwood floor in the living room (along with a 9-foot-tall stuffed bear), a marble floor in the kitchen, and designer bathrooms attached to each of the four spacious bedrooms. In the basement, there was a media room, a second full kitchen, and a hand-carved pool table that cost more than $120,000. The walls were a museum of taxidermy, with mounts of deer and all manner of wildlife, many of which Kevin had bought off eBay.

Still under construction was the building that was to house some of Kevin's garish hot rods and high-end snowmobiles on the first floor, with a cavernous second floor where he would keep his full video arcade.

To those who asked how they had come into the money, Angela spun a specific tale about being the CEO of seven small but highly profitable corporations. Kevin would joke that his job was "spending my wife's money." But most people assumed a different explanation. "Around here," said 81-year-old Bonnie Weston, who lives on the next farm over, "if you got a dollar, you must have won it somehow." The word went out: Angela and Kevin had scored big in Tri-State Megabucks.

Weston and her husband enjoyed their new neighbors, and benefited from their company. To expand their original 53-acre property, Angela and Kevin had bought 50 acres from the Westons, at $2,000 an acre.

Most of the neighborhood welcomed Angela and Kevin with warmth and evident curiosity, with a notable exception. Dale Pettis, a 42-year-old farmer, took an immediate disliking to Kevin and his bragging. "He threw it all away. People that make their money don't do that," Pettis said. "He didn't impress us hillbillies. He amused us hillbillies."

However they'd gotten rich, Angela and Kevin seemed excited to share. The invitations for the open house were printed on ornate scrolls, and Angela and Kevin made sure most people in town got one. The menu included whole lobsters, steaks, and rattlesnake meat. There was a kiddie land for the youngsters and an endless supply of booze for the adults. A cover band called Secret Service performed by the pool. Angela would later give a testimonial blurb for the band online in language that was part boardroom, part trailer park: "As a CEO of several corporations, I have been to many functions, but have never heard a band as talented as Secret Service. . . . Their utmost goal was to provide client satisfaction. . . . People will be talking about the Hendrix solo during the fireworks for years to come. . . . You truly ROCK!"

The only downside to the day was the theft of a few kegs of beer. Kevin would complain later, "Can you believe someone would do that?"

IN THE FALL OF 2005, as contractors put the finishing touches on their spread in Vermont and the bills came due, Angela and Kevin decided they needed another home. They wanted something closer than Vermont, but with more space than their place in Cumberland, where neighbors had complained about the traffic jams caused by their Halloween displays. They plunked down nearly half a million dollars for a four-bedroom Colonial on 5 acres in woodsy Foster, Rhode Island, loading it up with a truckload of new furniture and installing an in-house movie theater.

Around this time, Angela dispensed with her pattern of small checks, at times writing three checks a week that each exceeded $40,000. In October and November alone, she took nearly $1 million. While the embezzling had been relatively easy to hide in prior years because of the aggressive growth of Ferreira's companies, the combination of her more brazen check-writing and the cooling of the real estate market made the vanishing money more noticeable. With his cash flow constricted and the market beginning to slide, Ferreira pounced when he unexpectedly received a top-dollar offer to sell the Plymouth property where he'd built a J&J Materials store. Soon after, he closed his Bellingham store as well and sold the space. Fewer stores required fewer people in his corporate office, so he began to downsize.

Back at the Nantucket Pavers plant, Mike Albernaz's frequent complaints about Angela were finally addressed, though not in the way he expected. Angela, it was decided, would be moved on January 1, 2006, from the corporate office to Albernaz's plant a few buildings away. She'd relinquish doing the books and reviewing bank statements for three of Ferreira's companies and focus all her attention on one that Ferreira knew had major growth potential. The talk around the office was that Angela's head was next on the chopping block, and co-workers noticed that she seemed more stressed, and even took up smoking. "They're taking my job away," she complained.

But Ferreira continued to see Angela as part of his company's future.

In addition to her duties with his companies, Angela was the bookkeeper for Starr Quality Homes, which Ferreira's wife, Tricia, owns. When Christmas rolled around, and Ferreira reluctantly concluded he couldn't afford to hand out many bonuses, Tricia insisted that Angela make the cut and receive an extra $200. Angela, of course, had already done her own calculations. For 2005, she had decided she deserved a total bonus of around $3.4 million.

ON THE FRIDAY before Memorial Day 2006, everything changed.

Two months earlier, after tiring of Angela's stall tactics in moving to the Nantucket Pavers plant full time, Albernaz had brought in his own bookkeeper, an experienced 41-year-old named Amber Rebello. He was blunt when he hired Rebello, who has a face full of freckles and a throaty laugh. "We need to watch everything 'cause we're getting robbed."

During Rebello's first week, Angela trained her. Right away some of Angela's accounting practices struck Rebello as odd. When invoices and inventories didn't match up, Angela instructed her to simply override them to make them agree in the computer, rather than researching the discrepancy. In subsequent weeks, she noticed checks being cut on Wednesdays, when Rebello did that only on Fridays. Once when she asked Angela why the last page of a bank statement was missing, Angela told her that Punkie, the credit manager, had a habit of throwing those out.

For the first month after Rebello arrived, Angela cut back on her recreational check-writing. But by the end of April, she ramped it back up. She needed the money. Angela had hired a staff of professionals to arrange a spectacular June wedding reception for her brother and his fiancee at her Vermont retreat. A horticulturist was brought in to build an elaborate English garden for the day. A sound-and-lighting specialist was flown in from California. And an event planner was charged with arranging paid hotel rooms for 200 guests, limos, catering, and live entertainment. No cover band would suffice this time around. Instead, Angela had signed contracts promising a 20-minute performance by Riverdance's 30-member touring troupe (at a cost of $60,000 plus an estimated $200,000 in expenses) and a one-hour show by singer/composer Burt Bacharach (at a cost of $95,000 plus an estimated $300,000 in expenses).

As Angela was watching the wedding expenses climb past the million-dollar mark in Vermont, Rebello was growing increasingly suspicious back at the plant. Finally, in the week leading up to Memorial Day, Rebello spotted questionable records for three checks, totaling about $74,000. Each check was recorded as sent to a different Nantucket Pavers vendor. Rebello called each vendor, to see if the invoice number was valid, and if they had received the check. Three calls, three "no"s. On Friday, May 24, she called the bank. All three checks had been cashed, but instead of being made out to the vendors, bank records showed that they had been made out to one of Ferreira's dormant companies.

Ferreira dispatched his vice president, Sal Rao, to Slade's Ferry Bank, to examine copies of the cashed checks from that dormant company. A little while later, Rao called him from the bank. "I'm looking at a check here for $44,000, and it's made out to Angela Buckborough."

"Bring the check back here," Ferreira said. "I'll call the police, and call her in."

His mind was racing, but he was still hoping this was a one-time thing.

Around 4 p.m., Ferreira called Angela into the conference room. There she found Rao and two Rehoboth police officers.

After she waived her Miranda rights, Ferreira slid a copy of the $44,000 check across the table to her. "Angela, do you know anything about this?"

She didn't blink. "Yes. I've been stealing money."

"How much?"

"About $200,000."

"Two hundred thousand dollars! What have you done with it?"

Angela said she'd bought a horse for her daughter and a few other things. She said she'd been under a lot of stress, and had begun drinking.

The cops wanted to arrest her. Angela pleaded that she not be sent to jail, saying she would make things right.

"I can't believe that you stole from me," Ferreira said. "But I want it back. How much cash do you have in bank accounts right now that you can give me?"

She said she had $30,000 each in two local banks. And she

promised she would come in on Tuesday morning and sign over the deed to her house in Cumberland, which she said was worth $350,000.

Ferreira asked to speak with the cops privately. "Look," the former selectman chairman told them, "if you guys lock her up now, I get nothing. If she goes to the bank now, I get back 60 grand. And if she don't come in Tuesday with the deed, we can still lock her up, but at least I get 60 grand." The cops agreed.

Rao followed Angela to the banks and got the money.

At 10 o'clock on Tuesday morning, Angela walked into the conference room and told Ferreira and his lawyer, "I did some figuring over the weekend and it was a little more than I thought."

How much?

She slid a piece of paper over to Ferreira.

"A million, five hundred and thirty thousand?" He laughed. "This is a joke, right?"

Above the bottom line, she had itemized her purchases: the Vermont house, which she valued at roughly $900,000; four horses, at $100,000; four hot rods, at $60,000, and so on.

"You took that all from me?"

"Yeah, but I'm going to give it all back."

Rather than waste time on feeling betrayed, Ferreira shifted into recovery mode. He called in additional lawyers to preside over a massive transfer, with Angela signing over deeds to property big and small. He dispatched some of his guys, with a car carrier and horse trailers, to reclaim the assets. The next day he sent them to Angela's Vermont house. When they got there, they called and told him, "This isn't a normal house." The day after that, Ferreira's wife, Tricia, met a real estate appraiser at the Vermont house. The appraiser said there was too much in the house to determine value in one day, but estimated that it was well over $1.5 million. It was clear to Ferreira that Angela's staggering estimate was still too low.

Tricia was furious. "Send her to jail!" she told her husband. "I can't believe I trusted her and even gave her a bonus."

Ferreira countered, "Look, let's get our stuff back first."

He was determined not to end up like so many victims of embezzlement, who never get a dime back because all their money went up somebody's nose or all their assets were seized or hidden. But he had to act fast. It helped that he had friends in the right places, namely the police and sheriff's departments. Bristol County Sheriff Tom Hodgson got involved, persuading the FBI to hang back for a couple of weeks while he and Ferreira tried to bring order to the mess.

In his first meeting with Angela, which took place at Ferreira's accountant's office in Greenville, Rhode Island, Hodgson adopted a friendly rather than adversarial posture. It seemed to break through. He didn't see any signs of remorse, or nervousness, in Angela's face. But he did get the sense she was telling him the truth. Meanwhile, Ferreira stood outside the door, picking up bits and pieces of their discussion. He heard $4 million, $6 million, $8 million. He thought, "She must have been embezzling from somebody else, too."

Eventually, the sheriff emerged from the conference room. With Angela's help, he had a new estimate for Ferreira of her total take: $9 million.

"What, was she embezzling from the mob?" Ferreira asked. "That can't all be my money."

ON A BEAUTIFUL SATURDAY evening in June, John and Tricia Ferreira enjoyed a bottle of wine on the wraparound porch of their new Vermont log cabin.

The last few weeks had been a blur, as Ferreira turned his life over to uncovering—and recovering—assets. The list seemed endless: show horses, plasma TVs, the house in Foster, time-shares in Florida and the Bahamas, land in Maine. Still, much of the haul was the kind of bizarre crap you'd expect to find if you could journey through Christopher Walken's brain. A hot rod fashioned into a green monster with teeth the size of fence pickets. A 1931 Plymouth with the faces of Bonnie and Clyde and lots of bullet holes painted on it, bearing the Rhode Island license plate UMISED. Collections of rare guns and wretched movies. Talking trees inspired by *The Wizard of Oz*.

But at least the Vermont cabin had class, and Ferreira was happy to be its new owner. He and his wife had invited over some of their new neighbors. They began relating details of Angela and Kevin's life as Green Mountain high rollers, how they were treated like Hollywood stars every time they walked into the local restaurants. Angela and Kevin had been known to pick up the tab for everyone in the restaurant, and pass around $300 tips to each waitress.

As he listened to these anecdotes, Ferreira felt the anger boiling up—really for the first time since Angela's scheme had been exposed. With his money, Angela and Kevin were trying to buy friends, to buy fame. "That's something you just don't do," he said, "no matter how much money you have. It's having absolutely no respect for money." Then he wondered: "Is that why she thinks people like me?"

Just how much money Ferreira has, of course, had become a hot topic around his company and around his hometown. How do you lose $9 million and not feel it? In reality, Ferreira had felt it, without really knowing what he was feeling. And he insists that if business hadn't been growing so aggressively during much of the time when she was stealing, he would have figured it out much sooner. "I'm still in shock that I made that much money," he said, "that much *extra* money." Still, he's the first to acknowledge that he was far too trusting and that as far as victims go, he was pretty lucky.

Angela's adventure produced more victims than just Ferreira, and all of them had less to fall back on.

Employees lost their jobs after Ferreira closed stores and down-sized. Early in 2006, Angela and Kevin's neighbor in Vermont had quit his job at Sam's U-Save Fuels to become their full-time groundskeeper, at $850 a week.

A host of small-business people in Vermont devoted their lives to preparing for the over-the-top wedding Angela was bankrolling, only to find out 3½ weeks before the big day that it wasn't going to happen. Some never got paid by Angela. Others that did, like the horticulturist, who turned away all other customers for three months to meet Angela's massive challenge, now find themselves being sued by Ferreira. He is demanding that any money Angela paid them be given to him.

And then there's Sandy Brown. Despite her husband's warnings not to let her business become reliant on one customer, the horse trainer had done exactly that. On the Tuesday after Memorial Day, Angela called to confess that she'd been caught embezzling. She said that Ferreira would be sending someone to retrieve four horses, including one a 16-year-old girl had already paid Angela to lease for the year. Still, Brown forgave her. After all, Angela assured her she was making full restitution. Brown figured the expenses of the wedding had driven her to desperation. But, a week later, when Ferreira's guy showed up again, this time to reclaim the rest of the horses, there was no warning call from Angela. Brown realized Angela had been lying all along. The blow proved too much for her young business. On July 31, she shuttered it for good.

Like everyone else involved, Brown has been puzzling over what would drive someone with no hint of a criminal background to steal so much money. Was it smarts or luck that allowed her to keep it going for so long? Was it greed that kept her from knowing when to stop?

After several lengthy meetings with Angela, Sheriff Hodgson came to one conclusion: Her motivation was less greed than a need for control. She was more likely to be extravagant in gifts for others—her husband, her brother, her horse trainer—than in treats for herself. When Hodgson went to Angela's house in Cumberland, he found it barely passable, amid all the filth and clutter. "She did her embezzling in a very efficient way," he said, "when there was such disorder in the rest of her life." In the alternate life she created for herself, she was a success, she was popular, she was in control.

Of course, control is what Angela lacks most right now. Hodgson finished up as a friend-of-Ferreira fact-finder, and Angela and Kevin sat for depositions with Ferreira's lawyer. The FBI, US Attorney's office, and the US Treasury Department are now involved. Last month, Angela and Kevin signed a consent agreement in Rhode Island Superior Court, returning a vast inventory of property to the man whose millions had funded their shopping spree. Still, given the sums involved, it seems likely that Angela will go to jail.

As of a few weeks ago, though, she was still living in the Cumberland home that Ferreira now owns, awaiting her fate. She answered the door, with her Rottweiler mix at her side. When I asked her if we could talk, she shook her head vigorously. "Thank you. I'm not interested in talking. I'm going to close the door now."

She said more in a private letter she sent John and Tricia Ferreira in June, insisting they could trust what she was telling them. Then again, she'd made that claim before.

Dear John and Tricia,

I cannot say enough about how sorry I am that I stole money from you. As you are aware, Tom [Hodgson] has been working with me to not only sort it out but to find out why. Please understand I respect you both tremendously—to the point I never cashed the bonus check that Tricia gave me at Christmas because I felt so unworthy. Tom has asked me to delve deep within myself. I think I was trying to re-create your lives into mine hoping I would get the love and respect that I see so many people give to you. I know I was completely wrong in what I did. It never occurred to me that I was hurting anyone but myself. Last November I wanted it to end and I considered telling you myself but I was so scared.

Please know that I am deeply sorry for hurting you—the very people I looked up to and admired. I am being totally honest with you now in trying to correct this terrible action. I am so sorry that I did this to you.

Sincerely,
Angela

NEIL SWIDEY *is a staff writer for the* Boston Globe Magazine. *His story entitled "What Makes People Gay?" was included in the 2006 edition of* The Best American Science Writing, *and "The Self-Destruction of an M.D." was included in the 2005 edition of* The Best American Crime Writing. *He lives outside Boston with his wife and three daughters. His book,* The Assist, *about high school basketball and the narrow margins of urban education, will be published by PublicAffairs in the winter of 2008.*

CODA

Among Angela Platt's many outlandish purchases was a life-size ceramic statue of a cigar-chomping, white-suited Al Capone. As in Capone's case, the feds eventually caught up with Angela.

On February 12, 2007, Angela walked into a federal courthouse in Boston and faced her past.

After reviewing the final paper trail provided by John Ferreira's forensic accountants, prosecutors alleged her take had totaled $6.9 million. That figure was lower than what Angela had told the sheriff, but a staggering sum just the same.

As part of the deal she struck with the U.S. Attorney's office, Angela, who had by then moved to Pennsylvania, pleaded guilty to a single count of interstate transportation of stolen property. She would be required to pay back everything she had stolen, but the assets she had already returned to Ferreira—everything from the show horses and Vermont retreat to the 20-foot-tall, smoke-spewing "Slayer" and *Wizard of Oz* talking trees—would be deducted from her total tab. She would eventually be sentenced to four years in prison and ordered to pay $4.48 million, plus interest.

After the allegations against her were read in court, the judge asked her if she still wanted to plead guilty.

"Yes, your honor," Angela told the judge.

"Why?"

"Because I did those things."

STEVE FENNESSY

THE TALENTED
DR. KRIST

FROM *Atlanta* MAGAZINE

ONE DAY ABOUT 10 years ago, Andy Watry took a call from a man who was interested in becoming a doctor in Georgia. At the time, Watry was executive director of the state's medical board, and he had urged his staff to pass him any calls that sounded, as he put it, "fishy." In this case, the caller had explained to Watry's assistant, somewhat blithely, that he'd once had "a little trouble with the law." With the criteria for fishiness duly met, she transferred him to Watry.

"What's his name?" Watry asked his assistant.

"Krist," she said.

Watry picked up the phone, and the caller identified himself as Gary Krist.

"Gary *Steven* Krist?" Watry asked.

"Yes," came the reply.

"Your little problem with the law didn't have anything to do with burying Barbara Jane Mackle in a box for 80-something hours, did it?"

A beat. Two beats.

"Yes," the caller finally said. "How'd you know?"

"My dad was one of the FBI agents who dug her up. And let me save you some time. You can forget about Georgia, and I'm going to alert the other states now that you're looking for a license."

Technically, it was Watry's board—and not Watry himself—that had the authority to approve or reject an application for a medical license. But, he says now, "there's this little thing called no-brainers. In 25 years as an executive director of medical boards in Georgia and North Carolina, I don't think I ever told anyone, 'Forget it.' Except him."

Watry, though, was an exception. The fact is, Gary Krist's past is filled with people who gave him second chances—friends, lovers, teachers, patients, parole board members, even his victims. Out of Christian charity, out of faith in his stunning intellect and in the power of redemption, they forgave him, set him free, took him in, loaned him money when he was down. They believed, ultimately, what Krist himself had said—that a man should be judged as much by the second half of his life as by the first half.

And their faith was rewarded. Starting in 1979, when he was paroled after serving 10 years for kidnapping Barbara Jane Mackle and burying her alive in a box, Gary Krist was the picture of rehabilitation. He went to college. He went to medical school. He found God. He became a businessman, a world traveler, a missionary. And in 2002, in a little southern Indiana town called Chrisney, he leased a vacant storefront on Main Street and spent $17,000 to convert it into a doctor's office. A door in the rear of the office led to the little apartment he shared with his wife. Out front, he hung a shingle that said, "Chrisney Clinic, Steve Krist, MD." To the reporter of the weekly newspaper sent to cover the town's first doctor in decades, Krist announced that his sliding scale meant he would turn no patient away, no matter how poor. "Bring me a chicken, if that's what you've got!" he said. The transformation of Gary Krist from notorious criminal to pillar of the community was finally complete.

But it wasn't long before the past he'd tried so desperately to escape overtook him.

Today, instead of treating his patients in Indiana and living the quiet life he'd always dreamed of, Gary Krist is sitting in a jail cell in Alabama. He is 61 and overweight, his hair has gone gray, and he faces the prospect of living out his last days behind bars. He has nothing now but time to think about how it all went wrong.

> He sort of sat me up on the ground. My feet were dangling over the side into a hole or something.
>
> "I want you to slide down in there," he said, and he was pressing down on my shoulders.
>
> Up until then I thought it was a room; certainly a place big enough to stand up and walk around in. He put me down and he said, "Now straighten out."
>
> For the first time I could actually see. There was a light in there. I knew instantly this wasn't a passageway. It was a box.
>
> I was shaking, I was terrified. I was never so frightened in my life. I guess I became hysterical. I cried, "No! No! No! You can't do this!" And very calmly, the man stood there and said, "Don't be such a baby." Suddenly the top came down. It made a heavy thud. I could hear him screwing in the screws in the lid.
>
> Then I heard the dirt. I heard it falling. There are no words to describe it.

The passage above is from the book *83 Hours Till Dawn,* which Barbara Jane Mackle co-wrote with *Miami Herald* reporter Gene Miller in 1971. The book includes Mackle's first-person recollections of being kidnapped in Atlanta just before Christmas 1968 by Gary Steven Krist and his accomplice, Ruth Eisemann Schier. Aside from an 80-second press conference after her rescue, the book contains Mackle's only public comments about the three-plus days she spent buried alive as her father, Robert Mackle, a Florida real estate developer and major contributor to the Nixon campaign, frantically assembled $500,000 in ransom and waited for the directions that would lead him to his daughter, a 20-year-old Emory University student.

A year after Miller and Mackle's book came out, Olympia Press, a London publishing house, released *Life: The Man Who Kidnapped Barbara Mackle.* The 370-page memoir is described on the cover as a "breathless adventure of passion, madness and money. . . . Gary Krist tells the unique story of a life devoted to science and crime, love and hope."

Written from Georgia State Prison in Reidsville, where he was serving a life sentence for Mackle's kidnapping, the book would mark the first stage of Krist's transformation—from jailbird to published author. The 26-year-old writer spends pages baroquely recounting his sexual encounters ("Her responses were of the same dimensions, as impassioned and ardent as mine, and we spoke and felt love as we sagged slowly into the crater created by our threshings"), bragging about his intellect ("I could read light novels at a speed of three thousand words a minute"), and metaphorizing his state of mind ("Dejection, the bitter gall of rebellion, the ptomaine soup of anxiety all washed over me in a dull, mean storm of unreasoning emotion that would not crest").

But for all its ornate indulgences, *Life* also offers glimpses into how a neglected child evolved into the mastermind of one of his generation's most infamous crimes. Krist was born in Aberdeen, Washington, in 1945 but grew up in Pelican, a fishing village along Alaska's Alexander archipelago, a string of more than 1,000 islands stretching like a tail along Canada's western coast. Krist's father, James, was a salmon fisherman whose legs had been mangled in a plane crash years earlier. Krist's mother, Aline, was, he wrote, "a well-intentioned scatterbrain."

The prospects for the Krists' fishing business were as dismal as their surroundings were breathtaking. While his parents were out at sea, they'd leave Gary and his brother, Gordon, in the care of others. Once, a babysitter's bossiness made young Gary erupt in anger.

He fired a shotgun blast over her and his brother's heads before hiding in an abandoned doghouse. "I spent the night in that little structure, and this incident vividly illustrated one of my basic traits: an absolute hatred for authority," he wrote in *Life*.

The details of Krist's bleak upbringing were scrutinized by Georgia prison officials when he began his life sentence in 1969. Looking for clues to how his childhood shaped the man he became, officials drew on interviews with Krist's parents to augment the tales woven by the precocious new inmate. "The parents state that, as a young child, Gary had some tendency to pick up things around the community and bring them home," the report reads. "They describe Pelican as a place where everyone knows everyone else, so many people feel free to take on parental roles with children when they see them do something wrong." Still, it seems James and Aline Krist often chalked up to childhood exuberance some of their youngest son's activities that would have alarmed most parents. Yes, their son had blown up an empty oil drum at a Fourth of July bonfire. And yes, he did steal comic books from a store in town. No, he didn't steal money from the March of Dimes bank at school. Most disturbing to prison officials, perhaps, was the parents' blasé attitude toward reports that their youngest son had engaged in "frequent intercourse" with an 11-year-old girl in town. "The parents appear to take a very easy attitude towards sex on the part of their children and show little concern about episodes of sex play on the part of the children in the community," the report concluded.

Krist's teen years featured a series of ever-grander larcenies that led to his arrest in late 1959 at age 14 for a crime spree with a Norwegian friend named Teriji that included various burglaries, assorted sexual conquests, and much drinking. "Our crimes arose, I believe, more from an overpowering hungry curiosity coupled with excess physical energy than from any defined hostility or malice toward others," Krist wrote in his memoir.

In the early sixties, Krist stole a car while he was on probation.

He was sent to a reform school in Ogden, Utah, from which he would stage two unsuccessful escape attempts. Still, his academic performance convinced school officials to send him to the public school in Ogden, where he earned straight As and worked on the school paper. "I was accepted and I was happy," he wrote. Life at the reform school was unique of his time behind bars. To Krist, it was the first time he was encouraged to think that his future might hold promise. "The staff," he wrote, "was willing to chance a failure to gain a success."

IN 1967, HENRY KOLM, A SCIENTIST at Massachusetts Institute of Technology, met a lab technician named George Deacon. Forty years later, Kolm still recalls Deacon as one of the brightest lab technicians he'd ever worked with, especially considering his lack of formal training. Deacon operated the machinery, maintained the solenoids, and monitored the water pumps at MIT's National Magnet Laboratory, where Kolm was doing pioneering work on the technology that led to magnetically levitated high-speed trains. Deacon was resourceful and diligent, often coming to Kolm to chat—about the lab, his wife and two young children, his living arrangements in Boston. He tended to avoid talking about his past, but Kolm didn't think too much of it at the time.

Deacon, as Kolm learned later, was Gary Krist, who had been released from reform school in 1961, only to end up again on the wrong side of the law, serving stretches for crimes such as auto theft. In 1965, he married Carmen Simon, a woman he met at a roller rink. A year later, he was arrested again for auto theft. Just eight months into his five-year sentence, he made a daring late-night escape from the Deuel Vocational Institution in California. While Krist got away, his accomplice wasn't so lucky; he was shot to death by guards. A California law permitted capital punishment when an escape led to someone's death, and Krist worried that he'd get the gas chamber if he were found. So he moved his young family to Boston and reinvented himself as George Deacon, aspiring scientist.

One day, Kolm returned to MIT from the University of Miami, where he'd gone on a short cruise with the university's Institute of Marine Science. The Institute was looking for a technician. Krist, worried that he'd pushed his luck long enough at MIT, jumped at the chance. Before he left, his colleagues at the magnet laboratory treated him to dinner and gave him a beer stein engraved with the name George Deacon.

In September 1968, the 176-foot ship *Pillsbury* sailed for Bermuda on a marine science expedition. Deacon's job was to maintain the equipment. On board was a 25-year-old student named Ruth Eisemann Schier, born in Honduras but of German heritage. She pronounced his fake name *Shorrsh* and trilled her R's. Their shipboard flirtation grew into a full-blown romance, and soon Krist confessed his true identity and criminal past to her. On October 7, 1968, the ship returned to Miami.

During the next two months, Krist would leave his family and hatch a plot with Eisemann Schier to kidnap Barbara Jane Mackle, the daughter of a prominent Miami family, bury her in a home-made box, ransom her, and run away together to Australia, where they'd outfit a research vessel and Krist would "compile a world encyclopedia of oceanography." Such an endeavor, he wrote in *Life,* "would employ me the rest of my life."

This is where I'm going to die. Three or four times I thought this is going to be my casket.

And when I got morbid I would think of who would find me. Who and when and how? Maybe it would be a farmer. Or maybe someone building something. In 10 years? Twenty years? I wondered what I would look like and whether or not they could identify me. I was hoping that Mom and Dad wouldn't be alive when they found me. Because I wouldn't want them to think that was the way it was.

—Barbara Jane Mackle in *83 Hours Till Dawn*

Krist spent a month designing and building the box, "obsessed," as he wrote, with the idea that the capsule be sturdy enough to keep his victim alive for as long as a week. It was made of three layers of quarter-inch plywood and wrapped in fiberglass cloth. One end of the 8-foot-long box, partitioned off from the main compartment, contained a 12-volt motor to power a fan that would keep the victim from suffocating, as well as a pump that would drain the box in case it flooded. Even if the motor failed, he reasoned, there would be enough air movement through the intake and exhaust hoses leading above ground that the occupant could breathe on her own without the fan. "An intelligent person could not suffocate in the capsule," he wrote.

After Krist and Eisemann Schier snatched Mackle from the Clairmont Road motel room where she was sick with the flu, they buried her in a remote patch of woods near Berkeley Lake in Gwinnett County. By the light of a dim bulb inside the box, which was about 24 inches wide and 24 inches high, Mackle read a note Krist had left her, warning her not to use the fan continuously as it would quickly burn out the motor. Krist had installed screens at the ventilation system. "You risk being eaten by ants should you break these protection screens," he wrote. Krist had left her a pillow, candy, blankets, three gallons of water, a bucket for her waste, and some Kotex pads.

Ultimately, after he'd received his $500,000 in ransom, he called police, telling an operator where Barbara was buried. Krist's directions weren't exact, and the frantic agents weren't sure they were anywhere near her. But she heard their muffled searches from below ground and started screaming and punching the roof of the box. The agents clawed at the earth with their hands. They had tears in their eyes. As she waited for daylight, Barbara Jane Mackle began combing the dirt out of her hair with her fingers.

Agents cornered Krist in a swamp in southwest Florida. He gave up without a fight. All the money was recovered, except for 109 twenty-dollar bills he'd used to buy a getaway boat. Two months before his trial, Krist was interviewed by a psychiatrist named Dr. Morton Berger. Krist's mood varied but, as usual, he was eager to flex his intellectual muscles. "I am a superior human being," he told Berger. "I've never found anyone who could match me in any field or at any level." Among the subjects he discussed were thermodynamics, physics, history, philosophy, and his favorite Norse god, Thor. "He was cool," Krist said. "When he felt things weren't going right, he picked up a hammer and blew the shit out of it." Krist pegged the speed of light at 186,242 miles per second (he was off by 40 miles), recited the Celsius equivalent of absolute zero to the fourth decimal place, and offered opinions on Wagner, the Roman emperor Caligula, and the peripatetic nature of the Sophists. "I would gauge his IQ to be, if not at the genius level, then certainly in the near genius category," Berger wrote.

When he wasn't expounding on science and literature, Krist gave Berger glimpses into how his mind rationalized the life of crime he'd chosen. He told Berger that when he was 13 or 14, he suffered an attack of appendicitis while his parents were away. For 10 days, Krist lay in his own excrement, until he was finally able to make his way to a general store in Sitka, where the owner denied him food, claiming that Krist's parents had overdrawn their account by $300. "So later," Krist said, "I went back to [the] store and splashed it with gasoline and burned it down to the ground." Experiences such as this, he told Berger, taught him that "power and money are the only things that count."

Berger declared him fit to stand trial, classifying Krist as "having a sociopathic character disorder with no evidence of psychosis."

At his Decatur trial, in May 1969, Krist's court-appointed attorney, James Venable, called not a single witness after the jury heard testimony from dozens of witnesses for the prosecution. Still, Venable, whose family once owned Stone Mountain and whose night job was imperial wizard of the Ku Klux Klan, did manage to rail against the minorities who'd served as witnesses for the prosecution. Meanwhile, the 231-pound wooden box, which was rolled in as an exhibit, drew stares from everyone in the packed court-room. Only Krist seemed uninterested; on the trial's fourth day, he leafed through a science textbook called *The Origins of Pre-Biological Systems and Their Molecular Matrices.* At another point, the defendant, knowing things weren't looking good, told reporters, "Maybe after they electrocute me, they can bury me in that box." The penalty for kidnap for ransom, after all, was death.

As it turned out, the jury spared Krist the electric chair, citing not only Barbara Mackle's testimony, in which she expressed no hatred for Krist, but also the steps he took to keep her alive while she was underground. Although he called his trial "cracker-barrel justice," Krist knew he was lucky to escape the death penalty. Still, no one is prepared for life in a 5-by-9 cell. Not even Krist, who'd spent a healthy percentage of his young life in the custody of one law enforcement agency or another. He told reporters that he was "a different species." As such, he was particularly ill-suited to a con-fined existence and was quick to let everyone know just how ill-suited. A few weeks into his sentence, corrections officers reported that Krist "is always complaining about something. He complains about being confined, about his food, and always wants to see some high-ranking officer." In the fall of 1969, he even filed a lawsuit, claiming his solitary confinement amounted to "cruel and unusual punishment." But the judge threw out the case, saying that Krist's complaints—a small cell, no TV, no movies, too many turnip greens—"make the Book of Lamentations sound like a paean of thanksgiving." A year later, he was given 14 days of isolation and put on a restricted diet for digging a hole in the floor of his cell.

Inmate D-1473, as all his correspondence indicated, still man-aged to take classes to keep his mind limber. In January 1972, Krist attended a graduation ceremony at Reidsville state prison, where he received a certificate for completing the "motivational and emotional stability course, 'Guides for Better Living.' " Krist was also hammering away on his book and, at the same time, suing (unsuccessfully) to halt the serialization of Miller and Mackle's book in the Atlanta newspapers.

That same year, after just three years in prison, Eisemann Schier was released. J.O. Partain, a member of the Georgia Board of Pardons & Paroles at the time, remembers returning from a trip to find that Eisemann Schier had been paroled. Two FBI agents were waiting in his office.

"This comes straight from the president of the United States," one of the agents said. "He is a close friend of Mr. Mackle, and they don't want her out." But it was too late. Eisemann Schier was already out of state custody and traveling back to Honduras, banned from the U.S. for 50 years.

Partain's account makes sense. The Mackles were close to Nixon, and in her book, Barbara Jane Mackle has more sympathy for Krist than for Eisemann Schier. Why? Because he made the call. The Honduran woman just took off on her own, never bothering to confirm that Barbara had been rescued. Eisemann Schier was arrested several weeks later in Oklahoma, where she was working as a waitress. She told police that she went along with the plot in order to ensure Barbara's safety. But Barbara didn't think so. "I think she is quite a little actress," Mackle wrote in *83 Hours Till Dawn*. "And I think she was lucky. Very lucky."

AFTER HE READ MACKLE'S BOOK from his jail cell, Krist wrote her a letter of apology. "You were chosen from a list of 41 young women on the basis of emotional stability, intellegence [sic] and record of religious belief. I felt you were the one woman of means in the Miami area who would not suffer any lasting damage due to rigid confinement in a small space." He explained he needed the ransom money because his California prison escape made him a marked man and he had decided to undergo radical plastic surgery—"and even have my natural teeth pulled at a discreet clinic abroad"—to get the fresh start he'd longed for. "Of course my crime was evil, immoral, and cruel and I cannot excuse it, nor do I expect anyone else to excuse it. I don't *deserve* forgiveness but it would make me happy to receive it," he wrote. "The real violation of morality lay in the willingness I felt to harm you to save me. *That* attitude is cowardly."

But as penitent as Krist was toward Mackle in his letter, he remained eager to cut his prison sentence short. He started corresponding with Partain, telling the parole board member that life behind bars was no life at all. He alluded to how easy it would be for him to escape, but quickly added that he wouldn't do such a thing. What he failed to tell Partain was that his most recent escape attempt, two months earlier, had gone hilariously awry. Guards had gotten wind of an upcoming prison break, possibly via a barrel headed for the landfill. What's more, they'd received reports that Krist had been practicing standing on his head for 32 minutes at a time. On March 22, 1973, a garbage truck left the back dock of the prison at Jackson, under the watchful gaze of the guards. At the landfill, they found Krist, head-down in one of the garbage barrels. They pulled him out by his belt and doused him with water. On trial for escape, Krist said he didn't know how he ended up in the barrel.

Seemingly oblivious that his escape conviction might lessen the parole board's opinion of him, Krist petitioned the board to commute his sentence, appealing to their sense of logic and fair play. "To imprison [me] for the entire duration of [my] young adult/mature adult life will be both an insane waste and a crime far greater than any which [I have] committed." Krist went on to list his hobbies and interests, which included engineering, swimming, table tennis, roller skating, square dancing, and "attending films of educational nature."

Cecil C. McCall, the parole board chairman at the time, wasn't impressed. "Your attitude and conduct prior to and during your incarceration has been more apocalyptic than you apparently have taken the time to realize," McCall wrote. Krist, abandoning the polite tone in his petition, lashed out at McCall in equal measures

of anger and petulance. "I made Miss Mackle suffer for 83
hours. . . . So far you and the system have kept me in pain for close
to 45,000 hours. . . . I did not do what I did as revenge but to keep
you and others like you from catching me and hurting me."

Krist seemed to find a sympathetic ear in Partain, who urged
him to seek solace in religion. "Your sentence is not the end,"
Partain wrote. "You are young, and there is much to follow. . . .
[F]ind the joy of helping people and having Christ in your heart.
He is more than sufficient to sustain you." Krist seemed to give it a
shot, and he began reading his Bible. "The chemistry of faith will
defy my attempts at analysis," he wrote Partain, "but the result is
peace of mind."

J.O. Partain is 88 now, and during 15 years on the Board of
Pardons & Paroles, he learned two things: The only predictor of
future behavior is past behavior, and only a religious epiphany can
truly turn the heart of a criminal. He was skeptical about the gen-
uineness of Krist's conversion. "I thought he was a sociopath,"
Partain says simply.

That label and others were appended to Krist's file over the 10
years he would serve for Mackle's kidnapping. "Egotistical personality," wrote one counselor. "A man of little or no compassion," concluded another official. Even the warden chimed in. Krist, wrote Joe
Hopper, is "the most astute individual at manipulating others that I
have encountered during my 16-year career in corrections."

But by the late 1970s, Krist had learned to temper his letters and
muzzle his mouth. He enrolled in all the classes he could. He
worked as an orderly and an optometry technician. He took up
painting. He helped other inmates write letters. He talked of
becoming a doctor. In 1978, when deadly riots turned the
Reidsville prison into a tinderbox, Krist served on the Inmate
Unity Committee, which acted as a liaison between inmates and
prison officials. But the warden came to believe that the committee
was part of the problem and put Krist in solitary confinement for
allegedly advocating the torching of the prison chapel. To clear his

name, he volunteered for a lie detector test. After failing, he accused the state police of falsifying the results.

John W. Murphree taught English 101 and 102 to inmates at Reidsville. He remembers Krist. "He was singularly the most academically talented and gifted student I had in 40 years of teaching," Murphree says. Krist could be given an impromptu topic and, in 50 minutes, turn out an "absolutely flawless college-level paper." Krist even helped Murphree research and prepare a paper on prison dialects, a study for which Krist was named co-author. The young professor was so impressed that he wrote the parole board in 1978, advocating for Krist's release.

(Murphree didn't learn until recently that his prize student had authored a book years before. "He's a published writer and he's taking English 101 as a college freshman? That's a con game," says Murphree, who lives in Tennessee now. "I may have been one of the huge number of people who've been conned by him.")

Murphree's letter was just one of dozens that the board received as Krist's parole eligibility grew closer. Kolm, his former MIT colleague, wrote that to keep Krist in jail would only cause him "needless embitterment" and that Krist's crime was "committed very much in the spirit of a bad but harmless prank." Ray Moore, the news director at WAGA-TV in Atlanta who interviewed Krist during his trial, had come to know Krist well, even visiting him occasionally in jail. "I cannot overlook the terror of his deed," Moore wrote to the parole board. "But I can argue that he took many precautions to sustain her life. And a seven or eight year hunk out of his life ought to be a more than ample payment to society, and a lesson to him." Mary Hougland, from the Clearinghouse on Georgia Prisons and Jails, wrote that her two-year correspondence with Krist reflected a "remarkable change in his attitude. I have seen a shift from self-orientation to genuine concern about other people."

Despite the letters of support, Krist's parole denials piled up. By then he was in his early 30s and seemed to take the news in stride. "I believe to the limits of my soul that I can compete and win in free society if given a chance," he wrote. Even complete strangers were taking up his cause. Most notable was Joan Jones of Auburn, Georgia, who'd begun writing Krist while he was in jail. She informed the parole board that she'd be willing to give Krist a place to live if they sprung him.

"I am absolutely certain Mr. Krist is a gentleman and a friend if he accepts my offer," Jones wrote. "I hope you give him this opportunity."

Partain wasn't interested, but Krist kept pushing. In a letter to Partain, he called Jones a "really good woman, a woman of charac-ter (a rare find), and a Christian. There is nothing that could cause me to hurt her or make her suffer." Arguing his case, Krist reminded Partain that he'd found religion. "Prayer does wonder for my peace of mind and I pray at least daily."

Krist's prayers were answered, in the form of James T. Morris, who had become Georgia's parole board chairman. Morris was convinced that Krist's change-of-heart was genuine. Partain believes that, more than anyone else's letters of support, it was Jones' advocacy that finally paid off for Krist. "She'd come to the office frequently, and Morris seemed to be real friendly with her," Partain says. "I don't mean to intimate anything. But Morris seemed to fall into that. She convinced him that [she and Krist] were going to get married."

And on May 19, 1979, five days after Joan Jones picked up Gary Krist at Reidsville prison in a rental car, they did.

AFTER KRIST LEFT PRISON, parole officers hovered close. First in Sitka, where he put $6,000 down and paid $834 a month on a 45-foot fishing boat called the *Alcid*. Then at sea, where he shrimped the frigid waters of Glacier Bay and near Prince of Wales Island. Then in Seattle, where he and Joan lived in a seventh-floor apartment on 15th Avenue while he attended the University of Washington. Then back in Alaska, where, in the summers, he fished his beloved Lituya Bay, "one of the most scenic areas in the world and [where] the wildlife is a non-stop source of joy." By virtually every measure, Krist was a model parolee, reporting on time, keeping a positive attitude, building a new life. Still, the transformation wasn't complete. Occasionally, the old Gary would materialize, and the officers would take note. "I had the feeling that he was attempting to manipulate me through his clever verbage [sic]," wrote one. "He occasionally appears somewhat arrogant," reported another.

If anyone really knew him, it was his wife, Joan. Her loyalty was unflagging. One spring, from the Sitka Hotel, where she was a desk clerk, she wrote Morris back in Georgia to thank him again. "He is a very good husband and friend. . . . Thank you so much for making us happy. Believe me you will not regret your decision. Gary is A-okay."

For four years, Krist—eager now to go to medical school—lobbied for a pardon. And finally, his old ally, James T. Morris, came through for him. In 1989, freshly pardoned by the state of Georgia, Krist enrolled at Ross University School of Medicine in the West Indies. He loved medical school but wasn't kidding himself about his professional prospects. "I'm sure society is overpopulated with people who would never dream of letting a bad man 'go good'—much less letting him be a doctor," wrote Krist from medical school in 1990 to the now-deceased Morris. "I don't know what problems these people will give me, but I'm sure they will give me problems."

And problems there were. Around the same time he left Ross University with his medical degree, CBS aired a made-for-TV movie about the kidnapping. The notoriety forced the 46-year-old doctor to resign from a hospital in Connecticut. He went to Haiti, where he practiced among some of the poorest people on earth. In 1994, Krist took an internship at West Virginia University, which led to a residency in psychiatry there. He was depressed. He told his supervisor that he couldn't concentrate, couldn't sleep, was listless, and that his mood was in the "near paralysis range." He left West Virginia without completing his residency.

By then, he and Joan had bought a house in Auburn, Georgia. To pay the bills, he worked construction jobs. Around that time, he made a phone call to the Georgia medical board to see whether his past precluded him from getting a medical license, which is when he stumbled onto Andy Watry, the son of the FBI agent who'd worked on the Mackle case. Undeterred, Krist looked one state over, and in December 1996, he applied for a medical license in Alabama. He acknowledged his conviction, but his application was denied. He fell back on construction work and kept looking for an opportunity to practice medicine.

Then, finally, a chance. In December 2001, Indiana's medical board, aware of his criminal background, agreed to grant him a probationary license. Dr. Krist was in business.

OF CHRISNEY'S POPULATION OF 544, there's not one doctor. For years, one of the nearest was Cheryl Crawford, who practiced 12 miles to the north in a town called Dale. One night she was working late when a man dropped by and introduced himself. He said his name was Steve Krist. Although he was almost 60, he was looking to establish a practice in underserved Chrisney. The Indiana medical board had said he needed an established physician to supervise his work. Would Crawford be interested?

"You're going to hear it eventually, so I'll tell you up front: I have a criminal record," she recalls Krist telling her.

"What'd you do?" Crawford asked.

"I kidnapped a girl and held her for ransom."

On the Internet, Crawford read about the Mackle kidnapping. Horrible, she thought. *But he had kept her alive. Sure, it wasn't a buffet, but she had food and water. And Georgia had paroled him. Not only that, they'd given him a full pardon. He put himself through medical school, did missionary work. Who am I to judge?*

She agreed to help. Once a month, he'd drop by her office and, together, they'd review his cases. "He was a good doctor and he did a lot of work with people that others wouldn't," Crawford says. "He wasn't afraid to ask a question when he didn't know."

In Chrisney, word of the new doctor in town spread fast. Peggy Lawson, who owns Town & Country Hardware, two doors down from the clinic, would wave when she walked by. Sheila Roos, whose photography studio was two doors in the other direction from the clinic, saw him almost every day. Besides being Krist's neighbor, she was also his landlord. Across the street was the Adams Service Center, a little café and store owned and operated by Bob Adams, who serves as a town councilman.

Adams is 85, but he still gets up at 3 o'clock every morning to deliver newspapers in Chrisney. One day, he was walking up a hill with his stack of papers and felt out of breath. He dropped by the Chrisney Clinic, where Dr. Krist put a stethoscope to his chest and didn't like what he heard. He told Adams to see a cardiologist right away. Sure enough, three arteries leading from Adams' heart were blocked. He had a triple bypass, and Dr. Krist visited him at home every day for seven weeks while the councilman was on bedrest, to draw blood and send it off to the lab. "You won't get me to say anything bad about him," Adams says. "He saved my life."

Dr. Krist and his wife, Joan, settled on United Methodist Church, where the pastor, Reverend Stephen Ellis, came to know his new congregants well. They were quiet, unassuming. More than anything, Ellis was relieved that, for the first time in years, Chrisney finally had a doctor. "We were tickled to death to have him," he says. "And he made house calls! When's the last time a doctor made house calls?"

To Sheila Roos, Krist appeared soft-spoken and good-hearted. The doctor was full of enthusiasm for the adventure ahead and seemed grateful for the warm welcome. Only in retrospect, really, do the comments he made to the *Spencer County Leader* seem a little, well, patronizing. "It's not a hotbed of cultural diversity here, so it's an area that's been hard to get doctors to come to, but this is an area I consider to be real Americana culture," he said. "It's more like what America was in the fifties and sixties. I appreciate these people. This area probably doesn't suit most physicians, but I'm not your average physician."

Indeed he wasn't. While Crawford kept the story of Krist's past to herself, it didn't take long for the media to get word. In the fall of 2002, Krist's carefully constructed plan began to unravel. On November 13, a local TV station aired a story on Krist, who declined to answer reporter Jack Rinehart's questions, except to say, "Ambush journalists inflicting pain on people who are trying to do the right thing are almost as shameful as Osama Bin Laden." To an Associated Press reporter, he was a bit more politic. "I think a man should be judged as much by the last half of his life as by the first half."

To Kolm, his old colleague at MIT, who even loaned Krist money over the years, Krist expressed frustration that the media wouldn't let him be. "I do the best I can," he told Kolm. "I charge very little. I take care of poor people for free. I do all the good things a doctor can do. And the media keeps hounding me."

When news of his past reached the residents of Chrisney, Krist lost some patients. But others stood behind him. "There are worse criminals than him," Bob Adams says. The Mackle kidnapping "was more of a college prank," Adams says. "They talk about rehabilitating criminals and getting them back into society and making good citizens out of them, and when a man *does* try, they knock him down."

Krist was summoned before the Indiana medical board, which claimed that Krist wasn't adhering to the letter of his supervisory agreement with Crawford. In late February 2003, the board suspended his license for 90 days, and the state attorney general began a detailed investigation, not only into Krist's criminal past, but also his medical past. In April 2003, the board discussed Krist again, and in the gallery were several Krist supporters, including Reverend Ellis, who was escorted out for tossing (or rolling, depending on whom you ask) a stone at the board members. It was a Biblical reference.

Ellis believes Krist had truly repented of his past sins and was willing, in true Christian spirit, to give him a second chance. "Society seldom agrees with that," Ellis says. "It's hard for a con to get ahead on anything."

In an e-mail sent around that time to Cheryl Hurst, reporter at the *Spencer County Leader,* Krist fell back on the two themes that defined his latest incarnation—Christian love, coupled with a finely honed persecution complex. He kidnapped Barbara Mackle, he explained, because it was "the best way to survive" in a "predatory" society that never protected him. "At least I didn't do to her what has been done to me," he wrote. "What else could I be but a Christian? My sins are legion. Gotta love Jesus—they did him even worse than me and he didn't even do anything wrong. He paid for my sins because I never could. The Devil controls this earth and I am just looking forward to the next life. At least God has forgiven me."

As the summer of 2003 neared, Indiana's attorney general was digging up details on more than just the Mackle kidnapping. Of particular interest were reports from West Virginia, where Krist had worked as a resident. Once, investigators learned, Krist told a 13-year-old girl with an eating disorder that she had a "big butt." He told a woman who'd tested positive for HIV that "her boyfriend must be thrilled." One patient complained that Krist told her she had "big boobs" during a breast exam. Another complained of a sore throat and said Krist gave her a neck massage and a back rub. Even other medical students complained about the way he interacted with patients, saying he put his feet up on furniture, played with a deck of cards, and made inappropriate sexual comments.

Krist was supposed to have revealed such disciplinary actions on his medical license application. He'd also neglected to disclose his history of depression. On August 28, 2003, the board determined that Krist had "engaged in a pattern of fraud or material deception." His license was revoked.

"I tried to be a beneficial part of society," Krist told one local TV station. "They wouldn't let me."

RETIRED ATLANTA JOURNALIST Ray Moore has kept in touch with Krist ever since interviewing him in 1969 on the eve of his kidnapping trial. "I found him an interesting person," Moore says. "He was brilliant and yet he was dumb. On the brilliant side, he worked at MIT and the University of Miami without anything more than a high school education. To bluff his way through that is quite remarkable. Then he conceived of this idea to kidnap Barbara Jane Mackle. He studied her. He figured she could endure being confined. That was the brilliant part, I guess. The dumb part was he showed up at a Clairmont Road filling station right near I-85 with this big box in the [trunk] of a Volvo wagon and asked for directions to a remote place. So the guy at the filling station found it easy to remember him at the trial."

Through correspondence and occasional visits over the years, Moore saw Krist's arrogance replaced with a kind of humility. At his Sunday school class several years ago, Moore invited Krist to talk about his post-medical school missionary work in Haiti. Krist spoke of the horrible conditions, the lack of proper drugs and equipment. "He felt he was where God had led him," Moore says. "He was trying to make amends. His testimony was such that it was obvious he was sincere." Through his church, Moore even raised funds to help Krist build the Chrisney Clinic.

From Georgia, Moore watched with dismay as his old friend's medical practice—and his carefully constructed new life—fell apart. Krist moved back to Georgia but was getting too old for the rigors of construction work. He was also fighting prostate cancer. Occasionally, Moore would hear that Krist was off sailing in the Gulf of Mexico. "I was hoping desperately that he was just doing it to rest body and soul," says Moore, who, even as late as last November, was still writing letters of recommendation for Krist. On November 16, 2005, he wrote Doctors Without Borders, asking that they take a chance on Krist. "This man is stubborn and proud," Moore wrote, "but since winning his freedom and citizenship, there has been a long and strong commitment to honesty."

Nothing came of the letter. Even if something had, it would have been too late. Two days before Moore wrote the letter, Krist and Joan's son from a previous relationship—47-year-old Harry Greeson—chartered a 39-foot Beneteau Oceanis sailboat and left the Dog River Marina in Mobile, Alabama. Their lease agreement stipulated that they travel no farther than 200 miles from the home berth. On December 4, 2005, Krist returned with the boat and drove back to Georgia. On board the boat, authorities found that its GPS system had been erased, making it impossible to know precisely where the boat had been. But there were still some clues, such as the map of the southwestern Caribbean Sea; tubing that smelled of diesel fuel, which indicated Krist may have siphoned gas for a long journey; and seven rolls of Colombian toilet paper.

In January 2006, Greeson reserved the boat again. This time, agents from Customs and Border Protection and Immigrations and Customs Enforcement were ready. They installed a transponder on the boat. On February 6, Greeson and Krist drove to the boat, but only Krist set sail. Greeson drove back to Georgia. On February 21, Krist entered the territorial waters of Colombia. Five days later, he set sail for home.

On March 6, federal agents awaited his return. They weren't sure exactly where he'd dock, so they set up teams along a several-mile stretch of Alabama's Gulf Coast. The primary bust team was headquartered at Fairhope's Grand Hotel, closed at the time due to Hurricane Katrina damage. One of the agents' biggest worries was that Krist would be met by a speedboat miles out at sea, making the suspected drug transfer there. But they resisted sending a Coast Guard cutter out to meet him, figuring that if he had drugs, he'd just throw them overboard at the first sign of trouble.

So they waited. In the early afternoon, Greeson pulled up in a Mercury Marquis, looked around, then drove around the area, at one point waiting behind a mall as the minutes ticked by. Finally, at about 3 p.m., he returned to the dock near the Grand Hotel as Krist's boat was arriving. When they tied off the second line to the dock, a dozen agents swooped in, arresting the two. "Everything was fast and furious," says ICE Agent Dwight McDaniel. "They looked like most people do when they're arrested. They were shocked."

On board, agents found a cooler strapped to the rear of the boat. The cooler contained 38.6 pounds of cocaine and a bag of Quikrete. "If he'd seen anyone coming close," McDaniel says, "he could have cut that strap and the cocaine with the Quikrete would have sank. And it wouldn't have been easy finding a cooler at the bottom of the ocean."

Authorities figured the cocaine's street value to be more than $1 million. But that wasn't all. In the boat's hold, agents found two Colombians and two Ecuadorians, who, according to authorities, had agreed to pay $6,000 each for transport to the United States. Krist told agents that he'd felt sorry for them and wanted to make their lives better.

A few days later, cops searched Krist's home in Auburn, Georgia. On the floor of a storage shed in the backyard, they found evidence that, once again, Krist had devised and carefully constructed an underground crime scene. This time, instead of a subterranean prison, they opened a trapdoor to find a ladder that descended five to seven feet into an underground compartment. There, authorities say, they found chemicals necessary to convert cocaine paste into powder. A tunnel led from the lab to a patch of woods 30 to 50 feet away.

In a pre-trial services report, Krist explained that he'd been disabled since 1996, due to depression and suicide attempts. He also said he and Joan had separated, although his wife insisted to officials that they were still together. Judge Sonia Bivins denied parole to both Greeson and Krist. On May 15, Krist pleaded guilty to conspiracy to import cocaine and to smuggling illegal aliens into the country. He faces a sentence of 10 years to life.

"It was a terrible way to go, to bring drugs up that would kill people," Moore says now. "It's a terrible disappointment to me. I believed in him and I saw the monumental efforts he was making." Moore continues to pray for Krist, but he isn't optimistic that there will be any more second chances. "I just don't have any great hope now that he'll come out alive, or how much more he can take."

Kolm, the scientist at MIT, says Krist is basically a good man who never meant harm. "His fatal flaw was an excess of self-reliance," Kolm says. "He thought he was invincible and always right. He was a smart guy; it's just he had this unfortunate propensity to go against the establishment. He thought he was unjustly persecuted."

From her home in Auburn, Krist's wife, Joan, who, three decades ago, so successfully helped repair his shattered image, has little to say. "I have no comment, but I will say that I've been married to Gary for over 27 years and he's never touched me with a feather." As for Gary Krist himself, he seemed willing to sit for an interview and perhaps reinvent himself yet again, provided his attorney gave him permission to talk, which she did not. In a letter to *Atlanta* Magazine, he wrote, "You say you seek the truth. I wish you success. 'Fair and accurate' is not truth. Truth is complex, difficult, challenging, rare. Old lies are more comfortable than truth. Most people refuse to abandon comfort.

"Good luck."

STEVE FENNESSY *joined* Atlanta *magazine as articles editor in 2005. Before that, he spent five years as an editor and writer at* Creative Loafing, *Atlanta's alternative weekly. He has worked as a reporter and editor in his hometown of Auburn, New York, as well as in Cairo, Egypt, and at the* Rochester Democrat and Chronicle. *In 2006–07, he was awarded a Knight-Wallace journalism fellowship at the University of Michigan, where he was named the Mike Wallace Fellow in Investigative Reporting.*

Coda

Reporters learn to love documents, so when a woman at the Georgia corrections department handed me a stack of papers on Gary Krist last summer that was about as thick as the collected works of Dostoevsky, I figured I was on my way. I was convinced that somewhere amid the letters, the reports, and the psychological profiles were the answers to two questions.

The first question was simple: How could someone so smart be so stupid? Krist spent a month constructing the box that entombed Barbara Mackle for 83 hours, and yet he drove around Gwinnett County in the days before the kidnapping asking for directions to remote areas of the county with the box sticking out the back of his car. In prison, he studied science and medicine, and yet he practiced standing on his head to prepare for an escape attempt straight out of *Hogan's Heroes.* My hunch is that what matters to Krist are not the crimes themselves, but the elaborate steps he takes to commit them. Given a choice between lifting a bag of money from an unlocked car or stealing the same amount through a complicated series of steps involving six months of planning, I'm quite sure he'd choose the latter. To Krist, the payoff isn't in the payoff, but in the scheming. In this way, he reinforces his self-perception that he is superior to his captors.

The second question was more complicated and, ultimately, unanswerable: Was his redemption for real? I was raised Catholic, so I was taught to believe in the power of repentance. But as I've grown older, I've come to realize how rare a true change of heart can be. Still, Krist did enlist an impressive array of allies as he carved out a new life for himself. One of those allies was Ray Moore, who became friends with Krist. Moore hosted Krist and his wife for dinner, and even had him speak to Moore's Sunday school class. Moore is a former journalist, and he did not strike me as gullible in the least. Finally there was Krist himself, who put himself through medical school, an incredible endeavor at any age but even more remarkable for a man in his 40s. His patients in Chrisney only bolstered the argument that after inflicting so much pain in the first half of his life, Krist wanted to ease it in the second half. At the same time, his futile efforts to keep his medical license in Indiana left him even more bitter and self-pitying, leaving many to speculate that he reverted to a life of crime because that is precisely what society expected of him.

For a while, it looked like I'd be able to ask Krist himself these questions. We corresponded several times through the mail as he was awaiting sentencing. It was my intention to cover the sentencing and then talk to him afterwards. And he seemed agreeable. But the case kept getting postponed, while my deadline did not. When his attorney wouldn't give him clearance to talk before the sentencing, I was forced to go with what I had. In January 2007, two months after the story ran, he was sentenced to 65 months in federal prison, the low end of the sentencing guidelines, thanks in part to cooperation with authorities. But don't expect Krist to serve his five-plus years quietly. Four days after he was sentenced, he began the appeals process, claiming his court-appointed attorney had been ineffective.

Sean Flynn

The Case of the Killer Priest

FROM GQ

Prelude
Summer 1956

THERE IS A BOY in a cottage on the Lake Erie shore. The silver light of a streetlamp shines through the window, illuminates a priest, the fat rolling up the back of his neck and down under his chin, the blackheads speckling his face like pepper, the hair sprouting from his belly, his dark nipples.

There are two other boys in the cottage, one alone in another bedroom, the third in the library. The priest kept them late at the lake—too late to drive home to Toledo—called all their parents, and took one to bed. *Why did he choose me?* The boy doesn't know. He's only 13 years old. He turns away from the priest, nervous and queasy, exposed in his underwear beneath the covers.

The boy feels the priest reach for him in the half dark, pull him close, stubby fingers tugging at his underwear. Then he is weight-less, the priest lifting him, rotating him, bringing the boy's crotch to his face, the boy's head to his own. He takes the boy's penis in his mouth. He slips a finger into the boy's anus, and the boy is in awe. *Why would he do that?*

The priest tries to force the boy's mouth over his penis. The boy resists. He forces the boy to hold it. It is short and wide and repulsive. The boy will not stroke it. He comes in the priest's mouth, a purely physical reaction. The priest grabs his own penis, ejaculates.

And then it is over.

In the morning, the priest puts on his collar, and the boy watches his fingers. He wonders if the priest will wash his hands before performing miracles at the altar, before he turns wafers and wine into the body and blood of Christ.

The boy tells only one person, a friend. *Father tried to queer me.* No details, but even that is too much. His friend will hold the secret like a switchblade, will wither the boy with only a look.

No one else will ever know. There are rules, unspoken and unfair, but real, as real as the Resurrection and the Virgin Birth, as real as heaven and as real as hell. Those rules are taught to him every day: Mass and another hour of religious instruction five days a week at school, confessions on Saturday, Mass again on Sunday. He knows that he should be grateful for the blessed embrace of the church. He knows that Martin Luther is burning for eternity and that the Jews killed Jesus. He knows that crossing the threshold of the YMCA is a mortal sin, that dating a Protestant girl is a mortal sin, that God, for all His love and wonder, has laid temptation in the world to capture the wicked, and anyone who is not Catholic is damned anyway.

And what if he tells? What, even, if he is *believed?* The priest would disappear, shuffled off to some other parish. Yet the boy would be punished, too. He would be ostracized because he would have broken a code, one that has nothing to do with good and evil—and the boy now knows all about evil—and everything to do with the institution of the church. It is 1956, and the church and its servants are believed to be holy and pure. To say that is untrue, to suggest that a man of the cloth is neither holy nor pure, is to challenge the obedient faith of nearly everyone he has ever known.

"You just didn't question what a priest did," he will say many years later, in the lobby of a hotel in Toledo, when the priest is long dead. "They walked on water." There will be tears in his eyes even then, when that night in a cottage on the shore of Lake Erie is five decades in his past and yet still right there in his present, too.

"A priest," he will say, "was goddamned *God.*"

ACT I
APRIL 5, 1980, HOLY SATURDAY

A FOLDED WHITE CLOTH is on the floor just outside the chapel at Mercy Hospital, by a closet door. Sister Madelyn Marie picks it up on her way into the chapel and places it on a pew. She does not see the bloodstains between the folds.

Sister Madelyn walks to the front of the chapel, kneels, and says her morning office just before eight o'clock. She is one of nine nuns who live in a convent on the seventh floor of the hospital, which is operated by the Sisters of Mercy and which sits on the edge of a ghetto in Toledo. Sister Madelyn goes to the organ to begin arranging music for the evening service. She stops, decides she should call Father Gerald Robinson, the senior chaplain, and ask him which hymns to play.

There is a phone in the sacristy, a small room adjacent to the chapel where, because it is Holy Saturday, the Blessed Sacrament—a wafer believed to be the literal body of Christ transubstantiated on Holy Thursday—is being held until the celebration of the Easter vigil. It is, for those few hours, one of the holiest places in Catholicism.

The door is locked. Sister Madelyn opens it with her key. She steps inside and screams.

Sister Margaret Ann Pahl, who would have been 72 years old on

Easter Sunday, is lying on the floor. Her habit is pulled up almost to her throat, and her panty hose are around her ankles. Her girdle is twisted around her right shoe. Her arms are at her sides, and her legs are straight and close together, as if she'd been posed. There is a smear of blood curling from the center of her forehead across the bridge of her nose, and an altar cloth is wrapped around her right forearm. The left side of her chest is perforated with puncture wounds, and there are more on her neck and jaw. In all, she has been stabbed thirty-one times.

DEPUTY POLICE CHIEF Ray Vetter is at Bowman Park that morning, watching his son play baseball in a Catholic Youth Organization league. He has six kids, five boys and a girl, barely ten years between the eldest and the youngest—*My wife will get a high place in heaven,* he likes to think—and all born at Mercy Hospital. His parents received their last rites at Mercy; his wife studied nursing at Mercy; his daughter is an emergency-room nurse at Mercy.

A murder at Mercy is something he should know about immediately. Forget the personal history: Vetter is in charge of investigations for the Toledo Police Department, and the standing order is for him to be called for any major case, day or night, on duty or off. But none of his men call him until midday, after Sister Margaret's body has been taken away and the crime scene has been cleared. He'll chew some ass that afternoon.

Vetter's a good cop. A micromanager sometimes, but smart, honest. Lieutenant Bill Kina has worked with Vetter for sixteen years, including three in internal affairs, and Kina figures if he ever hits the lottery, wins a million bucks, Vetter's the one guy he'd trust to hold the cash. And Toledo is Vetter's town. He was born there in 1923, one of three children of good Catholic parents. He was schooled at Saint Mary's, and he'd sprint past the synagogue in his neighborhood rather than linger too long in front of a Jewish temple he knew would be a sin to enter. There was no meat on Friday and no candy from Ash Wednesday until the church bells rang at noon on Holy Saturday. He obeyed nuns and he confessed to priests, and he believes even now that they both stand as near to God as any mortal could hope. *Priests and nuns are on pedestals,* he says. *Right next to God, for God's sake.*

He left Toledo only once, to fire artillery shells at the Germans with the 87th Infantry Division, then came home and took a job with the Edison. The suits in the office started hiring college boys as junior engineers, promoted them up the line, passing over war veterans like Vetter. With a dead-end job and a wife and kids to feed, Vetter decided to become a cop, earn a decent salary, have the city pick up his insurance and pay a death benefit if the Good Lord takes him. Thirty years later, he is in charge of every criminal investigation in the city of Toledo.

MONDAY, APRIL 7, 1980

MURDER IS NOT an especially complicated crime. Civilians like to fret about "senseless" killings, but those are like campfire ghost stories—scary but almost never true. Every man makes sense of what he does, even if no one else will ever understand. Every killer has his reasons, and Ray Vetter knows that those almost always involve sex or money. Or both.

The immediate working theory had been money, that Sister Margaret had surprised a burglar. But nothing was missing from the sacristy, none of the golden chalices or Communion plates or even Sister Margaret's purse. By early afternoon on Holy Saturday, robbery had been dismissed as a motive.

On Monday, Lieutenant Bill Kina starts working the case with Detective Art Marx, who's been on it since Saturday morning. With money eliminated, they explore the second most likely motive: sex.

Kina goes to the coroner's office, where an autopsy is under way. There is a small scratch just inside Sister Margaret's vagina, but she has not been fully penetrated; in layman's terms, she has not been raped. The coroner has more: She was choked nearly unconscious before being stabbed, probably by a man with large hands who approached her from behind—Sister Margaret did not hear well— and squeezed so tightly that he cracked two bones in her neck and popped the blood vessels in her eyes. She was unconscious but not yet dead when the killer laid her beneath the Blessed Sacrament and stabbed her with a blade that was a half inch wide and at least three inches long.

This is something a stranger wouldn't do, Kina thinks. *Somebody coming in to rape and rob her, he's gonna stick her, gonna slice her throat. But this is overkill. And the way the body was posed. This isn't something your average street person is gonna do.*

WEDNESDAY, APRIL 9, 1980

AT TWELVE-FORTY in the afternoon, Marx sits down in a hospital dining room with a housekeeper named Shirley Lucas, whose job includes cleaning the convent.

Sister Margaret, Lucas tells Marx, was "a very fussy individual." Extremely devout, extremely strict in her Catholicism, and rather cold, at least to Lucas. The nun spoke to her once about opera, which apparently was her only interest outside of the church, and once about her concern that her fellow sisters, who live a spartan, almost ascetic, life, had so much while others on God's green earth had so little. Mostly, though, Sister Margaret told her what to clean.

Marx prods Lucas, asks her to remember any other conversations, anything unusual.

Yes, she tells him, there was one thing. On Good Friday, Sister Margaret was upset. One of the chaplains had shortened the service. Sister Margaret took Lucas's hands in her own and began to cry. "Why," she asked, "did they cheat God out of what was His?"

THURSDAY, APRIL 10—WEDNESDAY, APRIL 16, 1980

DETECTIVES INTERVIEW student nurses and cleaners, search rooftops and bushes for clues, chase away the specters of all those scary black men people seem to recall loitering around the lobby. By early the following week, they can account for the whereabouts of almost everyone in the hospital.

On Sunday, April 13, they talk to Wardell Langston II, who was cleaning the floors inside the main entrance, under a balcony. He tells the police that just after seven thirty on the morning of Holy Saturday, he heard footsteps above him, running across the balcony and down a hallway toward an exit door. But he didn't hear the slap of the panic bar against the door. Whoever ran through the hall stopped before he got to the exit.

After all of the questioning and searching, Kina and Marx narrow the time of the killing to a forty-minute window early on Holy Saturday. They eliminate all their potential suspects except one: Father Gerald Robinson.

Robinson has been assigned to Mercy for more than six years, though no one there claims to *know* him. He is a loner, and he does not like his job, cloistered among nuns and the sick and the dying, saying Mass in a tiny chapel without a permanent flock, muttering last rites over comatose patients. He would prefer to be a military chaplain, but his superiors have not reassigned him.

The police have already gotten a cursory statement from Robinson. He said he was buttoning his cassock when a nun called and told him Sister Margaret was dead, that he ran to the sacristy as soon as he'd heard, that all he saw was Father Jerome Swiatecki, the junior chaplain, anointing her corpse. Yet he does not appear distraught. In fact, he seems to know very little about a woman he worked with for more than half a decade, the sister who oversaw the chapel where he performed miracles at the altar.

FRIDAY, APRIL 18, 1980

FATHER ROBINSON arrives at the detective bureau of the Toledo
Police Department a few minutes after eight o'clock in the evening.

Kina has been eyeing Robinson for days. There's nothing solid,
but everything fits around him. The posed body, the overkill, everything that says the killing was personal. Robinson's weird affect and
Sister Margaret's tears after Good Friday Mass. The elimination of
every other potential suspect. And he has his gut. Kina's worked
more than two hundred homicides, and his gut usually isn't far off.

Still, Robinson's a goddamned *priest*. Kina's not Catholic, but he
knows the unwritten rules in a city that defers to those who are.
Priests are supposed to be nearly infallible, and Toledo police would
prefer not to shatter that illusion. Catch a priest driving half blind
on Jameson, grab a padre sucking cock in an alley, you bring him
downtown and call vice. Vice calls the monsignor, and the monsignor comes and drags out the wayward father by his collar. Case
closed. No charges, no records. But murder? Is there a rule for that?
None that anyone's told Kina.

But there is one strange thing. Toledo police reports are typed in
triplicate: a yellow sheet that stays with the investigator, a pink one
that goes to the supervising officer, a white copy for the records
room. Vetter wants all three. Not one to review—*all of them*. Years
later, Marx will say this is not unusual in a sensitive case; on the
other hand, Vetter will later deny ever making such a demand,
which he suggests would be unusual and improper.

Robinson is taken into an interrogation room. The plan is to
rattle him, get him to allow a search of his quarters at Mercy, then
give him a polygraph. If the results are bad—and Kina is almost
certain they will be—they'll try to parlay them into a confession.

Marx does most of the talking. He's a Catholic, used to be an
altar boy, understands the dogma. He's a bulldog with Robinson,
catching him in little fibs, tripping him up on basic priestly doc-
trine. Robinson tells Marx that the killer confessed to him and that

he can't violate the sanctity of the confessional. Marx tells him church law says he already did by giving up the *fact* of the confession. Robinson backtracks, admits that was a lie to get the cops off his back. *To protect myself,* he says.

Kina's leaning back, listening. *I've heard some interrogations before,* he thinks, *but nothing like this.* He's playing good cop, figuring he'll break Robinson with a little kindness after Marx finishes pummeling him.

It's too late for that. After midnight, Robinson signs a waiver allowing his room to be searched, but the lieutenant waiting with the polygraph says there's no point. Marx has gotten Robinson too worked up to get a baseline reading.

SATURDAY, APRIL 19, 1980

KINA AND MARX poke around Robinson's quarters, two sparse rooms on the second floor at the end of a hallway near an exit door. In a desk drawer, they find a letter opener that looks like a miniature saber: a small handle with a knuckle guard and a slightly curved blade about eight inches long and a half inch wide.

The detectives send the opener to the lab, which will discover that it is exceptionally clean: no fingerprints, no fibers, no dust, no residue of envelope glue. Later, the technician will pry off a medallion at the hilt, under which he will find a spot of something dark that could be blood—that the best test he has indicates *is* blood—but the sample will be too small for anything definitive.

In the afternoon, Father Robinson returns to police headquarters for his polygraph test. He does not perform well; the results, Kina is told, "indicate deception." Legally, this means nothing—polygraphs can't be used in court—but tactically they are a blessing. Kina and Marx believe they've found the murder weapon in Robinson's desk, and the priest admits it is his, a souvenir from a trip escorting some boys to Washington, D.C. When they confront him with the polygraph, when they call him a liar to his face, he'll break.

Kina and Marx start with their questions. Kina believes it's only a matter of time. After a while, Marx leaves the interrogation room—Kina won't remember why, only that the reason was innocuous—and Kina gets ready to play good cop.

There is a knock on the door. It opens, and Deputy Chief Vetter is standing at the threshold. Monsignor Jerome Schmit is behind him. A third man, whom Kina recognizes as an attorney working for the Toledo diocese, is there, too.

Vetter says, "Would you step out of the room, Bill?"

Kina says sure, gets up, walks out into the detective bureau. Father Swiatecki is there, Robinson's chaperone. They make small talk until the door opens again. Robinson, the monsignor, and the attorney file out, cross the bureau, leave the room, leave police headquarters. Kina looks at Swiatecki. "What are they doing?"

Swiatecki shrugs. "Well," he says, "they'll put him out on a funny farm, and you'll never hear from him again."

LATE APRIL 1980

RAY VETTER does not want to find himself on a witness stand, swearing to tell the truth so help him God, and testifying that a defendant charged with murder *could* have done it. No, he wants to be certain, wants to convince himself before he'll try to convince a jury that a man should go to prison forever. *You're toying with someone's life,* he reminds himself. *And when I lay my head down at night, it's me I have to be at peace with. Not some prosecutor, not some judge.*

Vetter is not certain Father Robinson is a killer. After weeks of investigating, his men have zero witnesses, no firm motive, no evidence at all except a letter opener that *might* be the murder weapon. He does not want to tell a jury that Gerald Robinson—a *priest,* for God's sake—murdered Sister Margaret Ann Pahl, because he does not absolutely believe it to be true.

Yet deputy chiefs do not decide who stands trial for murder.

Prosecutors do.Vetter has his men take their case against Robinson—
a weak alibi, an inadmissible polygraph, a sterile letter opener—to
the Lucas County prosecutor's office. An assistant prosecutor is not
impressed. He tells the police he won't indict any man on such thin
evidence. And a priest? Is this a joke?

Vetter is relieved. He isn't the one who's letting Robinson walk.
*Hell, it's the biggest murder case Toledo's ever had, and some lousy cop's
gonna make that decision? No, that's not gonna happen,* he thinks.

Yet he does not disagree with the prosecutor. *If I'd had to make
that decision,* he tells himself, *I would've made the same one.*

MAY 1980—NOVEMBER 1981

WITH THEIR CASE against Robinson dead-ended, the detectives
of the Toledo Police Department dutifully follow every crackpot
theory and lunatic tip that filters over the transom. They take a
statement from a woman who knows that a short, fat white man in
his forties who cooks with large pots killed Sister Margaret because
she's seen him in a dream. They listen to the convict who says his
cellmate confessed to him and he must be telling the truth because
he included all the details the police have never released, like how
the killer sawed off the nun's head and stuffed her vagina full of
jelly beans. In October 1981, Marx drives to Michigan to meet
with a psychologist at Ypsilanti State Hospital, who reviews the
case and develops a profile of the murderer—a poorly educated
Hispanic stranger in his midtwenties—which demonstrates only
that homicides in Toledo should not be investigated by psychologists in Ypsilanti.

As for Kina, he gives up. He's done his job, done it well. He
knows who killed Sister Margaret and believes he was close to getting a confession. *But after you get kicked in the balls a few times, you
stop fighting,* he thinks. *What the hell are we gonna do with this case if
our deputy chief isn't behind us?*

And what of his deputy chief, his friend? Why would Vetter interrupt an interrogation? Kina does not know, and he will never know because he will never ask; in fact, he will speak to Vetter no more than he is required to before retiring in frustration eighteen months later.

SUMMER 1992

KINA'S OLD PARTNER is renewing his wedding vows. There is a party, and most of the guests are Toledo cops and retired Toledo cops. Ray Vetter, retired since 1986, is among them. He sees Kina in the crowd, makes his way over. He does not exchange pleasantries but simply blurts out, "Hey, Bill, what was the name of that nun?"

Kina does not exchange pleasantries either. "Sister Margaret Ann Pahl," he says.

Vetter nods. "I can never remember that name," he says. He shakes his head. "That was the biggest mistake I ever made."

Then he walks away, and maybe he even erases the moment from his mind, because years later he will swear he can't remember ever saying such a thing.

INTERLUDE
JANUARY 2002

THE BOY IS NOW A MAN, and he is in a car on a snowy highway in the Northeast. He is in the passenger seat, and the radio is tuned to a news station that is broadcasting a report about the unfolding scandal of child-molesting priests in the Boston Archdiocese.

Forty-six years have passed since he was raped by a priest in a cottage on the Lake Erie shore. The boy grew up and went to war and came home and got married and had children and started a successful business and got divorced and then fell in love again. He has lived, in forty-six years, a life as normal as anyone else's.

And still no one knows what happened in that cottage. Other than that first friend, he told only his mother, devout and pious, and the dissonance between what she believed and the words her son spoke was so great that she never reconciled the two. Even now, when she is in her mideighties and still prays at Mass, the man does not remind her. When the priest who raped him beat him for stepping off the playground, he did not tell. When that priest went after a cop's kid, and the cop found out and loaded his gun and went to the church to blow his holy fucking head off—and he probably would have if another clergyman hadn't gotten there first—the boy did not tell. Even when the priest disappeared, bounced by the church from one parish to another to another to another, he did not tell. There were rules in 1956, and the boy knew not to break them.

Years later, when he was a man and he saw the priest in a small Ohio town, he did not tell anyone that he wanted to kill him, that he felt a *solemn duty* to kill him. And when the priest finally was dead, half naked and stabbed by some hustler he'd picked up in a Florida bar, and the church that knew he'd raped kids eulogized him as a benevolent servant of God anyway, the man still did not tell. It wasn't about the rules anymore. It was nobody's business.

The snow is blinding, tumbling from the night sky and blowing across the highway. The radio is playing, and a voice is telling him that church officials in Boston let pedophiles and rapists run wild for decades. The radio is telling terrible truths he's known since he was a boy. Only now everyone hears them, and most people will come to believe what they hear. Forty-six years have passed, and the world is suddenly very different. A man in 2002 can say what a boy in 1956 could not. He can say *Father tried to queer me,* and he will not fear being ostracized by a church that has lost its purity and its authority. The rules have changed. There are no more rules.

He looks at the woman steering the car, the woman he loves. He turns down the radio and starts to tell her about a night in a cottage so long ago.

ACT II
JUNE—NOVEMBER 2003

A WOMAN IN her late thirties types a four-page letter about being raped as a girl by Toledo priests in satanic rituals. They penetrated her with a snake, butchered her dog, aborted her baby, and pimped her out for S&M sessions.

True? Maybe: Four other women will eventually tell similar stories. Yet this particular woman carries some credibility because she is a nun, and she expects the Diocesan Review Board, a panel of laypeople who listen to such claims, will take her seriously. She is asking for $50,000 to pay her enormous counseling bills; moreover, the board must decide whether to notify the authorities.

There is nothing unusual about this process. The Roman Catholic Church has become quite practiced in listening to tales of abuse, and it has paid out millions to victims, though how much is unknowable because the church is also adept at burying settlements under confidentiality agreements. The scandal—the church likes to call it a "crisis," but that implies forces beyond its control—has been exposed most notably in bigger cities like Boston and Chicago and Los Angeles. But Toledo is an epicenter of its own. The Survivors Network of those Abused by Priests, or SNAP, was founded by Barbara Blaine, who was molested in the '70s by a Toledo priest who told her, "You're holier than the other kids." A Toledo woman named Claudia Vercellotti started the first Ohio chapter of SNAP in 2002, after she saw the lay minister who'd raped her as a teenager grooming other girls. And the Toledo *Blade* writes about all this. The paper's most damning piece is still two years in the future, a recounting of collusion between Toledo priests and Toledo police. "I can tell you that there was always somebody they could go to in the police department," a retired detective sergeant named John Connors will tell the *Blade* in the summer of 2005. "And I can tell you that, at one time, I was that man."

The review board listens to the nun, then consults a diocesan attorney who declares there is no *legal* reason to inform police or prosecutors. Dissatisfied with that decision and distrustful of the locals, the nun, with the help of Vercellotti and a dissenting board member, goes to the state attorney general. The AG's office doesn't have primary jurisdiction, but an assistant there finds the nun believable enough to kick the whole thing back to Toledo.

Wednesday, December 3, 2003

Detective Sergeant Steve Forrester hears about the nun's letter during the regular monthly meeting of the Cold Case Task Force. A copy is faxed to him. The satanic stuff is interesting, sure, but Forrester receives the letter because of an aside: "One of these S&M perpetrators was Fr. Gerald Robinson, a diocesan priest."

He knows the name. Didn't Robinson look good for a homicide back in 1980? Twenty-three years earlier, wasn't he the prime—no, the *only*—suspect in the murder of a nun?

What the hell, Forrester thinks. *Let's pull it out.*

Forrester and his partner, an investigator with the prosecutor's office named Tom Ross (who knew the case because he was a Toledo homicide cop in 1980), find almost everything they expect to in storage: Robinson's letter opener, the altar cloths, Sister Margaret's clothing, the autopsy report and photographs, file folders of reports and statements. It's a good stash. They'll discover later that there is only one significant gap in the historical record: There are no reports of Robinson's interviews with Kina and Marx, and there are no statements from Father Swiatecki, who's dead. Those reports would have been typed in triplicate—all of which, Marx remembers, were deposited with Vetter. Now they're missing, as if two priests had been excised from the investigation of a murder in their own chapel.

Forrester and Ross carry the old evidence into a conference room. They unroll an altar cloth, the one that was found wrapped around Sister Margaret's right arm. It had been checked into storage two days after the killing, before anyone knew about the letter opener. Ross and Forrester are the first people to see it in twenty-three years. They immediately see a stain, long and thin and gently curved like a sword, then thickening and splitting, a trail of dried blood swooping down and away. They look at the letter opener, the shape of the blade, the knuckle guard. *Holy fuck,* Forrester thinks. *It's the same pattern.*

That stain has been there for more than two decades. It's all been there, waiting. None of the facts of the murder of Sister Margaret have changed since 1980. The evidence, so obvious that it makes a veteran cop think *holy fuck* and so plentiful that it points to only one suspect, is all the same. The only thing different in 2003 is the Catholic Church—and not so much because it has changed but because it has been exposed. Toledo cops no longer care if murder suspects wear clerical collars, and juries probably don't either.

THURSDAY, DECEMBER 4, 2003

FORRESTER AND ROSS interview the nun, the first of five meetings they will have before the end of the year. She is lucid and credible, not at all a crackpot who would manufacture stories of demons and priests. She has no specific information about the murder of Sister Margaret, but because she claims to have an unfortunate knowledge of the priestly occult, she offers the investigators a suggestion.

Look for an upside-down cross on her chest, she tells them. On Sister Margaret's left side, a mark of satanic defilement.

One more thing: If this was a ritual murder, the killer likely penetrated her with a cross, which surely would have left a mark.

Forrester and Ross aren't aware of any crosses, upside-down or otherwise, on Sister Margaret's body. And the nun does not know that the coroner found a scratch in Sister Margaret's vagina.

FRIDAY, FEBRUARY 27, 2004

FORRESTER AND ROSS deliver the letter opener and altar cloth to detective Terry Cousino, who is attached to the scientific-investigations unit of the TPD. He's a crime-scene man, a collector and analyzer of evidence, a *CSI: Toledo* type. Cousino is also the department's sketch artist; the other cops like to say he has an artist's eye.

He examines the cloth, sees the same bloodstains as Forrester and Ross: the curve of the blade, a mushy blob sprouting a deformed stem that matches the decorative nut at the end of the handle. Then he finds more, all just as blatant and apparent once he points them out.

He studies the eighteen holes stabbed through the cloth. At first glance, they seem random, jabbed in a frenzy. Cousino stares at them. There's a pattern, he's certain of it. The tears are in two main clusters, one on the left side of the cloth and one on the right, and they appear to be mirror images. Cousino folds the cloth, and eighteen holes align into nine. And those nine seem to form a shape. Six of them are positioned in parallel rows of three. Two more are spaced farther apart, like the endpoints of a line perpendicular to the rows. The ninth is off by itself like a stray star.

See it all through an artist's eye. Lay a cross on the altar cloth and the holes transform into a connect-the-dots sketch, six along the length, two at the ends of the crossbeam, the ninth just off the bottom, as if the last stab had been badly aimed.

Cousino lays the altar cloth on Sister Margaret's habit, shifts it around, finds corresponding tears. They are on the left side, and the cross is upside-down.

FRIDAY, APRIL 23, 2004

FATHER ROBINSON is 66 years old and semiretired after serving in several parishes since he left Mercy Hospital in 1981. He lives in a house on Nebraska Avenue next to a police station, and there are liquor bottles in his garbage can when he pulls it to the curb.

The police have had him under surveillance for weeks as investigators build their case. While murder may be a simple crime in the act, proving it more than twenty years after the fact is complicated. Retired detectives and aging witnesses have to be reinterviewed. The bloodstains that are apparent to cops, plain to anyone with eyes, require the testimony of a credentialed expert to convince a jury. Forrester has already been to Memphis to enlist one of the best, Paulette Sutton, who has found even more connections between the letter opener and the altar cloth and, more creepily, Sister Margaret's forehead: The red curl across her nose apparently was left by an anointment of bloody last rites.

And what if this *was* a satanic ritual? That had to be explored, which meant going to Chicago for the counsel of a priest, Father Jeffrey Grob, who specializes in the occult. (He reviewed the evidence and concluded that whoever killed Sister Margaret was schooled in church ritual and that elements of her murder were meant to mock her and her God.)

All of those things take time, and Forrester is happy to have it. But he wants more.

His phone rings at five thirty in the morning. Reporters are circling Robinson's house. Someone leaked the damned thing.

They decide to move. At three o'clock in the afternoon, Forrester and Ross knock on Robinson's door. They are polite, friendly, offer him their business cards, tell him they only want to clear up a few things about an old case. *Just a couple of nice guys in suits coming to your house,* Forrester says to himself, hoping Robinson will believe it.

They ask Robinson what he remembers from Holy Saturday 1980. He promptly lies. He says he was toweling off after a shower in his room when a sister called and asked him to anoint Sister Margaret's body. *Father Swiatecki anointed the body,* Forrester knows. Robinson explains how he saw the body, how he cleaned up the sacristy. *No one saw him there. His absence was conspicuous.*

They ask him about a bottle of Valium, prescribed the day of the murder and found in his room by Kina and Marx. Did he usually take Valium? "No," Robinson says. "I had headaches from the stress of that day."

Back in 1980, they remind him, detectives overheard Swiatecki pleading with him to "just tell the truth." What was that about?

Oh, it was worse than that, Robinson says. Swiatecki confronted him in the sacristy before the body was even cold. "He said, 'Why did you kill her?' "

Whoa. That's new.

"What'd you say?" Ross asks.

"I didn't know what to say." Pause. "I just kind of walked out."

They talk for a half hour or so, until Ross tells the priest he wants to show him some photos. Which isn't what he wants to do at all: He wants to lean on a suspect. Ross is older than Forrester, white-haired, carries a physical gravitas. Between the two of them, Ross can play an authority figure to an aging priest more convincingly.

Ross lays out his glossies: the letter opener aligned with the blood stains, the holes in the shape of a cross. He's no longer a nice guy in a suit. "This is your letter opener," he tells Robinson. "We know it's your letter opener."

Robinson says nothing.

"Scientists are telling us a weapon like this was laid down on that altar cloth, a weapon like this made those wounds. And this weapon was found in your room."

Nothing.

"Even if somebody was going to set you up with this," Ross says, "why would they clean it and put it back in your room?"

Still nothing.

Ross and Forrester arrest Robinson, and walk him to the precinct house next door, run through the whole thing again in front of a video camera. Ross asks him again about Swiatecki confronting him, why he didn't lash back, why he'd just take it when a man accuses him of murder.

"Well," Robinson says, "I took a lot."

Ross asks him, too, about his relationship with Sister Margaret, a nun he worked with for more than six years.

"She was just someone I worked with," he says.

The interview ends. Twenty-four years and four days after he was rescued from a police interrogation room and a failed polygraph, Gerald Robinson is charged with murder.

Retired Deputy Police Chief Ray Vetter finds out later that night. "I'll be damned," he says.

ACT III
APRIL 21, 2006

IF A MURDER TRIAL is a high-stakes poker game, then the prosecuting attorney typically needs to draw the equivalent of a full house. A solid hand, hard to beat at most tables.

It's a respectable analogy that Dean Mandros has worked out to explain his job. He is the chief of the criminal division of the Lucas County prosecutor's office, a thin man of 52 with a graying beard and glasses, who, if he isn't wearing a suit, looks as if he'd be comfortable at a poker table.

His job is to convince twelve jurors that Gerald Robinson is guilty of murder. A full house will not do. When he first learned, more than two years earlier, that the defendant was a priest, he decided he'd need a straight flush. Oh, wait, a priest who killed a nun? *Twenty-four years ago?* And the evidence is entirely circumstantial? Mandros feared he needed a royal flush.

The deck isn't stacked so badly against him now. In the two years since Robinson was arrested, the case has only gotten stronger. In the spring of 2004, the county exhumed Sister Margaret's bones and found, in her jaw, a diamond-shaped divot into which the tip of the letter opener fits precisely, "like a key in a lock," as Mandros will put it. And there are three witnesses who swear they saw Robinson near the chapel at the time of the killing, and they will do heavy damage to Robinson's alibi of having been in his room.

Mandros has his bloodstain expert, and he also has Henry Lee, the forensic scientist from the O. J. Simpson trial, who will testify that the letter opener could very well be the murder weapon. Mandros enlisted Lee less for his theatrical value—juries tend to trust famous people—than as a preemptive tactic. What if Robinson had hired him? "This *could* be the murder weapon" sounds reasonably doubtful when an expert for the defense says it.

But Robinson is still a priest. When Mandros steps to the podium to begin his opening statement, Robinson is over his right shoulder, sitting there in his clerical collar. His hair is thin and gray, and as Mandros describes his victim—a nun since 1927, when she was 19, a registered nurse who ran two hospitals before retiring to look after the chapel at Mercy—Robinson's thin lips are drawn into a weary little frown. He looks like what he is, an old, frail priest.

"The defendant, as he sits before you, is 68 years old," Mandros tells the jury as he pivots to his right and gestures toward Robinson. He shifts to his left, toward a large electronic screen and pushes a button on the remote in his hand. The screen blinks; an image appears. "But this," he says, "was the defendant back in 1980, at the age of 42."

A younger Robinson appears. His hair is thick and dark, and

those lips are pursed in either a dry smile or a dull smirk. The picture is oversize, and Mandros lets it linger, maybe long enough that the jury will forget the frail old priest in the courtroom, replace him with a memory of a smirking young man.

He lays out the rest of his case, the time line of the crime, a synopsis of the original investigation, the list of witnesses and forensics, all the circumstantial evidence that he says will prove Father Gerald Robinson killed Sister Margaret Ann Pahl.

Yet Mandros offers no motive. Legally, he is not required to: He has to show only the fact of a murder, not the reason for it. But it is a risky hole to leave in his argument. Every man has his reasons, and juries want to understand them. Yet what can Mandros say? That it was a satanic killing? Really? And have a dozen jurors roll their skeptical eyes? The problem with even mentioning such a thing is that Mandros would then have to *prove* it. Besides, a ritual satanic killing would be a method, not a motive.

ALAN S. KONOP, a highly regarded Toledo attorney who wears his reading glasses at the tip of his nose, gives the opening statement for the defense. He talks a lot about how evidence is a puzzle and how all the pieces have to fit together; otherwise, he says, there is reasonable doubt, and any honest jury is obligated to acquit. He uses the phrase "reasonable doubt" many, many times.

He does not, however, say the word *innocent*. He does not say, even once, "My guy didn't do it," or even the safely nonperjurious "The evidence *will show you* my guy didn't do it." The omission is so glaring that the commentators on Court TV, which is broadcasting live, pounce on it. One of them calls Konop's opening "namby-pamby."

Everyone's a critic. But Konop's client is a priest, after all. If you can't say *that* guy's innocent . . . well, juries notice that sort of thing.

FRIDAY, MAY 5, 2006

KONOP CALLS HIS first witnesses to the stand, including three detectives who worked the original investigation in 1980.

Through his questions, Konop begins to attack the investigation, drawing out fine threads of discrepancy, tugging at strands of sloppy police work. He asks one retired cop, for instance, about a long-ago report that mentioned a pair of scissors missing from the sacristy. Couldn't that have been the murder weapon?

He calls retired detective Art Marx to the stand. Weren't certain reports written in 1980, certain reports that the police can no longer locate? The implication is clear: Critical, perhaps exculpatory, evidence is missing.

Yes, Marx tells Konop, reports are missing. "Unavailable," he says.

What happened to them?

"I have no idea," Marx testifies.

Mandros has played his hand well. He doesn't want to criticize the police, either those in 1980 or those who reopened the case in 2003. That's why he'd kept Marx off the stand for his case. Let Konop call him. Let the defense ask about those missing reports, open the door just enough for Mandros to make a single salient point. He asks Marx if Deputy Chief Ray Vetter was the last person with those missing reports.

"To my knowledge, yes."

"And is this the individual who brought Monsignor Schmit and interrupted your interview with the defendant?"

"Same person," Marx says. "Yes."

"Deputy Chief Vetter," Mandros says. "Do you know if he's Catholic or not?"

"Yes. A very strict Catholic."

WEDNESDAY, MAY 10, 2006

MANDROS MAKES HIS closing argument, focusing on the damning essentials. The letter opener that fits neatly into Sister
Margaret's jawbone, aligns neatly with stains on the altar cloth and
with a bloody imprint on her forehead. Three witnesses who saw
Robinson near the chapel. "If you believe what they say, then you
can't believe his story," Mandros tells the jury. "If you believe what
they say, you know who went into that chapel. You know who
killed Sister Margaret Ann Pahl."

The irony, Mandros knows, is that he is arguing almost exactly
what he would have argued in the '80s. There is no new evidence
save the tiny shifts in Robinson's alibi and, perhaps, a desiccated
jawbone that more clearly shows the fit with the letter opener.
Everything else, everything physical, is exactly the same. It just
wasn't enough in 1980, when priests were holy and pure, when
police reports disappeared and interrogations were interrupted, and
when the average Lucas County juror was obedient, or at least deferential, to a church of mercy and charity. Is it enough in 2006?

Mandros still hasn't given the jurors a motive. Truth is, Mandros
doesn't know why Robinson killed Sister Margaret. He believes
there were *rituals* involved, though not necessarily satanic ones. The
cross pattern, the way her body was posed, naked and humiliated,
beneath the Blessed Sacrament. He was mocking Sister Margaret—
Who's in charge now?—mocking the church—*You bastards want to
stick me in this hospital?*—maybe even mocking God Himself—*See
how angry You've made me?* Mandros can see Robinson stabbing her
corpse again and again, trying to draw out enough blood to soak
his weapon and anoint her forehead. All method, no motive.
Mandros has worked out a theory, though, and it is plain and boring and as good as any. A misfit loner priest who's *taken a lot* from a
dominating nun gets chewed out for trimming a Good Friday service. By a nun! A woman who dogma teaches is subservient to
him. He is humiliated. He stews. He fumes. He paces his cramped

quarters, relives every slight, replays and amplifies them. A rage builds, and then, as dawn is breaking, he decides: *I'm gonna whack the bitch.*

Pretty routine, really. Prisons are full of guys like that—only hardly any of them are priests, and most of the victims are girl-friends and wives. "This case is about perhaps the most common scenario there is for a homicide," Mandros tells the jury. "A man got very angry at a woman, and the woman died. The only thing different is the man wore a white collar and the woman wore a habit."

Thursday, May 11, 2006

After six hours of deliberation, the jury files into the court-room, and the bailiff hands Judge Thomas Osowik a slip of paper. The judge glances at it and begins to read aloud, so quickly that he has to stop in mid-sentence and tell Robinson to stand up.

Guilty.

The judge pronounces a mandatory prison sentence of fifteen years to life, and then the court officers are next to Robinson, pull-ing his arms behind his back, cuffing his wrists. As he is led out of the courtroom, the old priest looks back over his shoulder, his lips drawn again into a small, dry frown, and then disappears through the door.

The Lucas County jailers take away his collar and his rosary and put him on a suicide watch. In a few weeks, the state will lock him up in the Hocking Correctional Facility, a medium-security prison where he will stay at least until he comes up for parole in just over a decade—unless he wins his appeal.

EPILOGUE
JULY 25, 2006

RAY VETTER IS 82 years old, and most of his senses are failing. But he looks good, big and robust with a full head of white hair, and he walks eight miles a day unless it gets too hot in the afternoon and he cancels his second four miles.

He lives in a small house in a quiet neighborhood with his wife, and he still expects God will reserve her a high place in heaven. He no longer gives up anything for Lent, because there is nothing left to sacrifice. Except ice cream. "I can taste ice cream," he says. "I love ice cream. I ain't giving that up."

Vetter will surely be forgiven such a minor transgression. He is one of the remaining devout in a largely Catholic city that no longer believes as deeply, where the faith is no longer practiced with the same innocent obedience. The pedophiles and the rapists, the lawsuits and payoffs, have done tremendous damage to the church. "A hell of a kick in the ass," Vetter says. He can see it at Mass, where the pews are half empty, and in the collection plate, where there is only a miserly scattering of coins and bills.

"When I was a kid, you didn't hear about this happening," Vetter says, meaning the rapes. "I mean, maybe it happened, but I never heard of it." And he still can't get his head around it. "Priests," he says, "they're right up here—" he raises his hand above his white hair—"right below God."

He suspects now that Robinson is guilty. "If he didn't do it," he says, "then who did? That's my question." He doesn't have an answer, and he didn't have one in 1980. Yet he tells himself he couldn't have proved it so long ago, what with ancient technology and all. "We could have gone to court and said we *think* this is the murder weapon," he says. "In 2006 they could say, 'This *is* the murder weapon.' That's the biggest difference."

No, they couldn't say that in 2006. There's no difference at all.

Vetter was called by the defense, and he explained that he

brought the monsignor to the police station only to help. "I was a close personal friend of Monsignor Schmit," he testified. "I told him, 'All I want you to do is talk with Father Robinson, make him feel sort of at home. Whatever you can find out. And if you find out anything, let's talk.' And the monsignor said he'd be glad to do it."

But interrupt an interrogation? Break off an interview when his own men, good men, might be moments away from hearing a priest confess to murder? Allow a monsignor, a superior of his mystical faith, to escort a suspect out of a police station, back to the protective embrace of the church?

No, Vetter has no memory of that. "I wouldn't do it," he says. "I can't think of a reason why I would." But he hears the whispers. "They're coming up with the idea that I fixed the case, and that's bullshit," he says. "I would never do that. I wouldn't put my job at risk, my pension. I had six kids here to feed. I would never jeopardize that." He looks at his lap, looks up again. "And it's illegal. It's immoral."

Yes, it is both of those things. But every man has his reasons. And when he lays his head down at night, when he has to be at peace only with himself and his God, maybe then he begins to understand them.

SEAN FLYNN *is a correspondent for* GQ *and a contributing editor for* Parade. *He has also written for* Esquire, *the* New York Times Magazine, *and* Men's Journal, *among others. He is the author of* 3000 Degrees: The True Story of a Deadly Fire and the Men Who Fought it *and* Boston D.A.: The Battle to Transform the American Justice System. *He won the National Magazine Award for reporting in 2001, and his work has been anthologized in* Best American Magazine Writing 2001, Best American Sports Writing 2005, *and* Best American Travel Writing 2006.

Coda

There can be a certain familiarity to cold-case murder stories, a sense that they have been told before, if not in the details then in the broad outlines. Someone gets killed, the killer either gets away or goes undetected, years pass, and then the cops either find a critical, long overlooked piece of evidence or the killer makes a mistake that leads to his arrest. Typically, detectives become the protagonists of the narrative. Write about enough cold cases and eventually they become somewhat routine.

The murder of Sister Margaret Ann Pahl, after a cursory glance through the newspaper clippings, appeared to fit that general outline. The fascinating aspect, the details that elevated it into a magazine story (and several books) seemed to be only the particulars of the killer and the victim, a priest and a nun. And that is how I approached it. My job, then, was to convince the prosecutors and the cops to tell me their stories, to provide the anecdotes and the insight that would re-create the investigation, 24 years after the crime, that led to Father Gerald Robinson's conviction.

The first, most obvious step was to meet with Dean Mandros, the lead prosecutor. He was a bit wearied by people like me—reporters, that is; the case had already drawn an enormous amount of national media attention—but he agreed to have a beer in a strip-mall bar. He didn't say much, mainly because he was deciding if he wanted to be bothered with me at all. So I filled the awkward pauses. I mentioned to him that some people in Toledo believed that the prosecutor's office and the police were conspiring with the Catholic church, that Robinson was the proverbial tip of the iceberg, that diocesan scandals of sex and torture were being ignored, indeed covered up, by secular authorities.

He nodded and smiled a weary smile—he'd heard that all before—and took a sip of his beer. "The irony," he said, "is I could not have convicted this guy twenty years ago. No, I couldn't have convicted him *ten* years ago. *With the exact same evidence.*"

I had no idea what he meant, and I told him so.

"A priest?" he said. "You think I could've convicted *a priest?*"

Actually, I hadn't thought of it in those terms at all. Despite my aggressively Irish name, I wasn't raised Catholic; I held priests in no higher nor lower esteem in 2006 than I had in 1980. And yet what Mandros said was completely obvious: the killer hadn't made a mistake and the evidence hadn't changed. The Church, or the perception of it, had.

Which made the story not so routine. It was no longer about a killing—a rather mundane one, as Mandros said in his closing, simply about a man who got very mad at a woman—but about two investigations in two different contexts.

Matthew Teague

DOUBLE BLIND

*The untold story of how British intelligence
infiltrated and undermined the IRA*

FROM *The Atlantic Monthly*

I FIRST MET THE MAN now called Kevin Fulton in London, on
Platform 13 at Victoria Station. We almost missed each other in the
crowd; he didn't look at all like a terrorist.

He stood with his feet together, a short and round man with a
kind face, fair hair, and blue eyes. He might have been an Irish
grammar-school teacher, not an IRA bomber or a British spy in
hiding. Both of which he was.

Fulton had agreed to meet only after an exchange of messages
through an intermediary. Now, as we talked on the platform, he
paced back and forth, scanning the faces of passersby. He checked
the time, then checked it again. He spoke in an almost impenetra-
ble brogue, and each time I leaned in to understand him, he leaned
back, suspicious. He fidgeted with several mobile phones, one
devoted to each of his lives. "I'm just cautious," he said.

He lives in London now, but his wife remains in Northern
Ireland. He rarely goes out, for fear of bumping into the wrong
person, and so leads a life of utter isolation, a forty-five-year-old
man with a lot on his mind.

During the next few months, Fulton and I met several times on Platform 13. Over time his jitters settled, his speech loosened, and his past tumbled out: his rise and fall in the Irish Republican Army, his deeds and misdeeds, his loyalties and betrayals. He had served as a covert foot soldier in what has come to be called the Dirty War: a cutthroat and secret British effort to infiltrate and undermine the IRA, carried out in the shadows of the infamous Troubles. "It was a lot grayer and darker," Fulton said of the clandestine war. "Darker even than people can imagine."

But there's this: it worked. British spies subverted the IRA from within, leaving it in military ruin, and Irish Republicans—who want to end British rule in Northern Ireland and reunite the island—have largely shifted their weight to Sinn Féin and its peaceable, political efforts. And so the Dirty War provides a model for how to dismantle a terrorist organization. The trick is to not mind killing, and to expect dying.

This came clear to Kevin Fulton on the day his cover as an IRA man collapsed. It happened inside an IRA safe house in north Belfast, in 1994. Fulton sat facing a wall, blindfolded. Curtains shut out the pale light of winter. Bottles lay scattered on the floor, and the place stank of stale beer. An interrogator paced the room, his boots scuffing against the floor. He said, "I know what yer done, boyo."

He pressed a thick index finger against Fulton's temple, hard, then leaned in close to Fulton's ear and murmured a series of threats: *The IRA hunts down all snitches and executes them. Two quick bullets in the brain. Remember the boy from County Armagh who left behind the pregnant wife. Remember the boy from County Louth who left seven children mewling for a father. Remember them all.*

British authorities had recently picked up Fulton for questioning. Now the IRA, which had begun to suspect him of being a British agent, wanted to know why.

Again, the finger to the temple.

"What did you tell them?"

Fulton knew the voice, and its owner: Scap, one of the IRA's most feared interrogators. Fulton had once helped prepare safe houses for such interrogations, and knew that sometimes Scap's subjects survived. Sometimes not.

Colleagues called both men "hard bastards": true IRA boys, mothered by terrorism. They killed for the cause, time and again. But British spies had infiltrated the IRA, spreading deceit and rumors of deceit. The IRA had turned against itself. Scap couldn't say for sure who fought on his side.

The interrogation dragged on for hours. Fulton remained outwardly calm, and denied everything. Inwardly, though, he felt sick. He'd been spying on the IRA for a decade and a half, and he knew that if Scap broke him—if he admitted anything—he'd be a dead man. "Down a hole," in IRA slang.

So throughout the interrogation, Fulton sat stone-faced, blindfolded, and facing the wall. Double blind. He held tight to his secret: yes, he was a British spy.

But then, so was his interrogator.

As a boy, Freddie Scappaticci ducked and scuffled on the streets of Belfast, fighting Protestants to fit in with his Catholic friends.

His parents had immigrated to Northern Ireland in the 1920s with a wave of other Italian families and settled in the Markets area of south Belfast, where Freddie was born in 1944. The old neighborhood hummed; under historic Georgian terraces, families bustled from churches to butcher shops to apple stalls. The Scappaticcis sold ice cream and earned a reputation as "terrible nice people."

Belfast appealed more to the terrible than to the nice during Freddie Scappaticci's childhood. After thirty years of Protestant-Catholic strife, Catholic hatred for Protestants had grown so powerful that it enfolded all Irish Catholics, even those with Italian parents. As tension escalated in the 1960s and the Troubles began,

Scappaticci joined in schoolyard brawls and street fights, and at sixteen he received the ultimate mark of credibility: Protestant police on patrol beat him severely, leaving him bruised and proud.

In 1969 the British army blundered into Northern Ireland at the request of its overwhelmed government, to stamp out Catholic and Protestant animosity once and for all. Soldiers in armored Land Rovers patrolled city streets across the country; they wore uniforms and helmets, and brandished automatic rifles. They planned to bring peace to a troubled land. For a while the local population showered the troops with gratitude for helping separate the two black-eyed factions, but soon, in pubs and cathedrals across Northern Ireland, people began whispering "occupation." The whispers grew to shouts, and shouts became hurled stones. Before long Scappaticci—who had started to go by the less-Italian name Scap—took to throwing bricks at British squads. "Freddie was full Belfast," his childhood acquaintance Victor Notarantonio remembers.

Across the city, bands of jobless young men roamed the streets looking for a cause, or an excuse. And in 1971 they found one. After several murders by the IRA, the British instituted a policy of internment without trial, sweeping hundreds of suspects off the streets and taking them to an unused air base, called Long Kesh, several miles south of Belfast. It proved a spectacular bungle. The British had relied on outdated intelligence reports and arrested many people, including Scappaticci, with only a passing connection to the IRA, while the IRA's top people received tip-offs and went into hiding.

The roundup stirred up the peaceful majority of Northern Ireland's Catholics, and many of the moderates detained by the British quickly grew into extremists behind bars. Previously scattered rebels organized themselves at Long Kesh, forming leadership and rank. Scappaticci found himself interned alongside future notable Republicans like Gerry Adams and David Morley. The old IRA leadership in Dublin—relatively tame Marxists who spent more time writing than fighting—faded away, replaced by a more ferocious guard that called itself the Provisional IRA. The older generation had huffed and puffed against Protestant discrimination, but these younger men took up arms against a larger enemy: the British army.

When Scappaticci was released, three years later, he had become a hard-shelled IRA man. He switched from bricks to bullets. His colleagues marveled at his marksmanship, and rumor has it that he killed several soldiers. At the time, the atmosphere in Belfast was like Irish poteen liquor: boiled and fermented, distilled into something potent and unlawful. Protestants flew the Union Jack and painted their curbstones red, white, and blue; Catholics flew the Irish flag and painted their curbs orange, white, and green. Men in one part of the city wore bowler hats and carried silver-knobbed canes; men just a block away wore green and carried shillelaghs. Belfast felt more British than London, and more Irish than Dublin.

The IRA swelled in power, money, and numbers. Its members executed increasingly ruthless operations against Protestant groups and British forces, but Scappaticci gradually began to notice a disturbing pattern: hot-blooded young men were sent headlong into dangerous missions, but their leaders stayed safe in the pubs back home. And when these foot soldiers died or landed in prison, the leaders sometimes showed up around town with the missing men's wives. The leaders grew rich on cash pressed from the tills of working-class Catholic shopkeepers and tradesmen, and they splashed it around like mobsters. To Scappaticci, their behavior seemed more like robbery than revolution.

So did the IRA's assertion that the Protestant gangs were only a tool of the "real enemy," the British occupiers. It seemed a neat trick, summoning the banshee of a dying British Empire. The Catholics could conceivably stare down the Protestants at home, but they could never beat the British at war. A campaign against the British would ensure the IRA's necessity for generations to come. Scappaticci spoke out, mouthing off at pubs, questioning the

IRA leadership. One night in 1978, after an argument over IRA policy, IRA men beat him and told him to straighten up: *Don't cross the IRA*.

Scappaticci, the British intelligence services quickly recognized, had the makings of the perfect agent. A local man, born in Belfast. A credible IRA member. A disillusioned foot soldier. Beaten down. Ready.

Eventually, inevitably, an intelligence officer asked him: Would he spy?

ABOUT THAT TIME, in a small town called Newry, a teenaged Kevin Fulton was honing his shooting skills in the countryside, hunting foxes and rabbits. Newry lies about forty miles south of Belfast, in the rolling borderland almost midway to Dublin. It's a charming little seaport, with a linen mill and a city hall that straddles the drowsy Clanrye River on a three-arched stone bridge.

Growing up in the 1970s, Fulton heard songs of rebellion and stories of derring-do. He longed for adventure. Something grander than rabbits. But his family seemed determined to cling to the dullness of a balanced life, even during the chaos of the Troubles, even in a border town. They were Catholic, yes, but not political. They attended church, not rallies. They had another son who served as a priest, instead of a soldier. They kept to themselves.

Just after his eighteenth birthday, Fulton made his way to Belfast's Grand Central Hotel, which British soldiers had sandbagged and billeted as headquarters. There he enlisted with the British army's Royal Irish Rangers. It was an extraordinary move for a Catholic kid from a Catholic town—the British army! a miniature rebellion!—but it allowed him to shake off a sleepy home life and, as he put it, maybe "play around with guns and explosives." He expected to travel to distant lands, maybe the Falklands, and stare down foreign fighters.

He showed up for basic training, just a blue-eyed lad with no experience in the world. But his commanders saw unusual potential in him—or, rather, they heard it, in the snip and slur of his Northern Irish accent. In a matter of weeks he received a tap on the shoulder from a military intelligence officer. The British had a plan, the man said, and a proposition: Would he spy?

After the Long Kesh internment debacle, the IRA gained ground against the British. On patrol in Belfast, British soldiers dodged stones by day and firebombs by night. Troops in armored Rovers and protective helmets made no good friends; they only made good targets. They needed a better strategy, and a powerful personality to implement it. And they soon found the man for the job: Brigadier General Frank Kitson.

Kitson rolled into Northern Ireland in the early 1970s with considerable experience battling insurgencies in Kenya, Malaya, and elsewhere. He had learned valuable lessons, particularly in Kenya in the 1950s battling the Mau Mau, a band of rebels fighting for independence. He had rounded up suspected Mau Mau supporters, who then endured interrogation and torture at the hands of the British authorities. The Mau Mau couldn't match the British militarily, so they resorted to guerrilla tactics, hiding in the hills and striking from the shadows. But Kitson followed them there, recruited locals with money and idealism, and infiltrated the insurgent ranks. With layer upon layer of sabotage, subterfuge, and duplicity, he obliterated the Mau Mau.

Kitson's methods proved so effective that he wrote a now-classic counterinsurgency book, *Low Intensity Operations: Subversion, Insurgency, Peacekeeping,* which laid out principles now being followed by American forces in Iraq. By the time Kitson arrived in Northern Ireland, *Low Intensity Operations* had become his instruction manual for war there. He stayed for only about two years, but in that brief period he set a new course for the British army that, for better or worse, carried it through the Troubles. By 1978, using tactics endorsed by Kitson, the army had for years been regularly stopping vehicles at checkpoints and randomly arresting drivers to screen them. One of the men hauled in that year was Freddie Scappaticci, fresh from his beating by the IRA.

The account of why Scappaticci entered into intelligence work—whether he was driven by a desire for vengeance after his beating or wooed by his handlers over time—varies depending who recounts it. Regardless, he entered into it with vigor, ultimately signing on to work for a secret intelligence outfit called the Force Research Unit. Through the FRU, Scappaticci served a host of agencies, among them MI5, a paramilitary police unit called Special Branch, and army intelligence. Eventually he became one of the most important spies in Britain's history, working his way toward the IRA's heart.

His handlers gave him the code name Stakeknife.

FULTON RESISTED BRITISH intelligence work at first. After joining the army, he was sent to Berlin for Ranger training, where he learned to follow orders, to shoot, and to work with explosives. All the while, intelligence officers hovered nearby, whispering, promising, making appeals. Finally Fulton came around.

In 1981, two years after leaving his hometown of Newry, Fulton returned. If anyone asked about his absence, he rolled up his sleeves and showed them tattoos from his brief stint as a teenager in the Merchant Marines.

Evening after evening he showed up at the Hibernian Club, where IRA men unwound in their spare time. Fulton never asked where they went, or what they did. Never asked so much as the time of day, because questions made IRA men nervous. So he faded into the walls, just another son of Newry with working-class parents and a priest for a brother. He played pool. Drank pints. Laughed at tall tales. Drank more pints. Watched. Waited.

In time, with jokes told and pints drained, Fulton became one of the boys. And after several months, it finally happened: "Kevin! C'mere, boyo. Got an errand for you."

So it started. He delivered a package—a pistol and bullets—across town. He made another delivery, then another. Always on time and dependable. The jobs escalated in subtle increments, and as his errands reached farther, the packages grew deadlier. Bullets became pipe bombs, and pipe bombs became car bombs.

In carrying out his early errands, Fulton followed instructions handed down by his handlers in British intelligence. Whenever he overheard some tidbit of valuable information, some snippet about an IRA mission, he dialed a toll-free line and arranged a meeting. Usually his handlers told him to drive to an obscure parking lot, or a spot on a country roadside, and to wait there for a white delivery van. When it arrived, a side door would fly open and Fulton would climb in, typically greeted, he told me, by men representing the various agencies he served: MI5, military, Special Branch, all working with the secret Force Research Unit—the same group handling Scappaticci. They'd speed off to a safe house, often in a grand upscale neighborhood.

If the plan ever kinked—if his cover blew and he had no time for a phone call—he would follow an emergency plan. He'd drive out of town immediately and press a button that his handlers had installed under his dash. The button would send a tracking signal to British forces, who would then sweep in and extract him to safety.

Each night Fulton rocked himself to sleep repeating the mantra his handlers had given him: "The greater good. The greater good. The greater good." He and Scappaticci engaged in a difficult mathematics, a calculus of souls. If a man kills thirty people to save 3,000, has he done right? What about thirty for 300? Or thirty for thirty-one?

At one point I asked Fulton whether, in light of the human toll he would exact in the course of his career, someone could have served the greater good by killing him as a young man. I meant the question to be rhetorical. But Fulton just nodded.

"Yes," he said.

IN 1980, AFTER A COUPLE of years working as a British spy—
arranging meetings, handing over tidbits—Scappaticci joined the
IRA's internal security unit, which IRA men called the Nutting
Squad. "Nut" is Irish slang for the head. When the Nutting Squad
found a snitch or a British spy, its interrogators typically tortured
him, squeezed him for information, then "nutted" him with a pair
of bullets to the brain.

Scappaticci's history as an IRA sharpshooter gave him an advantage as an agent, and he quickly made his way to the top of the
Nutting Squad. The achievement reveals either a tactical brilliance
or a profound stroke of luck. The position gave him access to the
IRA's innermost secrets: missions completed and upcoming; arms
storage sites; travel and security details; bombing and assassination
targets. Over several years he helped foil numerous killings and kidnappings, and the information he provided to the British so daz-
zled his handlers that they passed it along to Prime Minister
Margaret Thatcher herself.

Moreover, his position atop the Nutting Squad made him
untouchable. If the IRA leaders ever suspected an infiltration, they
reported it to the Nutting Squad—and so to Scappaticci. If his own
activities ever drew suspicion, he could simply divert attention by
fingering an innocent man. Some British press reports estimate he
killed as many as forty people. A former British spy handler who
worked at the time of Scappaticci's rise—a man who now goes by
the name Martin Ingram—puts the death toll lower, but still "well
into the tens," including other agents. He said it all fit into the
larger British strategy. "Agents have killed, and killed, and have
killed," Ingram told me. "Many, many, many people."

Under Scappaticci's close direction, the Nutting Squad killed
dozens of people, including:

Seamus Morgan, 24. Abducted, shot in the head, and dumped by
a road in 1982.

John Corcoran, 45. Told his shooter, "Go easy," just before a bullet entered above his left ear, from behind, in 1985. He had eight children.

Paddy Flood, 29. Held captive for two months and tortured, then killed and left on a roadside. Twelve years later, it came out that Flood's murder was a mistake; he had been innocent.

The list goes on.

Scappaticci's handlers themselves went to extremes to protect their prize agent. Take the case of Francisco Notarantonio, the father of Scappaticci's childhood acquaintance Victor. In his day, the elder Notarantonio—who had been interned with Scappaticci at Long Kesh—had enjoyed a reputation as a tough IRA man. "Even when the queen came here," Victor told me, striking a certain triumphal tone, "before the Troubles started, my father got arrested and put away for a couple of days to make sure no harm came to the queen." But by 1987, the old man had mellowed and retired, both from driving his taxi and from the IRA. About that time, a powerful Protestant gang got a description of a man working high in the IRA. The gang suspected Scappaticci and dispatched a hit squad to execute him. As the squad moved toward Scappaticci, the alarmed British directed the killers toward another Italian IRA man: old Notarantonio. Shortly thereafter, Notarantonio lay dead in his bedroom, shot to death in front of his family.

I put it to Martin Ingram, the former spy handler, that in the case of Scappaticci, the British strategy had gone amok.

"No, I don't think so," he said. "I think it went very much to schedule."

"So you think—"

"I don't *think,* I know. He was acting to orders."

So the British government knew of Scappaticci's killings?

"Oh, yeah," he said. "The one preconception the IRA had is that if you are dirty—that is, if you have killed—then you cannot be an agent." Scappaticci exploited that misapprehension. "His best protection," Ingram continued, "was to keep killing."

If that's true, the British spy services beat the IRA by appealing to a belief that the United Kingdom wouldn't sacrifice its own subjects—especially its own agents.

In Belfast I met with Denis Donaldson, a Sinn Féin party leader and an IRA veteran alleged to have run the IRA's intelligence wing. He's a folk hero who led hunger strikes early in the Troubles, and British investigators say he traveled the world, cultivating terrorist contacts in Spain, Palestine, El Salvador, and elsewhere: a hard IRA man if there ever was one.

We sat at his kitchen table as he smoked, cursing British "interference" and "collusion." We had talked for a couple of hours before I noticed that the discreet television in the corner near the ceiling wasn't a television at all. It was a security monitor, and at the moment, it showed the front door through which I had entered. I noticed, too, a wrought-iron door that sealed off the upstairs, forming a redoubt.

When I mentioned the names of Scappaticci and Fulton, Donaldson's shoulders slumped. "I still can't believe it," he said, shaking his head. "My God."

His face seemed thin and gray, the face of a man who senses an end looming. A couple of weeks after we talked, the IRA laid down its arms, defeated by a confluence of circumstances: a change in the world's view of terrorism; apparent gains made by its political partner, Sinn Féin; and the steady infiltration of British spies.

FULTON WORKED as a painter by day, whitewashing the pocked walls of County Down, Northern Ireland. But secretly he made bombs, as part of a small team of demolitions experts who operated in both Northern Ireland and the Irish Republic. Some of their bombs blew up military targets. Others blew up civilians. Fulton could sometimes sabotage missions. Often he could not.

By early 1993, Fulton and his team of bombers had found something less clumsy than wires to use in bomb and rocket detonation. They rigged bombs with photo sensors, which they triggered by popping off camera flashes. The results were lethal. Trouble was, other lights—bright headlights, or a tourist's disposable photo flash—could set off a bomb prematurely.

British intelligence services, in an effort to control IRA techniques through collaboration, secretly passed along a solution for the problem: a new technology—the infrared flash—that could be acquired only in America. Fulton's handlers offered to facilitate an undercover IRA shopping mission to New York, and an MI5 officer flew across the Atlantic on the Concorde to make arrangements with American services in advance of Fulton's arrival. "This was a terrorist organization operating in the United States," Fulton told me, and it required cooperation. "It was a pretty big thing."

Fulton traveled to New York with several thousand dollars, met secretly with his handlers, arranged the purchase, and returned to Northern Ireland, ready to create a deadly new weapon. The IRA embraced the innovation, and it worked so well that other terrorist groups soon took notice and adapted the infrared photo-sensor bomb to their own wars. Today, Iraqi insurgents wield it against British and American troops in Iraq.

The British and American strategy—tracking insurgents by abetting them—seemed to follow a convoluted logic: that of a fighter who, trying to zero in on his opponent, waits for a few good shots to the nose. When Fulton traveled to New York with his handlers, he provided valuable inside information about the IRA's new tactics. But as each such step offered insight, it demanded another step, and another. The information came at a high price.

In Newry, for instance, not long before Fulton's trip to New York, a policewoman named Colleen McMurray and her colleague, Paul Slaine, were driving past the canal that runs through the center of town. Across the water, an IRA man triggered a flash unit, and a hidden rocket—called a "doodlebug"—burst from the grill of a car he had planted. It slammed into McMurray's car, injuring Slaine—he lost both legs in the attack—and killing McMurray on the spot.

As Fulton and I surveyed the bloody plain of his career, he said that McMurray's death was the only one he truly regretted. I asked why, and his hands traced the universal hourglass symbol for "woman." It seemed almost as though he didn't want to say it aloud: he had constructed a moral code as a bomber and spy, some unspoken list of atrocities he refused to commit, and apparently it included killing a woman.

Other people paid a price, too. Consider the case of Eoin Morley, a member of Fulton's bomb squad. After six years as a low-level IRA man, Morley quit and turned away from the IRA. Maybe he did it for the love of his girlfriend, and for her tiny children from a previous relationship. Maybe he did it because of an intra-IRA dispute. Maybe he did it because he already felt old at twenty-two.

That Easter Sunday night, Morley and his girlfriend put the children to bed and then turned their attention to a sink full of dishes. She washed, he dried. Someone knocked at the door. His girlfriend dried her hands, crossed the room, and opened the door. Two armed, masked men burst past her and grabbed Morley. They dragged him out into the garden and forced him to lie down. One of the masked men—Fulton, sources say—raised a high-powered assault rifle and shot Morley twice. The first bullet entered the back of his left thigh. Automatic rifles tend to rise as they're fired; the second bullet thumped into Morley's lower back.

As quickly as they had arrived, the men disappeared.

An ambulance took Morley to the hospital. His mother, Eilish, having gotten word of the incident, arrived soon after. Shootings were a way of life in Northern Ireland, and she expected him to rise from his bed and walk out—just like his relatives, just like his friends, just like Lazarus. But then a nurse burst into the waiting room and said, "Would you come quickly?"

Eilish moved to the door of the surgery theater, but someone stopped her at a red line painted on the floor. She wasn't sterilized and might infect the patient. Her son lay on a table in the center of the room. A doctor approached and said, "We couldn't save him. It's only a matter of minutes." She suspects now that the doctor kept her behind the line not because of infection but to spare her the sight of her son's body laid bare, bristling with instruments, tubes, wires.

Eilish told me this sitting in her living room, and throughout the story she stared at a spot on the floor just in front of her feet. Her voice strained. "I can see it here—a red line," she said. She moved her hand in the air just before her knees, as though tousling a small boy's hair. "I had to stand at that red line, and he died . . . it probably took five minutes, but to me it was five hours . . . I wasn't allowed over the red line."

She sat there for a long time after saying this, tousling an invisible boy's hair and staring at a nonexistent red line. At that moment, both seemed more real than anything else in Northern Ireland.

"I KNOW WHAT YER DONE, BOYO."

In the Belfast safe house, in 1994, Scappaticci continued to grill Fulton. The interrogation centered on something about a van. A phone. An assassination.

Fulton had pieced it together. In addition to his work as a bomber for the IRA, he specialized in procuring supplies: electronics, weapons, vehicles. Sometimes he stole the goods; other times, as in his trip to the States, his British handlers provided them. In 1994, when the IRA's leaders needed a "basher"—a mobile phone with no traceable bill—and a clean van, they turned to Fulton. No problem. Fulton got both from his handlers, who outfitted them with snooping equipment. Not long after, the IRA attempted to kill Derek Martindale, a senior police detective; but armed officers managed to arrest the would-be assassins in their van near Martindale's home. It was Fulton's van. The IRA, suspecting that a snitch had betrayed the mission, launched a massive internal investigation.

Meanwhile, the police arrested anyone who might have been even remotely connected to the case, including Fulton. "Who do you work for?" they demanded. Fulton sat silent.

Eventually the police released him, and right away the IRA ordered him to the Belfast safe house, where Scappaticci interrogated him. A close relative of Fulton's sat in another room, also awaiting time with Scappaticci.

The interrogator prodded Fulton: "What did you tell them?"

"Nothing."

Fulton was telling the truth. He hadn't known anything about the assassination attempt.

Scappaticci didn't believe him. He suspected Fulton of being involved in more than just the Martindale betrayal, in fact.

"You provided both the phone and the vehicle used in the job. Couldn't be a coincidence."

Fulton denied everything, because he had no other choice. To confess anything—anything at all—would mean instant execution.

The denials worked. Scappaticci wasn't sure. He needed more time. So he told Fulton to come back a couple of days later for a second round of interrogation. And to bring his relative.

Right away Fulton called for a meeting with his handlers and delivered what he thought was alarming news: Scappaticci was on to him.

"Oh, we've got the inside track," they told him. "Don't worry about it."

Fulton had no choice but to return with his relative for the second interrogation. Again Scappaticci pressed him hard. Again Fulton kept up his denials. Scappaticci released Fulton again and told him to come back one more time.

As Fulton and his relative drove away, Fulton complained about having to come back for a third interrogation. The relative looked at him blankly. "What third interrogation?" A siren sounded in

Fulton's head. He'd been called back for a third round, alone. Later that day a British handler, but not his own, contacted Fulton secretly to offer a private warning. "Don't go to the last meeting," he said. "You won't go home." Fulton blew out of Belfast and went into hiding.

AFTER SEVERAL MEETINGS on Platform 13, Fulton invited me to his home. It's an expensive flat, with heavy security, overlooking a well-known London landmark.

Inside the apartment, Fulton cooked a steak pie. While it baked, he put out laundry to dry. Then he took the plastic collar off a six-pack of canned beer and used a dainty pair of scissors to snip the rings. It's better, he said, for the "wee fish and creatures of the sea." He heard himself and grinned. "I'd make a fine housewife, wouldna?"

Over dinner he talked about New York, how he'd like to see it again. Outside the window, a construction crew worked near the entrance to the apartments. Fulton told me he won't go out while they're working, for fear one of them might be a boy from back home.

Some things he confesses, some he doesn't. "I can't admit to individual things," he said, for fear of prosecution. "But I won't lie to you." Over the course of our time together, he developed a winking non-denial answer: "No comment."

I asked if he had killed Eoin Morley.

"No comment."

I asked if it was true that he had personally killed eleven people, not mentioning the uncounted bomb victims.

"No comment."

I asked if that bothered him.

"You cannot *pretend* to be a terrorist," he told me. "I had to be able to do the exact same thing as the IRA man next to me. Otherwise I wouldn't be there."

Fulton harbors complex feelings about the British spy services.

His handlers in Northern Ireland abandoned him after his encounter with Scappaticci. His special toll-free number suddenly stopped working and eventually became the hotline for a forklift company. Fulton suspects that once the IRA loosed Scappaticci on him, his handlers decided he would make a good sacrifice: another mark of credibility for their prize agent, Stakeknife. His handlers betrayed him.

"He trusted the people he worked for," Jane Winter told me. She heads a human-rights organization called British Irish Rights Watch, one of the few authorities respected by people on both sides of the continuing conflict. "He believed that he was doing something that—although it was difficult and unpleasant—was necessary and right. And then he found out the people that he trusted were not worthy of his trust. I think that must be very difficult for anybody."

Scappaticci, too, eventually fell. In 2003, Francisco Notarantonio's family instigated a police investigation that soon exposed the existence of the agent Stakeknife. Like Fulton, Scappaticci fled Northern Ireland. Rumors circulated that he had gone to Italy, specifically to a certain Hotel La Pace in Cassino, a hillside town between Naples and Rome. The manager at La Pace told me that yes, he remembered Scappaticci arriving from England, but no, he knew nothing of his next destination. That's where Freddie Scappaticci's trail goes cold.

In Belfast, I met with Scappaticci's attorney, Michael Flanigan. In a neighborhood known as an IRA stronghold, we sipped coffee in a shop that had once been a Presbyterian church. I asked about Scappaticci's career as a spy, and Flanigan shook his head. He has previously called the allegations "misinformation" and told me it was all British propaganda. The British, he said, just wanted to embarrass the IRA by pretending they had penetrated it. When I suggested that the Stakeknife affair might reflect as poorly on the British as on anyone else, he smiled.

A few weeks later, back in the United States, I received a phone call early one morning from a source in the United Kingdom. He said, "Yer man Denis Donaldson"—the legendary IRA hunger-striker who had met with me in his kitchen—"has just been expelled from Sinn Féin, about three minutes ago. For being a British spy."

Donaldson, it turned out, had been spying on the IRA for two decades.

AFTER MY LAST VISIT with Kevin Fulton, we walked through London on a route that took us past Chelsea Barracks, a sprawling compound of bunker-like brick buildings not far from Buckingham Palace. The British army has stationed soldiers there for a century and a half, but the neighborhood has changed around it, and now Londoners consider it an eyesore. The Ministry of Defense plans to move its soldiers to another base and sell Chelsea Barracks for retail development. The site has outlasted its usefulness.

Fulton feels an affinity for the place.

In 1981, early in his stint as a terrorist, the IRA bombed the barracks, killing two people and injuring more than three dozen. As he and I approached the barracks, Fulton pointed out little strips of clear tape stuck to streetlights, electrical boxes, telephone poles—anything with a hinge or slot. Each piece of tape bore a serial number, he told me, and was meant to seal a potential hiding place for a bomb.

As we passed the Chelsea Barracks entry gate, Fulton noticed a sign announcing that this was Open Day, the annual recruitment day. Over the compound's high walls, I could see little boys inside, scurrying up a recreational rock-climbing wall. Fulton's eyes flashed. "You want to go in?" he said. "Let's go in."

We wandered in. Uniformed men and women staffed booths arrayed in the courtyard. As we picked our way through the displays, Fulton began looking for members of his original regiment, the Royal Irish Rangers. "Where're the Royal Irish?" he asked passersby. "Have ye seen the Irish?" I noticed that Fulton wore a tiny green pin on his collar that read ROYAL IRISH RANGERS.

At last we saw a group of men sporting green plumes and tending a booth that featured terrorist bombs. On display were explosive devices from insurgencies around the world: Algeria, Palestine, Iraq. Fulton picked through them with a certain efficiency, looking for something. He grew more agitated by the moment. "Jaysus," he grumbled to himself. "They've got nothing from Northern Ireland here." He was searching, I realized, for his handiwork.

He strode up to a smiling, broad-chested soldier with red hair. "Have ye nothing from Northern Ireland?" he barked. "Nothing? Nothing a-tall, then?"

Fulton's tone, his brogue, and the keenness of his interest focused the soldier, whose smile disappeared. "No, sir," he said. "We haven't." His eyes traveled down and back up Fulton's stocky frame.

Fulton caught himself and stuffed his hands into his pockets, and he turned to walk away. "Well," he said. "If they weren't such fecking terrorists, then maybe they could have a spot, aye?"

MATTHEW TEAGUE *is a native of Vicksburg, Mississippi, and now lives with his wife, Nicole, and two children in Pennsylvania, where he writes on staff at* Philadelphia *magazine. He has also written for* The Atlantic Monthly, National Geographic, GQ, Esquire, Men's Journal, *and other magazines.*

Coda

I researched this story for a long time, skipping between the United States, England, and Northern Ireland. I wrote it, filed it to my editors at *The Atlantic,* and began searching for a new story. But the characters in a nonfiction story continue living, long after that story is done.

This came to me in two reminding jolts. In the first, just as I finished this story's first draft, I received a call from the UK about Denis Donaldson, the IRA leader I met early in the story. He was, it turned out, a British spy: a stunning development because the Donaldson character, so to speak, had suddenly switched roles.

The second jolt came with another call, after the story had appeared on newsstands: Denis Donaldson had been found in a cabin in barren County Donegal. Someone had tortured and killed him, almost entirely severing his right hand from its arm.

In Belfast I had sat with Donaldson and his wife an entire night, at their kitchen table. I had watched him use that hand to smoke Irish cigarettes and eat oranges. Together we had eaten an entire bowl of oranges, and laughed about the leftover pile of seeds. And now someone had killed him.

Now, a year after the story first appeared, I still think about Denis Donaldson. I wish I had lingered with him a moment more, at his table, and maybe shaken his hand one more time. Because the characters in nonfiction stories aren't really characters at all.

They're people.

C. J. Chivers

THE SCHOOL

FROM *Esquire*

SEPTEMBER 1
AFTERNOON. THE GYM.

KAZBEK MISIKOV stared at the bomb hanging above his family. It was a simple device, a plastic bucket packed with explosive paste, nails, and small metal balls. It weighed perhaps eight pounds. The existence of this bomb had become a central focus of his life. If it exploded, Kazbek knew, it would blast shrapnel into the heads of his wife and two sons, and into him as well, killing them all.

Throughout the day he had memorized the bomb, down to the blue electrical wire linking it to the network of explosives the terrorists had strung around them hours before. Now his eyes wandered, panning the crowd of more than eleven hundred hostages who had been seized in the morning outside the school. The majority were children, crouched with their parents and teachers on the basketball court. The temperature had risen with the passing hours, and their impromptu jail had become fetid and stinking with urine and fear. Many children had undressed. Sweat ran down their bare backs.

His eyes settled on his captors. Most of the terrorists had left the gym for defensive positions in the main school building, leaving behind a handful of men in athletic suits or camouflage pants. These were their guards. They wore ammunition vests and slung Kalashnikov rifles. A few were hidden behind ski masks, but as the temperature had risen, most had removed them, revealing faces. They were young. Some had the bearing of experienced fighters. Others seemed like semiliterate thugs, the sort of criminal that had radiated from Chechnya and Russia's North Caucasus during a decade of war. Two were women wearing explosive belts.

Kazbek studied the group, committing to memory their weapons, their behavior, their relations to one another, and the configuration of their bombs. A diagram of their handiwork had formed in his head, an intricate map that existed nowhere else. With it was a mental blueprint of the school, in which he had studied as a boy. This was useful information, if he could share it, and Kazbek thought of fleeing, hoping he might give the Special Forces gathering outside a description of the bombs and defenses. Already Kazbek assumed this siege would end in a fight, and he knew that when Russia's soldiers rushed these rooms, their attack would be overpowering and imprecise. He knew this because he once was a Russian soldier himself.

He evaluated the options. *How does my family get out?* Escape? Passivity? Resistance? His wife, Irina Dzutseva, and their sons, Batraz, fifteen, and Atsamaz, seven, were beside him. Kazbek was a tall man with neat dark hair and a mustache, and Batraz, who was growing tall as well, had the hint of a beard. Kazbek had made him remove his shirt, exposing a boyish frame. He hoped this would convince the terrorists that, unlike his father, Batraz was not a threat, and he would not be rounded up with the men. Kazbek's mind was engaged in this sort of agonizing calculus, trying to determine the best way to save his children from a horror with too many variables and too many unknowns. How best to act? Yes, he had information to share. But even if he escaped, he thought, the terrorists might identify his wife and sons. And then kill them. They had already shot several people, including Ruslan Betrozov, who had done nothing more than speak. No, Kazbek thought, he could not run. He also knew that any uprising by the hostages would have to be swift and complete. There were few terrorists in the gym, but by Kazbek's count at least thirty more roamed the school. How could all of these terrorists be overcome by an unarmed crowd, especially when even before rigging the bombs the terrorists had created an immeasurable psychological advantage? "If any of you resists us," one had warned, "we will kill children and leave the one who resists alive." There would be no resistance. Who, after all, would lead it? Already the adult male captives were dying. Many had been executed. Most of the others were in the main hall, kneeling, hands clasped behind their heads.

Kazbek was lucky. The terrorists had overlooked him during the last roundup. He had been spared execution.

Now his mind worked methodically. He wanted no one to see what he planned to do. Slowly, almost imperceptibly, his hand moved over the floor to the blue wire. Kazbek was forty-three. He had been a Soviet sapper as a younger man. He knew how bombs worked. He also knew how to disable them. The bomb overhead was part of a simple system, an open electric circuit rigged to a motor-vehicle battery. If the terrorists closed the circuit, current would flow from the battery through the wires and detonate the bombs. But if Kazbek pulled apart the wire inside its insulation, no current could flow. Then, he knew, if the circuit snapped closed, the bomb above his family would not explode. Kazbek had spent much of the day folding the wire back and forth, making a crimp. It was only a matter of time.

He lifted the wire. Back and forth he folded the notch, working it, looking directly at the men who would kill him if they knew what he was doing. He would disconnect this bomb. It was a step.

Every step counted. His mind kept working. *How does my family get out?*

9:10 A.M. The Schoolyard.

Morning marked a new school year at School No. 1 in Beslan, beginning with rituals of years past. Returning students, second through twelfth graders, had lined up in a horseshoe formation beside the red brick building. They wore uniforms: girls in dark dresses, boys in dark pants and white shirts. The forecast had predicted hot weather; only the day before, the administration had pushed the schedule an hour earlier, to the relative cool of 9:00 A.M. Students fidgeted with flowers, chocolates, and balloons, waiting for the annual presentation, when first graders would march before their schoolmates for the opening of their academic lives.

Zalina Levina took a seat behind the rostrum and greeted the milling parents. Beslan is an industrial and agricultural town of about thirty-five thousand people on the plain beneath the Caucasus ridge, part of the Russian republic of North Ossetia and one of the few places in the region with a modicum of jobs. For the moment, work seemed forgotten. Parents had come to celebrate. Irina Naldikoyeva sat with her daughter, Alana, four, and glimpsed her son, Kazbek, seven, in the formation with his second-grade class. Aida Archegova had two sons in the assembly. Zalina was baby-sitting her two-and-a-half-year-old granddaughter, Amina. They had not planned on attending, but the child had heard music and seen children streaming toward the school. "Grandma," she had said, "let's go dance." Zalina put on a denim dress and joined the flow. Already it was warm. The first graders were about to step forward. The school year had begun.

The terrorists appeared as if from nowhere. A military truck stopped near the school and men leapt from the cargo bed, firing rifles and shouting, *"Allahu akhbar!"* They moved with speed and certitude, as if every step had been rehearsed. The first few sprinted between the formation and the schoolyard gate, blocking escape. There was almost no resistance. Ruslan Frayev, a local man who had come with several members of his family, drew a pistol and began to fire. He was killed.

The terrorists seemed to be everywhere. Zalina saw a man in a mask sprinting with a rifle. Then another. And a third. Many students in the formation had their backs to the advancing gunmen, but one side did not, and as Zalina sat confused, those students broke and ran. The formation disintegrated. Scores of balloons floated skyward as children released them. A cultivated sense of order became bedlam.

Dzera Kudzayeva, seven, had been selected for a role in which she would be carried on the shoulders of a senior and strike a bell to start the new school year. Her father, Aslan Kudzayev, had hired Karen Mdinaradze, a video cameraman for a nearby soccer team, to record the big day. Dzera wore a blue dress with a white apron and had two white bows in her hair, and was on the senior's shoulders when the terrorists arrived. They were quickly caught.

For many other hostages, recognition came slowly. Aida Archegova thought she was in a counterterrorism drill. Beslan is roughly 950 miles south of Moscow, in a zone destabilized by the Chechen wars. Police actions were part of life. "Is it exercises?" she asked a terrorist as he bounded past.

He stopped. "What are you, a fool?" he said.

The terrorists herded the panicked crowd into a rear courtyard, a place with no outlet. An attached building housed the boiler room, and Zalina ran there with others to hide. The room had no rear exit. They were trapped. The door opened. A man in a tracksuit stood at the entrance. "Get out or I will start shooting," he said.

Zalina did not move. She thought she would beg for mercy. Her granddaughter was with her, and a baby must mean a pass. She froze until only she and Amina remained. The terrorist glared. "You need a special invitation?" he said. "I will shoot you right here."

Speechless with fear, she stepped out, joining a mass of people as obedient as if they had been tamed. The terrorists had forced the crowd against the school's brick wall and were driving it through a door. The people could not file in quickly enough, and the men broke windows and handed children in. Already there seemed to be dozens of the terrorists. They lined the hall, redirecting the people into the gym. "We are from Chechnya," one said. "This is a seizure. We are here to start the withdrawal of troops and the liberation of Chechnya."

As the hostages filed onto the basketball court, more terrorists came in. One fired into the ceiling. "Everybody be silent!" he said. "You have been taken hostage. Calm down. Stop the panic and nobody will be hurt. We are going to issue our demands, and if the demands are implemented, we will let the children out."

Rules were laid down. There would be no talking without permission. All speech would be in Russian, not Ossetian, so the terrorists could understand it, too. The hostages would turn in their cell phones, cameras, and video cameras. Any effort to resist would be met with mass executions, including of women and children.

When the terrorist had finished, Ruslan Betrozov, a father who had brought his two sons to class, stood and translated the instructions into Ossetian. He was a serious man, forty-four years old and with a controlled demeanor. The terrorists let him speak. When he stopped, one approached.

"Are you finished?" he asked. "Have you said everything you want to say?"

Betrozov nodded. The terrorist shot him in the head.

9:20 A.M. THE ADMINISTRATOR'S OFFICE.

IRINA DZUTSEVA, Kazbek Misikov's wife, huddled near the desk, embracing Atsamaz, her first-grade son. Atsamaz was quiet and waiflike but dressed like a gentleman in black suit and white shirt.

Irina could feel his fear. They hid amid papers and textbooks, listening to the long corridor. Doors were being opened, then slammed. They heard gunshots. Atsamaz clung to a balloon. "Where are Papa and Batik?" he asked. "Were they killed?"

The first graders and their parents had been standing at the main entrance and were among the first to see the attack. Irina had turned back into the school and bolted down the corridor as the shooting began, charging down the hall in high heels, pulling her son by his hand. She heard screams and a window shatter. Glass tinkled on the floor. The corridor was long and still; their footfalls echoed as they passed each door, the entrance to the gym, the cafeteria, and the restrooms. At the end of the hall they rushed upstairs to the auditorium and crouched behind the maroon curtain on the stage with other mothers and students. Balloons were taped to the ceiling. Posters decorated the wall. Behind the curtain was a door, and they pushed in and settled into an office packed with books. *Short Stories by Russian Writers. Methods of Teaching. Literature 5.* Irina looked at the others: four adults and six children. They were cut off and could only guess at what was happening outside. They sat in the stillness, waiting to be saved.

After about half an hour, someone pushed against the door. A child called out hopefully: "Are you ours?"

The door swung open. Three terrorists stood before them, beards hanging beneath masks. "God forbid that we are yours," one said, and the group was marched down to the gym with terrorists firing rifles into the ceiling.

In the gym they encountered a scene beyond their imagination. Almost the entire student body had been taken captive, a mass of distraught human life trapped as if it were under a box. Children's cries filled the air. The gym was roughly twenty-eight yards long by fifteen yards wide, and its longer sides each had a bank of four windows, ten feet by ten feet, with panes made from opaque plastic. Light came in as a glow. A wide streak of blood marked the area where Betrozov's corpse had been dragged. Irina hurried with Atsamaz to the far corner and found Batraz, her older son. She understood that their lives would be leveraged in a test of wills against the Kremlin. Hope rested with negotiations, or with Russia's security forces, not known for tactical precision or regard for civilian life. The last time a Chechen group had seized hundreds of hostages, at a theater in Moscow in 2002, Russian commandos attacked with poisonous gas. At least 129 hostages died.

Two young women wearing explosive belts roamed the wooden floor, wraithlike figures dressed in black, their faces hidden by veils. Irina shuddered. Russia has an enduring capacity to produce ghastly social phenomena; these were the latest occurrence of the *shahidka,* female Islamic martyrs who had sown fear during the second Chechen war. The Russian news called them black widows, women driven to militant Islam and vengeance by the loss of Chechnya's young men. The hostages noticed an incongruity: The black veil worn by one *shahidka* framed the neatly sculpted eyebrows of what seemed a teenager who had recently visited a beauty salon.

Two terrorists entered the room with backpacks and began unloading equipment: wire and cable on wooden spools, bombs of different sizes, including several made from plastic soda bottles and two rectangular charges, each the size of a briefcase. With pliers and wire cutters, they set to work, assembling the components into a system. Their plans became clear. Many of the small bombs would be daisy-chained together and hoisted above the crowd, and a line of larger explosives would be set on the floor. The hanging bombs served two purposes: They were a source of mass fear, forcing obedience from the hostages underneath. And elevation ensured that if the bombs were to explode, they would blast shrapnel down from above, allowing for no cover. Virtually everyone would be struck by the nuts, bolts, ball bearings, and nails packed inside. The terrorists assigned the tallest hostages, including Kazbek, who is six foot three, to lift the bombs. The choice of suspension showed malign ingenuity: They strung cables from one basketball hoop to the other, dangling the bombs on hooks. Kazbek realized the terrorists had inside information. Not only had they planned the basketball hoops into their design, but the cables and wires were precut to size, as if they knew the dimensions before they arrived. The bombs were a custom fit.

The weight of the rig at first caused bombs to sag near the children's heads. "Do not touch them," a terrorist warned, and then instructed Kazbek and others to pull the slack out of the system. The network was raised higher, higher, and then nearly taut, until the deadly web was up and out of reach. Kazbek assessed the trap: It was like a string of Christmas lights, except where each bulb would go was a suspended bomb. A terrorist stood on the trigger, and the system was connected to a battery. If the triggerman were to release his foot, Kazbek knew, the circuit would close. Electricity would flow. The bombs would explode.

AFTERNOON. THE MAIN HALL.

ASLAN KUDZAYEV carried a chair through the long blue hall under the watch of his guards. He was hurrying through his tasks. He had been put in a work gang the terrorists formed from adult male hostages and ordered to barricade the classroom windows. The terrorists worried that Russian Special Forces would attack. The hostages proved to be a useful labor pool. Aslan wore white pants, a white shirt, and white shoes. He was thirty-three and lanky, with short brown hair. As he lugged the chair, a terrorist with a bandaged arm pointed a Makarov 9mm pistol in his face. Aslan stopped. "You have short hair," the terrorist said. "You are a cop."

Aslan shook his head. "No," he said. "No."

The terrorist told him to empty his pockets, and Aslan showed him a wallet, money, and keys. He owned a building-supply store. Nothing about him said cop. The terrorist signaled him to return to work.

Once the windows were blocked, the men were ordered to sit in the hall, hands behind their heads. By now the terrorists were emerging as individuals; the hostages were forming a sense of their captors. There were the leaders and the led, and the led were organized into teams. Some specialized in explosives. Others were jailers, controlling the hostages in the gym. The largest group was in the main building: a platoon preparing to fight off a Russian assault. They had come with packs of food, coffee, and candy, as well as sleeping bags, gas masks, and first-aid kits. Each had a rifle and wore a vest bulging with ammunition. Some had hand grenades. A few had 40mm grenade launchers mounted under their rifle barrels.

Aslan began to understand their command structure. All of them deferred to a light-footed and muscular man with a bushy reddish beard whom they called the Colonel. He paced the corridor with a cocky strut, his shaved head topped with a black skullcap, exuding the dark charisma of the captain of a pirate sloop. He was charged with energy and power and seemed fired with glee. Beneath him were midlevel commanders, including a Slav who used the name Abdullah and had pointed the pistol at Aslan's face. Aslan grudgingly marveled at their discipline and skill. They had taken the school, laced it with bombs, and made it a bunker in half a day. *Say what you want about these bastards, but they are not stupid,* he thought. *They know what to do.*

He and two other hostages were ordered to their feet and taken down the hall to the library, where they were given axes and picks and told to tear up the floorboards. Aslan wondered whether the terrorists had a cache of weapons under the planks, but he could see nothing in the hole he made and was led back to sit. Captive in the corridor, growing tired and cramped, Aslan realized he had come to the end of his life. He fell to reverie. Slowly he reviewed the things that made him what he had been: his marriage, the birth of his two daughters, the success of his business. He felt regret that he had not yet had a son. An Ossetian was supposed to have a son.

Now and then he was startled by nearby rifle fire, but he could not tell where it came from. He returned to daydreaming. He thought: *What will they say at my funeral?*

EARLY AFTERNOON. THE GYM.

THE TERRORIST WAS sick of Larisa Kudziyeva. She had been shouting, even after they had ordered everyone to be quiet. She was lean and beautiful in a quintessentially Caucasus way, with fine skin and dark hair and brown eyes, a look intensified by her black blouse and skirt. She did not look her thirty-eight years. The terrorist was one of the young men guarding the hostages. He wore his mask. He walked toward her to quiet her, for good.

Larisa had spent the first hours of captivity tending to Vadim Bolloyev, a father who had been shot near the right shoulder. He lay on the basketball court silently, holding in his pain. His white shirt was soaked red. He was growing weak. "Why did they shoot you?" she had asked him.

"I refused to kneel," he said.

Larisa urged him to lie back and placed her purse under his head. She inspected his wound. The bone had been shattered. Blood flowed freely. She tried using a belt as a tourniquet but could not position it. Sweat beaded his forehead. His son, Sarmat, six, sat beside him in a white shirt and black vest, watching his father slip away.

Larisa had not wanted to come to school that day. Her six-year-old son, Zaurbek, was starting first grade, but she had asked Madina, her nineteen-year-old daughter, to bring him. Her husband had died of stomach cancer in April. She was in mourning and felt no urge to celebrate. But after they left, Larisa looked outside at the crowds moving to the school. *Go with them,* a voice told her, and she rushed to her balcony. "Wait for me!" she called down.

Now she leaned over a bleeding man, struggling to save him.

Her daughter was enrolled at a medical academy. "You are a future doctor," Larisa whispered. "What do I do?"

"There is no way to save him," Madina said. "His artery is damaged. He needs an operation."

Larisa felt fury. She would not let him die. She shouted at a terrorist across the room. "We need water and bandages!" she said. No one answered. She shouted again. She was breaking rules. The terrorist approached. "Why are you yelling?" he said.

"I need bandages," she said.

"Are you the bravest person here, or the smartest?" he said. "We will check." His voice turned sharp: "Stand up!"

Bolloyev grabbed her shirt. "Do not go," he said. Larisa slipped free and stood, and the terrorist shoved her with his rifle toward a corner where confiscated cameras and phones had been piled and smashed.

"What are you doing?" she demanded.

He ordered her to kneel. "No," she said.

For this Bolloyev had been shot. "I told you," he said. "Get on your knees."

"No," she said.

For a moment they faced each other, the terrorist and the mother, locked in mental battle. She looked into his mask; freckles were visible near his eyes. A hush fell over the gym. The hostages had seen Betrozov's murder. Now came Larisa's turn. The terrorist raised his Kalashnikov, past her chest, past her face, stopping at her forehead. He pressed the muzzle against her brow. Larisa felt the circle of steel on her skin.

Bolloyev propped himself on an elbow. Larisa's children looked on. She reached up, grasped the barrel, and moved it away. "What kind of spectacle are you playing here, and in front of whom?" she snapped. "There are women and children here who are already scared."

The terrorist paused. Thinking quickly, she tried to convince him that Ossetians were not enemies of Chechens, a difficult task, given that enmity between Ossetians, a Christian people with a history of fidelity to Moscow, and the Islamic Chechens and Ingush, who have long been persecuted, is deep. "Your children rest in our sanatoriums," she said. "Your women give birth here."

"Not our wives and children," the terrorist said. "They are the spawn of Kadyrov."

The word stung. *Kadyrov*—the surname of former rebels who aligned with Russia and became the Kremlin's proxies. The separatists despised them with a loathing reserved for traitors. Larisa was stumped. Abdullah had been rushing across the gym; he stepped beside them. "What is happening here?" he said.

"This guy wants to execute me because I asked for water and bandages for the wounded," she said. Abdullah studied the two: his young gunman, the woman who stared him down.

"There is nothing for you here," he said. "Go back and sit down and shut up."

She pointed to his bloodied arm. "Your arm is bandaged," she said. "Give me some of those bandages."

"You did not understand me?" he said. "There is nothing for you here. Go back and sit down and shut up."

Larisa returned to her place. Her children stared at her. Bolloyev lay back down. His lips were violet, his forehead coated in sweat. His death could not be far away. She was enraged.

AFTERNOON. THE GYM.

ZALINA LEVINA could not console her granddaughter, Amina, and did not know what to do. She had stripped the pink skirt and red shirt from the toddler's sweaty skin. It was not enough. Amina cried on, filling Zalina with dread. The terrorists had grown more irritable, and their threats were multiplying. "Shut your bastards up or I will calm them down fast," one had said. Zalina worried the child would be shot.

Zalina knew Chechnya firsthand, having lived in Grozny, its capital, before the Soviet Union collapsed. She remembered its mountain vistas and orderly atmosphere. The city had industry, a university, an oil institute, a circus, a soccer stadium, and rows of apartment buildings on tree-lined streets. She also remembered its brutality. Nationalism had sprouted anew as Moscow's grip weakened. Old animosities reemerged. In the early 1990s, before the first Chechen war, a group of Chechen men had stolen her brother-in-law's car. "We give you a month to leave," one had said, "or we will return and burn down your house." The family fled to Beslan, sixty-five miles away, across what would become a military front. Zalina thought she had escaped the war.

Now Amina kept crying and Zalina's anxiety grew. There seemed no reason for hope. The terrorists were demanding a withdrawal of federal troops from Chechnya, and if the hostages knew anything about Vladimir Putin, Russia's president, they knew he was unlikely to do this. Putin's success rested in part on his reputation for toughness. He was not one to grant concessions, certainly not to separatists, for whom his disdain was well-known.

As they waited, the hostages were miserable in the heat. The gym was too crowded to allow for much movement, which forced them to take turns extending their legs. Others leaned back-to-back. The terrorists gave little relief. Sometimes they made everyone display their hands on their heads, fingers upright, like rabbit ears. Other times, when the gym became noisy with crying children, they selected a hostage to stand, then warned everyone: Shut up or he will be shot. But silence, like a federal withdrawal, was an almost impossible demand. Children can stay quiet for only so long.

Amina cried and cried. *I have to save this child,* Zalina thought. She opened her dress and placed a nipple under Amina's nose. Zalina was forty-one years old and not the toddler's mother. But she thought that maybe Amina was young enough, and a warm nipple familiar enough, that any nipple, even her dry nipple, would provide comfort. Naked and sweaty, Amina took the breast. She began to suck. Her breathing slowed. Her body relaxed. She fell asleep. *Be still,* Zalina thought. *Be still.*

AFTERNOON. THE GYM.

LARISA KUDZIYEVA'S defiance made her known to her captors, and in the hours after she was nearly shot, she noticed a terrorist staring at her. He was not wearing a mask and often turned his eyes toward her. He was just less than six feet tall, thick-armed and meticulous, possessing a seriousness the other terrorists seemed to respect. His camouflage pants were pressed. His black boots were laced tight. He had a freshly trimmed beard and eyes that lacked some of the bloodlust evident in the others. Larisa thought he must be in his early thirties, old enough to have waged guerrilla war for ten years. He was a negotiator and spent much of the time talking on a mobile phone with Russians outside. Between calls his eyes settled on Larisa.

Her anger had not subsided. She had kept working on Bolloyev, pressing rags to his wound. Each came away soaked. The blood grew sticky and spoiled in the heat; Larisa never knew a man's blood could smell so bad, like a butcher's drain. She shouted for aid again, for water, for bandages, but no one listened. As he was dying, Bolloyev asked for his daughters, who were also in the gym, and Larisa called to them. The terrorists punished her by posting a *shahidka* beside her with a pistol and instructions to shoot if she made another noise. Bolloyev weakened further and asked his son, Sarmat, to recite his address and names of relatives, as if he knew he would die and wanted the boy to rehearse his lines to rescuers, should they find him alone.

As Bolloyev faded, pallid and shivering, Abdullah ordered him dragged away. "Where are you taking him?" Larisa demanded.

"To the hospital," he said.

She knew it was not true, and fumed. Later, as the temperature soared, she took a group of children to the bathroom. Returning, she sat beside the one who stared. There was a connection here. She intended to use it.

"You are probably the only person who can tell us something about our fate," she said.

He looked at her, up close for the first time. She had washed away Bolloyev's blood. "You will stay here until the last federal troops leave Chechnya," he said.

"That is not a one-day matter," she said.

"Once negotiations start, you will have everything," he said. "Food. Water. Everything."

He sat with his rifle and phone, an underground fighter who had stepped into view. Men like this lived in Russia's shadows, biding time, praying, emerging on occasion to kill. Once a constant presence on television, they had disappeared into their insurgency. Now the hostages' lives were under his control. "What is your name?" she asked.

"Ali," he said. It was not a name common to the mountains.

"Is that a name or a nickname?"

"I see you are a wise woman," he said.

"Answer the question," she said. "A man should have a name. This is what differentiates him from an animal."

"It is a nickname," he said. "Now I am Ali. In the previous time, I was Baisangur."

"And your real name?" she said.

"I no longer need it," he said. "There is not a person left alive who can call me by my name."

Baisangur—a legendary Chechen warrior who had fought Russia in the nineteenth century, part of a generation revered in separatist lore. The most famous of these fighters had been Imam Shamil, whose name passed through generations to Shamil Basayev, the one-footed separatist commander whose wisecracking practice of terrorism made him Russia's most wanted man. Basayev planned hostage seizures and recruited *shahidkas;* the terrorists in this gym prepared under his command. Baisangur's martial pedigree was more pure. The original Shamil had been captured and accepted a pardon from the czar. Baisangur fought to his death.

Yes, once he had been Baisangur, and before that he used his real name. But years ago, Ali said, as Russia was trying to quell their rebellion, a warplane took off from this area and dropped bombs on a Chechen village. There were no men where the bombs landed. But the village was not empty. It was crowded with families. Those bombs, he said, exploded among his wife and five children. Everyone who loved him was dead. He looked at Larisa, the incandescent one. "My wife looked just like you," he said. "Even twins do not look so alike."

Larisa needed information; she pushed. "What is the name of your village?" she asked.

"You do not need to know it," he said. "You do not know what is happening in Chechnya."

AUGUST 30
SHORTLY AFTER DAWN. CHECHNYA.

THE ROAD TO GROZNY runs southward across a plain toward the sparkling and snowcapped Caucasus ridge, a setting so empyreal that had history been different it might be a land of fable. As the road continues on, crossing the swirling Terek River, bunkers and checkpoints appear, first occasionally and then frequently, from which sunburned Slavic soldiers look wearily out. Chechnya is a dot on Russia's vastness, an internal republic the size of Connecticut. But the Kremlin covets and fears it, and has flowed soldiers and police over its borders, ringing it with layers of security and denying most access to outsiders. It is a war zone and a region whose recent inner workings are largely unknown.

Short of the capital, the terrain becomes steep and scarred with artillery trenches, from which Russian batteries long ago fired their barrages. The city beyond these hills is a ruin, a warren of rubble and shattered buildings in which many of the remaining inhabitants camp in the wreckage of their homes. In the annals of recent conflict, few places have seen such a multiplicity of horrors and then fallen so swiftly from the public discourse. After Chechnya declared independence in 1991, prompting Russia to invade three years later, the Chechens became a source of fascination in the West. They were tribesmen who merged mountain traditions with modern life, an Islamic people speaking their own language, bound by ancient codes of honor and hospitality, and seeking independence as they fought armored columns in front of their homes. Their symbol was the wolf, but they were underdogs, local people who seemed to win skirmishes against a world power with little more than rifles and the force of will.

No matter those moments of military success, the Chechens' separatist urges have led nearly to their destruction. Russia and the rebels signed a cease-fire in 1996, and the Russian military withdrew, leaving behind a rebel-led government. Chechen independence and self-governance had been born. The result was disastrous. The young government, which inherited formidable problems and had little aid or revenue, was largely abandoned by the Kremlin, which seemed eager for it to fail. Inexperienced and prone to internal quarrels, it proved barely capable of governing and flashed an affinity for ancient notions of Islamic law, going so far as to show public executions on TV. Crime soared, corruption was unchecked, and ransom kidnappings became common enough to have the feel of an approved line of work.

Whatever the merits of the conventional portrait of the Chechen rebel, war and rackets warped many of them out of popular form, leading them to lives of thuggery and organized crime. Chechnya's people waited for autonomy to improve their lot. But nationalism led to warlordism, and warlordism to more sinister associations. Some prominent commanders, including Shamil Basayev, allied themselves with international Islamic movements that had taken root in Pakistan and Afghanistan, steering the republic deeper into isolation and attracting foreign jihadis to the slopes of the Caucasus. With Basayev's blessing, a dark-maned Arab field commander who used the name Ibn al-Khattab and had fought in Afghanistan and Tajikistan opened training camps in the mountains. Recruits arrived from Chechnya and elsewhere in the Caucasus, especially from nearby Ingushetia, and from Turkey, Central Asia, and Arabia. They studied weapons, tactics, and the manufacture of bombs. Under the sway of fighters, autonomous Chechnya was recognized by only one foreign government: Afghanistan's Taliban.

Spurred by Prime Minister Putin, who was soon to become president, Russia sent its armor back to Chechnya in 1999. This time Russia fought unsparingly. With little regard for life or property, its military surrounded Grozny and pounded the capital with rockets, artillery, and aircraft, collapsing the city around the rebels. Sweeps and barrages destroyed villages and towns. The destruction was of an order not seen since World War II; Grozny's sagging hulks invited comparisons to Warsaw, 1944. The city fell early in 2000, and Putin, by then president, declared the battle ended. A new policy took shape. Russia would garrison troops and equipment and provide money, instructions, and political support. But local administration was to be handed over to Chechens deemed sufficiently loyal, a formula flowing from the institutional memory of a weakened empire. The appointment of proxies was accompanied by a message that became more hollow the more it was repeated on state TV: *There is no war. We have won.*

No verified casualty counts exist for the wars, but all agree the human toll has been vast, ranging from tens of thousands of Chechens killed to more than two hundred thousand. Setting aside the numbers, the years of violence and atrocities made clear that as public policy, little could be less wise than extensive killing in Chechnya, where tradition asks blood to be washed in blood. Chechens are bound by *adat,* an oral code that compels families to avenge the killing of their relatives. By the time President Putin claimed victory, enough blood had been spilled for a fury lasting generations. It mixed not just tribal urges for revenge and independence but racism and militant Islam.

The war that did not exist continued. Unable to defend Grozny conventionally, the rebels formed guerrilla bands, hiding amid the local populace and in nearby Russian republics and traveling between Azerbaijan, Georgia, and Turkey, where the Chechen diaspora is large. Islamic unrest expanded through Russia's territory in the Caucasus, and underground *jamaats* with connections to the Chechens formed in at least six of the region's internal republics. A rhythm emerged. Almost daily the separatists or their allies would stage small attacks or plant mines, and occasionally they would mass for large raids. In response to a spreading insurgency, the Russians set out to annihilate it, raiding homes in search of young men and generating complaints of rape, torture, robbery, and abduction. Macabre profiteering took hold, including sales of corpses back to families for burial.

Terrorism had been part of the separatists' struggle since before the first war. Basayev's debut was as an airplane hijacker in 1991; mass hostage-taking began in 1995. But as death tolls rose and separatists were driven further underground, more turned to terrorism, then suicide terrorism. The rebels destroyed Chechnya's seat of government with a truck bomb in 2002 and assassinated the Kremlin-backed president in 2004. At the center was Basayev, sardonic and lame. His terrorist group, the Riyadus-Salakhin Reconnaissance and Sabotage Battalion of Chechen Martyrs, included ethnic fighters from the Caucasus and foreigners, including Arabs and a few Europeans.

A nationalist turned nihilist, Basayev made clear he thought Russian civilians were fair targets. After scores of hostages died at the theater in Moscow, he suggested Russia suffered what it deserved. "It turned out that these were innocent civilians who had gone to the theater for recreation," he wrote. "In this regard, you have to ask yourself: Who are the more than three thousand children aged under ten who died during the three years of the brutal and bloody war in Chechnya? Who are the more than four thousand children who lost their legs, arms, eyes, who ended up paralyzed? Who are the thirty-five hundred missing people who have been abducted from their homes or detained in the streets by the Russian occupiers and whose fate remains a mystery? Who are the two hundred thousand slain women, elderly, ill, children, and men? Who are they?"

Blood meets blood. Such were the rules in Basayev's war. And this time he was not sending terrorists to a theater. He had ordered them to a school.

EVENING. THE EXECUTION ROOM.

SOMETIME AFTER 5:00 P.M., while sitting in the hall with other male hostages, Aslan Kudzayev overheard the terrorists listening to the news on a radio. The announcer was discussing the siege, and Aslan understood that the world knew the students of Beslan were hostages. It was his first taste of the outside world since the siege had enveloped them, and it gave him a vague sense that they would be helped.

A few minutes later the Colonel appeared and ordered him and Albert Sidakov, another hostage, down the hall. Their walk ended in a literature classroom on the second floor, where eight dead men, broken by bullets, lay in a pool of blood. A portrait of Vladimir Mayakovsky, the revolutionary poet, hung on the far wall, which had been chipped by bullet impacts. Aslan understood. Throughout the day, men had been led off in small groups. Those who had not returned had been taken here and shot. As he and the others had sat downstairs, fingers interlocked behind their necks, the terrorists had realized the job of fortifying the school was done. Male hostages had become expendable. They were being culled.

"Open the window and throw these corpses out," the Colonel said.

Aslan and Albert lifted the first body to the sill and shoved it out. They moved to the next. So this is how Aslan would spend the last minutes of his life: When the eighth body was pushed onto the grass, he knew, he and Albert would be shot. Time was short. He glanced around the room. The Colonel was gone. A lone terrorist guarded them. Aslan assumed the terrorists would not throw out the bodies themselves, for fear of snipers. He and Albert were valuable for a few minutes more. They pushed out two more of the bullet-riddled men, including one who seemed to still be alive. Aslan leaned and pretended to retch.

The terrorist had removed the magazine from his Kalashnikov and was reloading it, round by round. "Let's jump out the window," Aslan whispered to Albert.

Albert was silent. "Let's jump," he whispered again.

"How?" Albert said, looking overwhelmed.

Aslan realized that if he was going to leap, he was going to leap alone. Their guard's rifle was unloaded. This was it. He bent to another corpse, then rushed toward the bloody sill. He hit in a push-up position and propelled himself out. The drop was eighteen feet, and he descended and slammed onto the bodies in a crouch. A bone in his foot popped. He rolled toward the school wall, reducing the angle the terrorist would have to fire at him, and began crawling away from the window. He worried the terrorist would drop a grenade. Gunfire sounded.

The terrorist's mask appeared in the window. The wall was nearly two feet thick, making it difficult for him to fire near the foundation without leaning far. He opted to try. His barrel blasted. Bullets thudded near Aslan. Bits of soil and grass jumped beside him. He scurried to the building's corner. Before him was a parking lot. He crawled on, putting cars between him and the window. The terrorist did not know where he was and fired into several cars, searching.

Aslan heard shouts. At the edge of nearby buildings, local men with the police and soldiers waved him to safety. He was so close, but an instant from death. The police had been told that if they harmed a terrorist, hostages would be executed in return. They held their fire. More bullets struck cars. A soldier threw a smoke grenade, hoping to obscure the terrorist's line of sight. It sent up a plume, which drifted the wrong way. Someone threw another, and a third, and a cloud rose between Aslan and his tormentor. He crawled with all of his speed and reached a railroad ditch in front of the school. He rolled in and lay still on the dirt. His white outfit was covered with grass stains and blood. Aslan was out. His wife, two daughters, and mother-in-law were still inside.

EVENING. THE MAIN HALL AND EXECUTION ROOM.

KAREN MDINARADZE was not supposed to be here. He kneeled in the hall, his nose near the plaster, hands behind his head. Male hostages were lined up the same way to his right. To his left was a thin older man. Beyond him stood a *shahidka,* keeping watch.

Karen's luck was worse than bad. He was not a resident of Beslan. He was a videographer, hired to videotape Aslan's daughter Dzera during her role as bell ringer. He had not wanted the job, but Aslan persisted, and finally Karen gave in. He had been framing the girl in his viewfinder when the terrorists arrived. So far he was untouched, but he suffered a banal affliction. Karen was highly allergic to pollen, and many children had come to school with flowers and had carried them to the gym when they were captured, surrounding him with irritants. His eyes had reddened. His breathing was short. He felt luck running down. At about 3:00 P.M. a terrorist ordered him to the hall. Although he looked strong—he was built like a wrestler—his allergies drained him. Fatigue settled over him with the arrival of dusk.

The woman near him exploded.

There had been no warning. One second she was standing there, a veiled woman in black. The next she was not, having been torn apart in a roaring flash. The explosives cut her to pieces, throwing her head and legs into the geography classroom. Much of her flesh splashed along the walls. Shrapnel and heat shot out from the belt, striking the men in the corridor as well as another terrorist who guarded them, who was knocked to the floor. The other *shahidka* was also pierced with shrapnel. She fell, blood running from her nose. Karen felt heat and debris smack his left side. His left eye went dim. But the older man between him and the *shahidka* had absorbed much of the shrapnel, creating a shadow in which Karen was spared the worst. He was briefly unconscious, but came to, slumped forward against the wall. He thought he was dying and traced his palms along his face and head. His eyelid was torn, and he had shrapnel in his face and left calf. Heat had seared his salt-and-pepper hair, making it feel like brittle wire. Someone handed him a handkerchief and he wiped his face, pulling out plaster. "If I die, tell my mother and wife I love them very much," he told the man.

He surveyed the gruesome space. The thin man beside him, who had shielded him, breathed fitfully. His hips and legs faced the wrong direction, as if his lower spine had spun around. Karen knew he was in the last minutes of life. The injured terrorist had been set on a door removed from its hinges, and Abdullah knelt beside him, reading in Arabic in the lilting rhythm of prayer. Someone produced a syringe. The terrorist was given an injection, became still, and was carried away. After a few minutes a terrorist addressed the wounded. "Go to the second floor and we will provide you medical assistance," he said.

Karen stood with those who were able and limped upstairs to the Russian-literature classroom, and saw dead hostages piled on the floor. The injured men were given an order: "Lie down."

Their lives ended in an instant. A masked terrorist stepped forward, shouted, *"Allahu akhbar!"* and fired bursts from fifteen feet away, sweeping his barrel back and forth. The air filled with their cries and the thwacks of bullets hitting heavy flesh. The men rolled and thrashed. Errant bullets pounded the wall. At last the hostages were motionless, and the terrorist released the trigger. He pulled a chair to the door and straddled it with the hot barrel resting in front of him. He was listening. A moan rose from the pile. He fired again.

He remained for a few minutes, watching, listening. The room fell still. The night was warm. He rose and walked away.

NIGHT. THE PALACE OF CULTURE.

OUTSIDE THE SCHOOL, Russia's local and federal authorities struggled to react to the hostage crisis, whose scale and ferocity had overwhelmed them.

Although the main Beslan police station was practically next to the school, its officers had not mustered a coordinated effort to aid the women and children. Federal soldiers from the 58th Army in Vladikavkaz, North Ossetia's capital, had flowed into Beslan during the day, joined by commandos from the former KGB, members of the famed units known as Alpha and Vympel. But so far the most anyone had done was form a disorganized perimeter, a cordon with uncertain orders and under uncertain command. The tactical leaders on the ground, in fact, seemed so unschooled in tactics that their cordon's outer limit was within range of the terrorists' small-arms fire, and families of the missing, who roamed the edges, were occasionally exposed to the 40mm grenades the terrorists fired out. A sense of logistics escaped these officials as well. No fire-fighting equipment was staged. There were few ambulances. Many of the soldiers were lightly equipped, without the helmets or body armor they would need in a close-quarters fight.

Just beyond the window from which Aslan Kudzayev had leapt,

within earshot of the executions, a vigil had formed. Relatives massed at the Palace of Culture, a grandly named Soviet movie house, consoling one another and worrying over the possibility of a Russian assault. They were a living picture of fear. Some were numb. Some were despondent. Hundreds paced. Many displayed the deflated calm of the helpless, people whose families were at stake but who had no influence over what came next. Now and then gunfire would sound. There would be a collective flinch. A few women would wail. Every few hours, Russian and local officials would leave the administration building, walk past the statue of Lenin, and brief the families in the palace. Each time they assured them they were doing all they could. And each time they said the terrorists had seized roughly 300 hostages, which was a lie.

NIGHT. THE EXECUTION ROOM.

KAREN MDINARADZE lay in the spreading pool of blood. It was dark. The room was quiet. The terrorist had fired without taking precise aim, relying on the automatic rifle to cut through the pile of men, and had missed one man. As bullets killed everyone around Karen, he fell behind a man who must have weighed 285 pounds. This man had been struck. Karen was not. He survived his own execution. After his executioner walked away, he lost sense of time. He saw the chair in the doorway and the open window and wanted to leap out. But he heard footsteps and was afraid.

In time the terrorist returned with two more hostages and ordered them to dump the bodies. Corpse by corpse they lifted the dead to the sill and shoved them out. The pile grew on the grass below. Three corpses remained when they came to Karen. He did not know what to do. He assumed the two men would be shot when their task was done and assumed he would be shot if he was discovered alive. But he knew he could not be thrown out the window; the drop was eighteen feet. The men bent to lift him. He felt a pair of hands clasp behind his neck and hands tighten on his ankles. He rolled forward and stood.

The men gasped. Karen rocked on his feet.

The terrorist told Karen to come near and stared at him, eyes moving under his mask as he surveyed his intact frame. "You walk under Allah," he said.

"Now throw out the rest of the corpses and I will tell you what to do next."

Two bodies remained, including that of the heavy man behind whom Karen had fallen. He lifted him by the belt as the other two took the legs and head and pushed him out. Another terrorist appeared, and the two captors pointed excitedly; Karen realized they had decided not to kill him. The three hostages were ordered downstairs to wash, then led to the gym.

Karen sat. His head was cut and bruised, his left eye blinded, his clothes drenched in blood. A woman near him whispered—"Did they hit you with a rifle butt?"—and he passed out.

SEPTEMBER 2
BEFORE DAWN. THE BATHROOM.

ZALINA LEVINA rose at midnight. Rain was falling. Many of the children slept. The terrorists had not granted bathroom privileges for hours, but now the gym was quieter, and she wanted to try again. The bathroom was not lined with bombs; she thought she might hide with her granddaughter there. None of the terrorists stopped her, and she carried Amina into the room and sat. Her neighbor Fatima Tskayeva was already there, cradling her baby, Alyona, as rain pattered outside.

Whispering in the darkness, Fatima told of signs of dissent in the terrorists' ranks. The *shahidkas,* she said, seemed to have been deceived, as if they had not known they would be targeting children. One of them had used the bathroom in the evening, and was menstruating and upset. Now, Fatima said, the *shahidkas* were dead, killed in an explosion hours before. Fatima also said that some of their captors were capable of compassion. Her other daughter, Kristina, ten, whose heart was weak, had fainted earlier. Abdullah had picked up the girl and given her a tablet of validol, an herbal medicine for tension and heart pain. None of this made sense to Zalina, and she wondered about her own daughter. What would she think of Zalina bringing Amina to the school? Amina was not a student. There was no reason for her to be here. *I have to save this child,* she thought.

Under a desk stacked in the barricade she saw a lump of dried chewing gum. Zalina peeled it free, rolled it into a ball, and put it in her mouth. Slowly she worked it between her teeth, softening it with saliva. A faint taste of sugar spread on her tongue. It was food. She kept pressing and rolling it between her teeth, restoring it to something like what it had been. The gum absorbed more saliva and softened. It was ready. She plucked it from her lips and fed it to the toddler in her arms.

Morning. The Gym.

The Colonel stormed onto the court. Negotiations, he said, were failing. Russia was not responding, and was lying, saying only 354 hostages were in this room. "Your president is a coward," he snarled. "He does not answer the phone."

For these reasons, he said, he had announced a strike. There would be no more water and no food for the hostages. Bathroom privileges had ceased. The terrorists had told Russia's negotiators, he said, that in solidarity with their cause the hostages had agreed to these terms.

LATE MORNING. THE GYM.

ABDULLAH PULLED ASIDE Larisa Kudziyeva, the commanding presence in a gym full of fear. He wanted to know who she was. A Chechen, or perhaps a member of another of the Islamic mountain people in the Caucasus?

"Do you have your passport with you?" he asked.

"Why should I bring my passport to a school?" she said.

"Are you Ingush?" he asked.

"No," she said.

"What is your last name?"

"Kudziyeva."

He studied her black clothes. "Why are you dressed like that?" he asked.

"It is how I choose," she said. Her defiance was almost reflexive.

Abdullah proceeded with his offer. The *shahidkas* were dead, but an explosive belt remained. This hostage, who could look into her executioner's barrel without flinching, was a candidate to wear it.

"We will release your children, and if you have relatives, we will release them, too," he said. "But for this you will have to put on a suicide belt and a veil and become one of our suicide bombers."

Larisa wondered about the *shahidkas*. "Where are yours?" she asked.

"Yesterday your soldiers tried to storm the building and they died," he said. It was a lie.

"I am afraid I may spoil everything—I am not a Muslim," she said. "How much time do I have to decide?"

"You have time," he said. "Sit down and think."

She returned to her children. The women nearby were curious. The temperature had risen again. The crowd was weak. "What did he want?" a woman asked. Larisa told them. "Do it," the woman said. "Maybe they will let us go."

AFTERNOON. THE GYM.

KAZBEK MISIKOV FELT the wire separate between his fingers. His task was done: Inside its insulation, the wire had broken. But chance contact, he knew, might still allow a spark to jump across, and he needed to be sure the two ends could not meet incidentally. This required a finishing touch, and Kazbek grasped the blue plastic on either side of the crimp and stretched it like licorice, putting distance between the severed ends inside.

Now a new problem presented itself. Stretching the plastic had turned it a whitish blue. The defect was obvious. The terrorists had inspected the wires and bombs several times, and if they checked again, they would discover his subterfuge.

He felt a surge of worry. He and his wife had made it this far and had agreed on a plan: If the Russians attacked, Irina would help Batraz, their older son, and Kazbek would help Atsamaz, their first grader. Atsamaz was exhausted and dehydrated. Kazbek often looked into his eyes, and at times they seemed switched off. But he had found a way to keep him going. Other adults had whispered that it was possible to drink small amounts of urine. Kazbek had collected their pee. "I want a Coke," Atsamaz had said when told to drink it.

"After we leave, I will buy you a case of Coke," Kazbek said. The boy drank.

Now Kazbek had put them in fresh danger and would have to take another risk. When a terrorist strolled past him, he addressed him politely. "This wire lies across the passage," he said. "They are tripping on it. Neither you nor we need these to explode."

"What can be done?" the terrorist said.

"If we had a nail, the wire could be hung," Kazbek said.

The terrorist returned with a hammer and spike. Kazbek stood and drove the spike into the wall. He lifted the wire from the floor and laid a few turns around the shank, taking care to wrap with the whitish-blue section. He put a wooden spool on the spike and pressed it tight. The severed portion of wire was hidden. Kazbek had succeeded. He sat back with his family beneath the disconnected bomb.

AFTERNOON. THE BATHROOM.

ZALINA LEVINA AND Fatima Tskayeva hid in the bathroom with their small children. Hours passed; more breast-feeding mothers with babies pushed in, seeking relief from the heat. The place became a nursery.

Abdullah passed by and taunted them. "Maybe we have something to tell you," he said. Fatima begged for information. He laughed. Two hours later he offered a hint. "If they let him come in, maybe we will let the breast-fed children out," he said.

Zalina's mind whirled. *Who was coming?*

At about 3:00 P.M., a new man passed the door. He was tall and well built, with a thick mustache and graying hair. He wore a clean gray sport coat. They recognized him at once: Ruslan Aushev, the former president of Ingushetia, a republic bordering Chechnya, and a decorated Soviet veteran from Afghanistan. Aushev commanded respect among both his people and Chechnya's separatists. But he had been ousted by Putin, replaced by a loyalist from the KGB. Aushev's career stalled. In the nursery, he was the most important man in the world.

Zalina felt hope. *Aushev!* she thought. *We will be let go!* Applause sounded in the gym. Aushev stopped before them. A terrorist pointed in. "Here are the women with breast-fed children," he said.

"Do you know who I am?" Aushev asked.

"Of course," a mother said. He turned and left. The women rose, holding their babies, shaking with anticipation. They had been captives for more than thirty hours, without food, with little water, and with no sleep. There had been shooting and explosions. Their babies could take no more. Soon they might start to die. Abdullah stood at the door. "We will release you," he said. "But if you point out our photographs to the police, we will know immediately, and we will kill fifty hostages. It will be on your conscience."

"Now," he said, "one breast-fed child with one woman." He motioned for them to go.

Fatima was near the door. She did not move. "Let me take all of my children," she pleaded, reminding Abdullah of her two others, including Kristina, with the weak heart. "You helped her yourself," she said. "Let us all go."

"No," he said.

"Let my children out. I will stay."

"No."

Fatima sobbed now. "Then let Kristina leave with my baby," she begged.

Abdullah's anger flashed. "I told you, bitch, no," he said. "Now I am not releasing anyone because of you."

He looked at the other women. "Everyone back to the gym," he said. Panic flowed through Zalina. Sweeping up her granddaughter, she stepped past Abdullah. Rather than turning left for the gym, she turned right, toward the main school. She had decided. *I am leaving,* she thought. *Let them shoot me in the back.*

Another terrorist blocked her. "Where are you going?" he said.

She tilted her head at Abdullah. "He allowed me," she said, and brushed past. The main hall was a few yards away. The walk seemed a kilometer. Zalina passed through the door and saw Aushev by the exit at the end of the hall. She moved toward him. He waved her on.

Zalina walked barefoot in quick strides, Amina's cheek tight to her own. Her heart pounded. Would she be shot? She did not look back. The corridor was littered with bits of glass. She did not feel it nicking her feet. Behind her the other women followed. A chain of mothers and babies was making its way out, twenty-six people in all.

Zalina focused on the door. She passed Aushev, who stood with the Colonel. "Thank you very much," she said. The exit was barricaded with tables, and a terrorist slid them aside and opened the door. Air tumbled in, and light. She stepped out.

Behind her in the corridor, Fatima Tskayeva wailed as she carried Alyona, her infant. She could not go any more. Sobbing, she handed the baby to a terrorist in a black T-shirt and mask. She had two more children here. She had decided to stay. The terrorist carried Alyona down the hall to Aushev and handed him the child. Fatima's cries pierced the corridor.

Outside, Zalina rushed Amina past the place where the assembly had been the day before. Discarded flowers were on the ground. A man shouted from a roof. "There are snipers," he said. "Run!"

The line of women followed, and together they approached the perimeter. An aid station was waiting with medicine, food, and water. Zalina knew nothing of it. She trotted for her apartment, which was inside the perimeter, reached the entrance, climbed the stairs, and stood at her door. She had no key. She banged. It had been a mistake to bring Amina to school. It had been a mistake to have been taken hostage. But the terrorists had mistaken her for a breast-feeding mother. It was their mistake that she was out. They were free. Amina was alive. Who had a key? She descended the stairs to the entrance. Four Russian troops approached.

"Give me the child," one said, extending his arms. Amina saw their camouflage and began to howl. "Do not touch her," Zalina snapped. "No one will touch her."

EVENING. THE GYM.

KAREN MDINARADZE slipped in and out of consciousness. Once he awoke to see a woman over him, fanning him, another time to find children cleaning his wound with a cloth soaked in urine. He awoke again. A teenaged girl thrust an empty plastic bottle to him and asked him to urinate in it.

"Turn your eyes away," he said, and he pressed the bottle against himself and slowly peed. He finished and handed the bottle back. The girl and her friends thanked him and quickly poured drops to wash their faces. Then each sipped from the bottle, passing it among themselves, and returned it to him. Karen's dehydration was advanced; his throat burned. He poured a gulp of the warm liquid into his mouth and across his tongue, letting it pool around his epiglottis. The moisture alleviated some of the pain. He swallowed.

He looked at the bottle. A bit remained. A very old woman in a scarf was gesturing to him, asking for her turn. He passed the bottle on.

September 3
Past Midnight. The Weight Room.

Irina Naldikoyeva picked her way by the hostages dozing on the floor. Her daughter, Alana, was feverish. The gym was connected to a small weight-lifting room, which had become an informal infirmary. Irina asked permission from a terrorist to move Alana there. He nodded, and she carried the drowsy child and laid her on the room's cool floor. Perhaps fifty people rested in the space, mostly children and elderly hostages.

A water pipe was leaking, and, unsolicited, a small boy came to them and gave Alana a cup of water. She drank thirstily and lay down. Gradually her breathing slowed and deepened. She drifted to sleep. Irina returned to the gym, retrieved her son, and placed him beside his sister.

After several hours caressing the children, Irina dozed off, the first time since they were taken hostage that she had slept. Her father appeared. He had died several months earlier, but his face hovered before her, an apparition with gray hair. He did not speak. Nor did she. They looked into each other's eyes.

After perhaps twenty minutes, she woke. Her father, Timofey

Naldikoyev, had been a gentle man, quiet and kind. She had never dreamed of him before. She wondered: *What does it mean?*

MORNING. THE GYM.

FORTY-EIGHT HOURS after the hostages had been taken captive, the survivors were sliding to despair. They were beginning their third day without food, and their second without water. Almost all had slept only in snatches through two nights. They were dehydrated, filthy, weak, and drained by fear. They slumped against one another and the walls. The terrorists seemed tired, too, frayed and aware that their demands were being ignored. They had become nastier and drove the hostages out of the weight room to the gym, shoving some with rifles.

As the sun climbed and the temperature again began to rise, the two terrorists who specialized in explosives roamed the court. Their explosives were arranged in at least two circuits—the more visible one connecting the hanging bombs. A second circuit wired together a string of bombs on the floor, including two large bombs. The terrorists moved this second chain near one of the walls. Irina Naldikoyeva watched, struggling to stay alert. She was massaging her son, waiting for a sign.

MINUTES AFTER 1:00 P.M. THE GYM.

THE EXPLOSION WAS a thunderclap, a flash of energy and heat, shaking the gym. Twenty-two seconds later a second blast rocked the gym again. Their combined force was ferocious. Together they blew open the structure, throwing out the plastic windows, splattering the walls with shrapnel, and heaving people and human remains through the room. One of the blasts punched a seventy-eight-inch-wide hole through a brick wall twenty-five inches thick, cascading bricks and mortar onto the lawn. It also lifted the roof and rafters above the hole, snapping open a corner of the building like a clam before gravity slammed the roof back down. Much of the ceiling fell onto the hostages below.

Scores of hostages were killed outright. Their remains were heaped near the fresh hole and scattered across the basketball court. But most survived, hundreds of people in various states of injury. At first they hardly moved. Many were knocked senseless. Some were paralyzed by fright. Others, worried about another blast, pressed to the floor. At last they began to stir, and escape.

Dzera Kudzayeva, the first-grade girl who was to have been the bell ringer, had been near the blast that knocked out the wall. She had been asleep under her grandmother, Tina Dudiyeva, whose body had seemed to rise above her with the shock wave. The child stood now, and seeing sunlight through the hole, she scampered out, over the shattered bricks and onto the lawn. She began to run. She had arrived on Wednesday in a dress with a white apron and ribbons; she left now in only panties, filthy, streaked in blood, sprinting. She crossed the open courtyard and lot and came to the soldiers who ringed the school. She was free. The sound of automatic weapons began to rise.

The hole was only one route. The pressure of the explosions had thrown the windowpanes clear of their frames, exposing the room to light and air. The hostages reacted instinctually. A desperate scramble began. The sills were a little more than four feet above the floor, and throughout the room many of those who were not badly injured rushed to the sills, pulled themselves up, and dropped out to the ground.

Karen Mdinaradze had been unconscious on the floor and had not been struck by shrapnel. He woke, heard moaning, and found himself surrounded by gore. Human remains had rained down; two girls near him were covered by a rope of intestine. He saw people hurdling the windows, mustered his energy, stumbled to the sill, and followed them out.

He landed in the courtyard and ran in a panicked human herd. A mother weaved in front, pulling her small boy. Bullets snapped overhead. They dashed across the courtyard toward the far corner, following those in front toward a gap in the fence. The mother went down. Her son stopped. "Mama!" he screamed. Karen bent and scooped the boy with his right hand as he ran past, pulling him tight like a loose ball. He charged for the fence opening and passed through it and out of the line of fire. Beside him was a small metal garage. He placed the boy inside. The mother ran around the corner. She had not been shot. She had stumbled. She fell atop her boy, sobbing. Soldiers, police officers, and local men were hunched and running toward them; Karen stumbled on, one-eyed and bloody, until a man hooked an arm under him and steered him down the street to an ambulance, which drove him away.

The first rush of escapes was over. Back in the gym, Aida Archegova had been leaning against the wall opposite a large bomb and had been stunned by the explosions. A piece of ceiling had fallen on her. She woke to glimpse her older son, Arsen, eleven, scrambling out. She recognized him by his blue briefs, which she had folded dozens of times. She did not see her younger boy. She pushed aside the ceiling and scanned the room. *Where is Soslan?* Gunfire boomed. A terrorist stood at the door, shouting. "Those who are alive and want to live, move to the center of the gym," he said.

Aida picked her way through the corpses and mortally injured, looking for Soslan. He was not among them. A boy about four years old told her he was looking for his brother. She took his hand and led him to the door and told him to wait. Another boy approached her, and a girl about twelve. "I am scared," the boy said. The girl said her sister was dying. Bullets zipped through the gym, the tracers glowing red, smacking walls. "Lie down here and wait," she said. "You may be killed."

Terrorists clustered in the hall, and Abdullah approached and ordered the hostages to follow. They formed a line, and he led them down the long hall to the cafeteria, a light-blue room where perhaps forty hostages were sitting or lying on the floor. Terrorists ducked behind barricades at the windows, firing out. Buckets of water rested on the table, with cookies and salted cabbage. The children took bowls and dipped them. Some drank six or seven bowls, unable to slake their thirst, and then began to eat with their hands.

Abdullah ordered the women to the windows. "Put the children there as well," he said. Aida froze. Bullets buzzed and popped through the air, pecking the brick facade, pocking the plaster walls. "If children are there, then they will not shoot and you will be safe," Abdullah said.

Six large windows faced the front of the school, each with steel bars, which prevented escape. Aida stepped to a middle window, lifted a boy who appeared to be about seven, and laid him on the sill. She took her place beside him. She made a highly visible target, her black hair falling on a red blouse. Her feet were on broken glass. The Russians were advancing. Abdullah ordered her to shout to them. She found a piece of curtain and held it through the bars, waving it. Other mothers were being used the same way. Beside her, Lora Karkuzashvili, a waitress at a local restaurant, frantically waved a strip of cloth. They were human shields. "Do not shoot!" the women screamed. "Do not shoot!"

1:10 P.M. THE GYM AND THE WEIGHT ROOM.

ATSAMAZ STOOD OVER his unconscious father. "Papa!" he shouted. "Papa!"

His father, Kazbek, was stunned. Inside his haze he heard the boy and remembered his agreement with his wife. He was to get Atsamaz out. He opened his eyes. The bomb overhead had not exploded. It still hung there. He saw Atsamaz and looked for his wife, Irina, crawling to Batraz, their older son, who was curled life-lessly on the floor. She rolled him over. "Batik!" she screamed.

Both of her eardrums had been ruptured, making even her own voice seem muffled. "Batik!" she shouted. He did not move. He was wearing only black pants. Blood ran from his left knee. "Batik!"

Batraz stirred. Irina cradled him, urging him toward alertness.

The survivors were in motion. At the opposite wall, children were going out the window, using the body of a fat old woman as a step. One by one they scrambled over the corpse, becoming silhou-ettes in the window frame, and then were gone. Tracers zipped in; Kazbek worried his family would be shot.

He wrapped Atsamaz with his arms and lurched to the weight room. Putting Atsamaz down, he saw that the boy was covered in someone else's blood. Kazbek inspected himself. A chunk of his left forearm was gone, as if it had been cut away with a sharp scoop. Blood pulsed from the wound. His right arm was injured, too; a bullet, he thought, must have passed through it.

He felt weak. If he were to keep bleeding like this, he knew, he did not have much time. He pulled a bright orange curtain toward him, made bandages, and tried to stop his bleeding. His head was injured, too, with cuts and burns. After dressing his arms, he tied a piece across his scalp, making a garish turban, and sat down. There were three windows, each covered with bars. They were trapped.

About a dozen hostages were in the room, including Larisa Kudziyeva and her family, and Sarmat, Vadim Bolloyev's small son. Larisa had been at the entrance to the weight room at the instant of the first explosion, standing beside Ibragim, one of the terror-ists. The blast had knocked them to the floor together and entan-gled their legs. Ibragim had seemed surprised. After the second blast, he rolled free of Larisa and stood. "Are you blowing us up?" she asked him.

"No, it is yours," he said.

Ibragim disconnected a bomb at the doorway and rested it on

the floor. "Make sure the children do not touch it," he said to her, and left.

The terrorists had staged equipment in the weight room, and Larisa rummaged through their backpacks, finding candy, raisins, dried apricots, and cookies. She handed food to the hostages. The battle flowed around them; they devoured the terrorists' supplies. A boy came to Larisa. "Where is my mother?" he said.

"At this moment I am as good as your mother," she said. "Sit. Eat."

Kazbek was slumped on a wrestling mat, fighting for consciousness. His bandages were soaked. Shooting roared at the windows. He knew Russian soldiers were closing in. *Soon they will be tossing grenades through windows,* he thought, *and then asking who is inside.* His wife was nearby. Blood ran from her ears. A bone in her neck had been cracked. The building shook from explosions, and he was falling asleep. He saw Irina's face, her soft cheeks and warm brown eyes. It was beautiful.

"Do not die!" she said.

1:25 P.M. THE GYM.

IRINA NALDIKOYEVA had been lying among corpses for at least twenty minutes, covering her son, Kazbek. Her niece, Vika Dzutseva, fifteen, was beside her, in a sleeveless blue dress, with Alana. Flames were spreading in the ceiling. The children wore only soiled briefs.

The children had been asleep on the floor at the moment of the first explosion, and were protected. But the first blast sent shrapnel into Irina's leg; the second sent more metal into her neck and jaw. She was light-headed and unsure what to do. Helicopters thumped overhead. She worried one would be disabled and slam into the gym. She had watched other hostages being led away and was wary of following the terrorists, but was running out of choices. The gym was afire.

Abdullah entered, looking for survivors. "Those who are alive, stand and go to the cafeteria," he shouted. His eyes met Irina's. *This means you.*

She took Kazbek by his hand and told Vika to take Alana, and they made their way to him. Broken bodies were packed in a wide arc around the hole in the wall, so many that Irina and Vika had trouble finding places to put down their feet. Several times they had to lift the children over the tangle.

In the main hall Vika collapsed with Alana, but a terrorist drove Irina on to the cafeteria, where she looked in and saw bloodied hostages and terrorists firing through the windows. Her instinct was to hide. She kept moving, heading upstairs to the auditorium and slipping behind the maroon curtain on the stage. Perhaps twenty hostages were there. A girl came to Irina, tore off a piece of her black skirt, and bandaged her leg. Irina held Kazbek and waited. Bullets pecked against the school's outer walls.

Before 2:00 p.m. The Coach's Office.

With so many armed terrorists inside, School No. 1 was difficult for rescuers and the Special Forces to approach, especially because they had been caught unprepared. At the moment of the first explosion, two T-72 tanks had been parked with engines off on Kominterna Street, one block east of the school. Their crews had reacted with as much astonishment as the civilians clustered nearby, and argued over what to do. Inside a five-story apartment building overlooking the gym from the northeast, a Russian sniper team had also been taken unaware, and rushed to a balcony to see what had happened. They began to provide covering fire to hostages climbing out. A group of Special Forces soldiers, who had been rotated from the perimeter to a training range at a nearby army base, began speeding back, scrambling to a fight that had started while they were out of position.

Along the uneven perimeter, held by a disorganized mix of Ossetian police officers, traffic cops, conscript soldiers, local men with rifles, and Special Forces teams, disorder and confusion reigned. Some men were ordered to advance, while men beside them were ordered to hold their fire. Gradually, however, a sense that the final battle had begun took hold, and the men moved forward. Volleys of bullets smacked into the school, kicking up red dust. Litter bearers followed.

After an hour the Russians were pressing near the gym, and the volume of their fire, coming from so many directions, had begun to reduce the terrorists' numbers and push them out from many rooms. Several terrorists were injured, and others were dead. The gym, with flames crackling on its ceiling, had become untenable to defend. The terrorists were making a stand in the cafeteria, where the windows had iron bars.

For this they wanted hostages as shields, and Ibragim returned to the weight room to retrieve the group hiding there. He was a dark-haired young man, appearing younger than twenty-five, wearing a T-shirt and an ammunition vest. He entered the room and shouted at the hostages on the floor. Kazbek was there, wrapped in orange bandages, looking near death. Others looked capable of walking out. "Those who want to live, come," he shouted. No one complied.

"Get the people out!" he shouted. "The ceiling is on fire."

"You leave," Larisa said. "We will stay."

"The roof will collapse," he said.

Larisa worried that if they did not follow his orders, Ibragim would begin to kill. She led a group to the door and was joined by Ivan Kanidi, the school's physical-education instructor. Ibragim signaled for them to move low along the wall, ducking at windows so no one would be shot. Heat radiated from above. Flaming pieces of ceiling fell. Larisa's daughter, Madina, held three children by the hand, but a boy shook free to hide among the dead.

Ibragim forced them on, mustering more hostages he found alive on the floor. At the far end of the gym, he directed them to the coach's office, where he looked out the window to see what he could of the Russian advance. When he turned, Ivan Kanidi lunged.

Ivan was seventy-four years old, but he retained the muscularity of a lifelong athlete. He seized Ibragim's rifle with two thick hands, trying to rip it from his grasp. The rifle barrel swung wildly as they struggled and spun. "Get the children out!" Ivan shouted.

"Let go, old man, or I will kill you!" Ibragim snarled.

Back and forth they fought, pushing and pulling each other around the room by the rifle. Basketballs and other sports equipment littered the floor. After what seemed a minute, Ivan fell backward with the rifle in his hands. He was a nimble man, big-chested but lean, with a finely trimmed gray mustache. Before he could turn the rifle, Ibragim drew a pistol and shot him in the chest. He was motionless. Ibragim leaned down, retrieved his rifle from the dead man's hands, and looked at the group. "Everybody out," he said.

They began the walk to the cafeteria. Kira Guldayeva, a grandmother Ibragim had rousted from the gym, was suspicious, and when Ibragim looked away, she pulled her grandson, Georgy, six, into a classroom. Larisa and Madina remained under Ibragim's control, arriving at the cafeteria under his escort.

The place was a horror. Each element of the siege—from the capture of the children to the enforced conditions of their captivity among the bombs to the murders of their fathers and teachers in the literature classroom to the explosions that ripped apart people by the score—had been a descent deeper into cruelty, violence, and near-paralyzing fear. Now they had reached the worst. Women stood at windows, screaming and waving white cloths. Bullets struck the walls. Dust and smoke hung in the air. Glass covered the floor, much of it splattered with blood. The room stunk of gunpowder, rotting food, and sweat. Terrorists raced through the haze, bearded, whooping, firing, and yelling instructions. Larisa had her son, Zaurbek, by the hand, and apprehended their new conditions; Madina had the two children she had brought from the weight room. She did not know their names. They rushed around a corner near the dish-washing room, where at least twenty other hostages were massed tight. Two girls were trying to squeeze themselves into a massive soup pot. Dead women and children were strewn on the kitchen tiles. The Kudziyeva family took a place on the floor.

Just after 2:00 p.m. The Weight Room.

Kazbek Misikov tried to focus. He had fainted from blood loss, but Atsamaz revived him by dumping water on his face. He knew he had to rally himself. Roughly a dozen hostages remained in the weight room, but only three were adults, and he was the only man. Heat and orange glow emanated from the gym. Sounds of battle boomed outside. They were in a seam, forgotten but alive.

The barred windows offered no escape. Irina found paper and made a sign with red lipstick. *DETI,* it read, Russian for "children." She held it up at a window so they would not be shot. Kazbek staggered beside her, put his head at the window, where it was exposed. "There are children here!" he shouted. "Do not shoot!"

He was wearing a bloody turban and wondered if he would be mistaken for an Arab. Peering into the narrow alley, he saw the district prosecutor looking back. They both were startled. "Alan!" Kazbek said.

The prosecutor rushed to the window. "What can we do?" he said.

He was accompanied by a man with a rifle, and Kazbek asked him to aim at the door, in case a terrorist returned. He was weak but managed to lift a barbell and pass it between the bars. The men outside used it as a lever and popped the frame free. An escape route was open. Irina started handing out children: First the little ones, and then the adults helped her with a badly burned teenage girl. When the last child was out, the adults followed.

The Misikovs emerged behind the school. Soldiers passed them going the other way, rushing to penetrate the building through the hole they had made. The fire in the gym roof, which had spread slowly, was now a conflagration. Smoke rose over the neighborhood. Kazbek moved woozily to a stretcher, lay down, and slipped out of consciousness.

The children were handed from rescuer to rescuer in a chain. Atsamaz was passed along with the others until he ended up in the arms of Slavik, his uncle, a face he knew in the chaos. Slavik embraced him. Atsamaz realized he had been saved. He clung to the man. "Papa promised me I could have a Coke," he said.

AFTER 2:00 P.M. THE CAFETERIA.

LESS THAN FIFTEEN MINUTES after Irina Naldikoyeva and her son found refuge in the auditorium, the terrorists forced them downstairs to the cafeteria and its tableau of misery. Hostages crowded the room, partially dressed, soiled, riddled with shrapnel, shot, burned, dehydrated, and stunned. Irina saw her niece, Vika, slumped beneath a window, her long black hair matted with sweat. "Where is Alana?" she asked.

"Here," Vika said, pointing to a child, naked except for dirty panties, curled under a table.

Bullets were coming in from the Russians firing outside. Irina grabbed her children and scrambled with them along the floor, stopping against a large freezer, panting. A terrorist handed her a bucket of water, and she tilted it and gave each child a drink. They gulped voraciously. At last it was her turn, and she put the bucket to her lips, poured the cool water onto her tongue, eager for it to hit her parched throat. But instead the water splashed onto her floral blouse. Irina did not understand and reached under her chin and felt the place where shrapnel had passed through. The bottom of her mouth was an open hole. Blood and water soaked her torso. She put the bucket aside.

Around her were at least six dead children, and she knew this place was not safe. She crawled to the dish-washing room, pushed the children under the sinks, and lay her body across them. Bullets kept coming. Some skipped off window frames or iron bars and whirred by, ricochets. One plunked the sink above her son.

A terrorist was on his back on the floor, motionless with his mouth open, showing gold teeth. His head had been bandaged. In the cupboards along the floor were more small children, hiding with pots and pans. The terrorist stood and lurched back to fight. On the other side of the door, Lora Karkuzashvili stood at a window. Aida Archegova was to her right. Abdullah was ducking and shooting, moving between them. Ibragim was in the corner, firing through the bars, his arms streaked in blood. Volleys of bullets came back in. Lora was struck in the chest, dropped, and did not move. Aida was standing, shouting and waving a cloth. A boy sat beside her, exposed. "Do not shoot!" Aida screamed.

Aida had been at the window for at least twenty minutes; somehow the bullets missed her and the child. She did not know his name; only once had he spoken. "I do not want to die," he said. Every chance she had, she put him on the floor. Always Abdullah told her to put him back. But Abdullah looked away again, and Aida swung the boy off the sill and placed him under a table. She stood upright and felt a tremendous slap on the left side of her face. The impact spun her head. Much of her jaw was gone. She had been hit. She looked at Abdullah, who was using her for cover. "May I sit now?" she tried to ask. "I am bad."

"I do not care if you are bad or good," he said. "Stand if you want to live."

She was dizzy. There was an explosion. Aida fell.

Everyone was wounded, cowering, or dead. A creaking and rumbling sounded outside, and the turret of a T-72 tank appeared near the fence bordering the school grounds. Its barrel flashed. There was a concussive boom. The entire facade shook. Dust fell from the ceiling. The shell had struck another room.

MIDAFTERNOON. THE GYM.

PUSHED AWAY BY FLAME, sniper fire, and charging infantry, the terrorists yielded the gym. The place in which they had confined more than eleven hundred people, the pen with its matrix of bombs, was no longer theirs. Flames rolled along its ceiling and roof. Beneath the fire, on the basketball court, corpses and gravely injured hostages were spread across the floorboards, partially dressed or nearly naked, twisted into unnatural shapes. Heat seared the room.

For a long time almost no one moved, but at last Marina Kanukova, a first-grade teacher who had been feigning death with a third-grade girl, stirred. The heat had become too much, and she had heard a soldier's voice telling those who were alive to crawl to safety. The bodies were too thick to crawl over, so she took the child by the hand, crouched, and with flames roaring overhead they stepped across the dead to the weight room, where they were met by soldiers and local men, who directed them out a window. Behind her, bit by bit, coals and the flaming roof were dropping onto the injured and the dead. The air filled with smells of burning plastic and roasting hair and flesh.

Flanked by the Special Forces, a BTR-80 had arrived on the gym's western side. An eight-wheeled armored vehicle with a 14.5 mm machine gun on a turret, it rolled toward the door where the hostages had first been forced into the school, its gun firing as it advanced, and rammed the wall and windows.

Soldiers and local men climbed into the bathroom and freed a group of screaming, terrified hostages, many slicked in blood and shit. Teams of soldiers pushed into the school. The Russians were inside at last, possessing opposite ends of the gym. Their storm had come late. On the basketball court, burning bodies were before them by the score.

MIDAFTERNOON. THE CAFETERIA.

THE SURVIVORS SLUMPED in the corner by the dish-washing room, perhaps twenty-five people crammed in a tiny space. Still the bullets kept coming. A crash sounded along the outside wall; they noticed that the iron bars on the window in the left corner were gone. Three Russian commandos climbed in.

They were a fit and nimble trio, carrying rifles and wearing body armor and helmets. They stood among the dead and the injured, weapons ready, blood, broken glass, and spent shells around their feet. One of them bled from his hand. "Where are the bastards?" one whispered.

A door to the storerooms swung open. Ibragim was there. Simultaneously, the commandos and the terrorist opened fire over the hostages. Ibragim stepped aside, then reappeared, holding two hand grenades. Bullets hit him as he let them go.

Time seemed to slow.

Larisa Kudziyeva watched one of the grenades, a smooth metal oval about the size of a lime, as it passed over her, fell to the floor, and bounced off the kitchen tile toward the soldiers. Her son was beneath her and her daughter beside her. She squeezed the boy, threw her leg and arm over him, and swung her other hand over her daughter's face.

A hand grenade is a small explosive charge surrounded by a metal shell, whose detonation is controlled by a fuse with a few-second delay. When the charge explodes, it shatters the metal exterior, turning it into bits of shrapnel that rush away at thousands of feet per second, accompanied by a shock wave and heat. It can kill a man fifteen yards away. The nook was less than six yards across.

The grenade exploded.

After the wave of metal hit her, Larisa was encased in something like silence, a state in which the absence of sound was overlaid by the ringing in her ears, leaving her to feel an effect like a struck crystal glass. *How easy it is to die,* she thought. But she did not die, not immediately, and as if in a dream she ran an arm over her son, who was beneath her. He was alive. "Mama," he said. "Mamochka."

The shrapnel had blasted the right side of her face, tearing part of it off, and ruined her right arm. Larisa did not want the boy to see what had become of her and turned away and raised her left hand to her face. Her fingertips felt wet flesh and exposed bone. The bone fragments were sharp enough to prick. She passed out.

Her daughter crawled to her. A teacher beside Larisa was missing a leg. One of the commandos was dead. The children Madina had escorted in were dead. One of Larisa's neighbors was dead. Another teacher was dead. The grisly mess extended through the room.

Larisa looked dead, but Madina checked her pulse, finding life. More commandos climbed in. They told the survivors to follow them out. "My mother is still alive," Madina said.

"We will take care of her," a soldier said.

Madina picked up her little brother, handed him out the window to a man outside. The man helped her down, too, and the brother and sister ran out into the neighborhood. They were saved.

Inside the dish-washing room, Irina Naldikoyeva had felt the wall shake, but she remained on top of her children, holding them down, unsure what had happened. There were two doors into the tiny room, and after a few minutes a man's head appeared along the floor at one of them. It was a commando, crawling. He wore a helmet. His face was sweaty. Irina understood: Russians were inside. The children hiding with the pots understood, too. The cupboard doors flew open and they scuttled out and bounded past him, looking for a way out.

Irina followed with Kazbek and Alana, out the door, past the mangled corpses, to the window. She handed out the children and then shinnied down. She was out, in autumnal air, standing on grass. She walked unsteadily and turned the corner at the first house on Kominterna Street. She did not know where her children had gone. She sat on the ground. Someone came and led her away.

Late Afternoon. A Classroom.

Kira Guldayeva hid with Georgy in the classroom as the sound of gunfire rose and fell. Six Kalashnikovs were stacked against the wall. Camouflage clothing was strewn on the floor. The walls were streaked with blood, as if during the battle injured terrorists had congregated here. Kira pulled Georgy close. He was a small boy, wearing only underpants. She checked him for injuries and found tiny holes where shrapnel had entered his back, buttocks, and one of his feet. Blood beaded from each wound. Her injuries were worse, a catalog of the afternoon's hazards: She had been shot twice, and one bullet had passed through her arm. Shrapnel had struck her shoulder. She had been burned.

She sat for a long time, afraid the terrorists might return and wondering when the rescuers might reach them. "Stay here," she told the boy, and crept to the door.

A Russian soldier stood across the hall. They appraised each other, two faces in the chaos. He dashed toward her.

As he crossed the open, gunfire boomed. A bullet slammed into his head. He staggered into the room, dropped his rifle, grasped for his helmet, and collapsed. He did not move. His dropped rifle pointed at Kira and Georgy; she pushed it away with a board.

Another soldier followed him in and leaned against the wall. He was injured, too. "Lie down," he said to them, and began applying a bandage to his leg. A microphone hung at his throat, into which he spoke in clipped tones. More soldiers entered. The school was falling under Russian control.

They put Kira and Georgy on stretchers, and she was handed through a window. Litter bearers ran with her, tripped, and dropped her to the ground. "Where is the boy?" she screamed. "Where is the boy?"

LATE AFTERNOON. THE CAFETERIA.

LARISA KUDZIYEVA AWOKE, unsure how much time she had spent on the floor. The hostages near her were all dead. She tried to move, but her right arm felt as if someone were atop it.

Much of her face was gone; soldiers stepped past her as if she were a corpse. They seemed calmer, having for the moment taken control of the room. One stood above her, a blurry form. She raised her left hand to wipe blood from her eyes. He glanced down, surprised. "Girl, be patient," he said. "They will bring stretchers."

His voice sounded kind. *If he can call me girl when I look like this,* she thought, *then I can wait.* She drifted to sleep.

LATE NIGHT. A HOSPITAL ROOM IN VLADIKAVKAZ.

NIKOLAI ALBEGOV ARRIVED at the door and surveyed his son's wife. He was sixty-six, a retired truck driver, fidgeting where he stood. The thin frame of Irina Naldikoyeva, his daughter-in-law, was extended on the bed. Her head and her neck were wrapped in gauze. She was foggy from painkillers. An IV snaked into her arm.

Throughout Beslan and Vladikavkaz a fresh horror was descending. The morgue in Beslan was overflowing, and bodies were laid on the grass. Vladikavkaz's morgue also had a growing display of corpses waiting to be claimed. The dashes out of the school, and the rescues, had been so spontaneous and disorganized that many families were not sure whether their spouses and children had survived. The families also heard of blackened remains encased on the basketball court under the collapsed roof. The living roamed among the dead, peering at the unclaimed, looking for their own.

Nikolai's family had been spared this. For nine years Irina had lived in his home. She had borne the family a son and a daughter and performed much of the daily labor. Nikolai kept one of the most traditional households in Beslan, and under the mountain customs he observed, he was the *khozyain,* the elder of his domain. Irina was not allowed to address him. She had never spoken to him unless he had asked her a question. They had never embraced.

He stood at the door in a suit, a leathery, strong-handed old man in his very best clothes, assessing the woman who had come into his home. He did not yet know what had happened in the school. But she had brought his family out. Tears ran down his dark face. He walked to her bed, found a spot on her face where there was no bandage, and gave her a kiss.

SEPTEMBER 4
EVENING. A HOSPITAL ROOM IN
VLADIKAVKAZ.

THE DOCTOR ASSESSED Larisa Kudziyeva. Twice they had operated on her, but she had remained in a coma. Shrapnel had cut too many holes through her; blood transfusions leaked out. Her blood pressure had sunk. She was near death. The hospital was overwhelmed with patients, and at last Larisa was triaged. Nurses washed her and put a tag on her toe.

But Larisa Kudziyeva would not die, and hours later another doctor found her alive where she had been left for dead. Early on September 4 she was put back on an operating table. Much of her eye socket was gone. The right side of her face was mashed. Her right arm was shredded and broken in three places. Her middle finger was snapped. Her side had absorbed a shock wave and shrapnel blast. But the metal had missed her main arteries and her right lung. She stabilized before sunrise.

Now she was awake, barely. The surgeon questioned her, running through a simple neurological exam.

"What is your birthday?" he asked.

"The fourteenth," she said.

"What month?"

"May," she said. It was true. But it was not.

"No, forget that day," the doctor said. "Your birthday is September fourth."

EPILOGUE

THE BESLAN SIEGE claimed a greater toll of human life than all but one act of modern terrorism, the destruction of the World Trade Center. The terrorists' actions and the bungled rescue efforts ended with the deaths of 331 people, not counting the 31 terrorists the Russian government says were killed. Among the dead were 186 children and 10 members of Russia's Special Forces, whose individual acts of courage were undermined by the incompetence of their government's counterterrorism response. More than seven hundred other people were injured, most of them children.

The siege ended with no victor. Faith in Russia's government, and the ability of its security agencies to protect its citizens, has been shaken. Sympathy for Chechen independence has shrunk. Even some of Chechnya's separatist fighters, men claiming loyalty to Shamil Basayev, have questioned the utility and rationale of such tactics, although the underground rebel government, unwisely, has not distanced itself from Basayev, who was appointed its first deputy prime minister in 2005. His retention of such a post, no matter his earlier guerrilla prowess, discredits the separatists and is grounds for shame.

The Russian and North Ossetian parliaments have opened investigations into the terrorist act, which thus far have led to inconclusive findings and drawn accusations of cover-ups from survivors and the bereaved. Official lies have eroded public confidence, including the insistence during the siege that only 354 hostages were seized, and an enduring insistence that the T-72 tanks did not fire until all the survivors were out, which is false. It remains unclear, and a source of acrimonious debate, what caused the first two explosions and the fire in the gym, although the available evidence, on balance, suggests that the blast damage and the majority of the human injury were caused by the terrorists' bombs. There is similar uncertainty about the reason behind the explosion of the *shahidka*. Other points of contention include what help, if any, the terrorists received from inside Beslan, whether the terrorists hid weapons in the school before the attack, how many terrorists were present, and whether several of them escaped. A third of the dead terrorists have not been publicly identified, and their names are officially unknown. Ibragim was killed; this is clear. But many hostages, including Larisa Kudziyeva and Kazbek Misikov, have studied the known pictures of the dead terrorists and insist that Ali, previously known as Baisangur, and others were not among the dead and were not seen on the last day of the siege.

Almost all of the surviving hostages remain in North Ossetia, and many continue to receive treatment, including Larisa, who had endured fourteen surgeries through early April 2006 and is expecting two more. Aida Archegova, who became a human shield after searching for her son Soslan, was rescued and later learned that Soslan escaped. Her face has been rebuilt, with bone from her hip grafted to fashion a replacement jaw. She has never again seen the boy who was a human shield with her and does not know whether he is alive. Sarmat Bolloyev survived. Lora Karkuzashvili, the human shield shot in the chest by rescuers, did not. Alina Kudzayeva, the wife of Aslan Kudzayev, who jumped from the window of the literature classroom, was freed with their nineteen-month-old daughter and other breast-feeding mothers; the remains of her mother, Tina Dudiyeva, who shielded Dzera, the bell ringer, were found in the gym. Albert Sidakov, who opted not to jump with Aslan, was killed, as were both sons of Ruslan Betrozov, the man who stood to translate the terrorists' instructions. Fatima Tskayeva, who sent out her infant but stayed behind with her two other children, died with her daughter Kristina. Makhar, Fatima's three-year-old son, was saved. Karen Mdinaradze, who survived execution, was questioned by a detective at the hospital, who thought that he might be a terrorist masquerading as a fleeing hostage; he was eventually treated properly. His ruined left eye has been replaced with an artificial one. Even up close it looks real. Kazbek Misikov and his family recovered from most of their injuries, although Kazbek's arms remain damaged and he is classified an invalid. On January 22, 2006, his wife, Irina Dzutseva, gave birth to a third son, Elbrus, who is named, like his father, for a mountain that soars above the others on the Caucasus ridge.

C. J. CHIVERS *became a Moscow correspondent for the* New York Times *in 2004 after covering war zones in Iraq, the Palestinian territories, Israel, Central Asia, and Afghanistan. Prior to that he covered crime and law enforcement in New York City, including the attacks on the World Trade Center on Sept. 11, 2001. He is a regular contributor to* Esquire, Field & Stream, *and* SaltWater Sportsman. *He lives in Moscow with his wife and four children.*

Coda

Beslan had become like the Kennedy assassination, a mystery burdened with nonsense, conjecture, and lies. I became interested in finding what actually could be known and demonstrated as fact, and I wanted to create a narrative in real time, a museum of words, of the hostages' experience inside that claustrophobic space.

Two more adult victims died of their injuries after the story was published, bringing the death toll to 333. That count does not include the terrorists. Nurpashi Kulayev, the terrorist that Russia has said is the only surviving hostage-taker, was convicted of murder and other charges in May 2006 and sentenced to imprisonment for life. Shamil Basayev, the one-footed fugitive who ordered the school seizure, was killed by an explosion in Ingushetia in July. In December 2006 the Russian federal government issued the final report of the Parliamentary investigative commission into the circumstances of the siege at Beslan. The report strongly and appropriately condemned the terrorists but whitewashed the failures of the Russian government's handling of the counter-terrorism response and its use of indiscriminate weapons, including tanks.

Pamela Colloff

A Kiss Before Dying

FROM *Texas Monthly*

WHEN FOOTBALL SEASON ENDED and there was nothing much to do on Friday nights except drink beer and stare up at the wide-open sky, teenagers used to park their pickups across the street from Odessa High School and wait to see the ghost they called Betty. According to legend, she would appear at the windows of the school auditorium at midnight—provided that students flashed their headlights three times or honked their horn and called out her name. The real Betty, it was said, had attended Odessa High decades before and had acted in a number of plays on the auditorium's stage. But the facts of her death had been muddled with time, and each story was as apocryphal as the last: She had fallen off a ladder in the auditorium and broken her neck, students said. She had hanged herself in the theater. Her boyfriend, who was a varsity football player, had shot her onstage during a play.

So many teenagers made the late-night pilgrimage to see Betty that the high school deemed it prudent to paint over the windows of the school auditorium. During a later renovation, its facade was covered with bricks. But the stories about Betty never went away.

Students still talk of "a presence" in the auditorium, one that is to blame for a long list of strange occurrences, from flickering lights and noises that cannot be explained to objects that appear to move on their own. Some claim to have seen her pacing the balcony or heard her footsteps behind them, only to find no one there. Rumors have flourished that a coach who knew the real Betty is visited by her, on occasion, in the field house and that a former vice principal who once caught a glimpse of her after hours was so spooked by the encounter that he refused to be in the school again by himself. "I hear her name on a daily basis," says theater arts teacher Carl Moore, who has taught at Odessa High for four years. "Whenever something unexplained happens—a book falls on the floor in my classroom or the light board goes out during a technical rehearsal—someone always jokes, 'It's Betty.' "

What may be nothing more than just a ghost story can also be seen as something more complicated—as a metaphor, perhaps, for the way that one crime has lodged, uneasily, in Odessa's collective memory. The teenagers who pass down stories about Betty are too young to remember the Kiss and Kill Murder, as it was christened by the press in 1961, but it was the most sensational crime in West Texas in its day. The notoriety of the case has long since faded, yet 45 years later, something lingers. When Ronnie White, who graduated from Odessa High the year that the murder took place, returned to his alma mater to teach history, in 1978, he was astonished to hear students talking about the former drama student named Betty whose spirit supposedly haunted the auditorium and the popular football player who had had a hand in her killing. "I couldn't believe what I was hearing," he says. "I thought, 'Good Lord, they must be talking about Betty Williams.' "

SEPTEMBER 23 [1960]
STUDY HALL

. . . Well, I've finally made the rank of Senior and I can hardly believe it! I really don't feel much different. We get our Senior rings Wednesday. I'll be glad.

It sure does feel funny to be on the top of everything looking down. Seems strange to think that this is really all of high school. Next year???

We had our pictures made last week. If they turn out half-way decent, I'll send you one. Send me another picture if you have it.

Well, the bell is about to ring so I'll write more later.

Love,
Betty

WHAT MOST PEOPLE remember about Betty Williams is that they hardly noticed her at all. She lived in a small, well-worn frame house on an unpaved street not far from the oil fields west of town, where gas flares burned and drilling-rig lights illuminated the desert at night. Her father, John, was a carpenter who had difficulty finding steady work, and her mother, Mary, had taken a job at J.C. Penney to help make ends meet. A strict Baptist, her father often preached to Betty about sin and eternal damnation, and on more than one Sunday morning, he prayed that she might learn to be a more obedient daughter. At seventeen, Betty was pretty in an unremarkable way, with sandy-blond hair that brushed her shoulders and big, expressive blue eyes that could feign sincerity when talking to authority figures but were alive with irreverence.

Betty disdained conformity and reserved particular contempt for the girls with matching sweater sets and saddle shoes who seemed to look right through her. She fancied herself an intellectual and put down her opinions on everything from boys to religion in dozens of letters and notes that she passed in study hall. She read Jack Kerouac's *On the Road* and the poetry of Allen Ginsberg, and she listened to records of Lenny Bruce's stand-up routines, in which he railed against racism and skewered middle-class hypocrisy. She too liked to get a rise out of people, and she thrived on attention, whether she got it by arriving at Tommy's Drive-In dressed entirely in black but wearing white lipstick or in jeans and a T-shirt, under which she didn't bother to put on a bra. She freely expressed opinions that went against the grain, like her belief that segregation was unjust and that blacks should not have to attend a separate high school across the railroad tracks. In bedrock-conservative, blue-collar Odessa—where the John Birch Society's crusade against communism and other "un-American influences" had struck a chord—she was seen as an oddball. "Most people do not understand me," Betty wrote to a friend her senior year. "There are people willing to be my friends, but mostly they [are] either too ignorant to understand why I'm like I am, and consequently offer my mind no challenge; or they haven't the wits to match mine."

At the top of Odessa High School's rigid social hierarchy were the "cashmere girls," as one alumna called them—the girls with perfect complexions from West Odessa's better neighborhoods who were perennially voted most popular, best personality, and class favorite. At football games, they sat in the stands wearing the ultimate status symbol: their boyfriends' letter jackets. They belonged to the informal sororities called Tri-Hi-Y clubs—Capri, Sorella, and Amicae—which cherry-picked the most popular high school girls. Betty was hardly Tri-Hi-Y material; in the high school pecking order, her classmates remember her as "a nobody," "a nonentity," and "someone on the outside looking in." But while she struck an antiestablishment pose, the rejection she felt from the other girls still stung. "Betty wanted to be liked," says her first cousin Shelton Williams, whose memoir, *Washed in the Blood,* chronicles his coming-of-age in Odessa through the prism of Betty's murder. "She wanted what we all want—to be totally unique while being completely accepted."

In a place where fun on a Saturday night might mean deciding to take only right turns while cruising around town, Betty dreamed of her escape. She hoped to one day become an actress, and in her bedroom, where movie posters and playbills covered the walls, she devoured magazines like the Hollywood scandal sheet *Confidential*. She loved the thrill of the spotlight and was gifted enough that she landed parts in three school plays when she was just a sophomore. During her junior year, when the speech team performed the balcony scene from *Romeo and Juliet* at the University Interscholastic League competition, Betty played the doomed, lovesick heroine.

But as desperately as she wanted to propel herself out of Odessa, she was fatalistic about the future. The oldest of four children, she knew that her parents could not afford to send her away to college, and her part-time job at Woolworth's barely paid enough to finance any kind of getaway. While she aspired to one day appear on the Broadway stage, in the meantime she planned to live at home after graduation and attend Odessa College, just up the street.

Some nights, Betty would slip out the back door after her parents had gone to bed and walk the four blocks to Tommy's Drive-In, where there were always boys to talk to. Plenty of girls were flirts, but few of them were as assertive as Betty. She made no secret of the fact that she was not a prude and that she was willing to prove it. At the end of an evening at Tommy's, it was not unusual for her to end up parked in a secluded spot somewhere with a football player—after, of course, he had taken his girlfriend home to meet her curfew. While boys were free to do as they pleased, "good" girls were expected to obey an unspoken code of conduct. "If a girl had a steady boyfriend, then she could have sex, as long as she didn't advertise it," says Jean Smith Kiker, a Capri who was a year below Betty. "But if she did it with someone who wasn't her boyfriend, then she was a pariah." Betty chose to disregard the rules, and if she had earned herself a reputation, she hardly seemed to care. "Eisenhower had been president during most of our years of growing up, and kids were kept on a very short leash," remembers classmate Dixon Bowles. "You got the feeling with Betty that she was always straining against that leash, even when it choked her. Maybe *especially* when it choked her."

> *Mack,*
> *Well, I guess you accomplished what you set out to do. You hurt me, more than you'll ever know. When you handed me that note this morning, you virtually changed the course of my life. I don't [know] what I expected the note to say, but not that. I'll not waste time saying that I didn't deserve it because I guess I did. I've never been so hurt in my life and I guess your note was the jolt I needed to get me back on the straight and narrow. I've done a lot of things, I know, that were bad and cheap, but I swear before God that I didn't mean them to be like that. I was just showing off. I know it's much too late with you, Mack, but I swear that another boy won't get the chance to say what you said to me. You've made me realize that instead of being smart and sophisticated like I thought, I was only being cheap and ugly and whorish.*
> *Forgive me for writing this last note and thank you for reading it. I'll not trouble you again, and Mack, I haven't forgotten the good times we had. I really have enjoyed knowing you and I'm awfully sorry that it had to end this way. . . .*
> *Best of luck with your steady girlfriend. I hope she's the best.*
> *Betty*
> *P.S. When you think of me try to think of the good times we had and not of this.*

MACK HERRING WAS not one of the elite football players at Odessa High School on whose shoulders rested the hopes for the 1960 season. As a back for the Bronchos, and one of average abilities, he was just another guy on the team. Tall and good-looking, with jet-black hair that framed a long, contemplative face, Mack was "a guy's guy," his classmates remember, who was quiet and self-contained. The oldest son of a homemaker and a World War II veteran who owned an electrical-contracting business, Mack grew up in the solidly middle-class neighborhood that was home to many of his teammates and the Tri-Hi-Y girls they dated. An avid hunter, he was happiest when he could spend a few days bagging dove or quail on his father's hunting lease north of town or ramble around the oil fields with his .22, plinking jackrabbits. "If Mack wounded an animal when we went hunting, he would pursue it and dispatch it," says Larry Francell, who grew up across the alley from him. "A lot of kids were cruel—they would shoot something and watch it hobble off—but Mack was different. He didn't like to see things suffer. If he was going out there to hunt, he was going to kill."

Although Mack was near the top of the high school caste system and Betty was at the bottom, they managed to strike up a friendship when she was a junior and he was a sophomore. Betty thought she sensed in him a kindred spirit; he seemed more sensitive than the other boys she knew, and she thought there was something lonely and romantic about him. In the summer of 1960, they started dating, and Betty wondered if she might be falling in love; Mack, she told friends, really *listened* to her. But Mack was careful to be discreet about the time they spent together. He never took Betty to his neighbor Carol McCutchan's house, where the in crowd gathered for dance parties and rounds of spin the bottle. He never gave her his letter jacket or brought her home to meet his parents.

Perhaps because he had wounded her pride, or maybe just to make him jealous, Betty tried to even the score one night when she parked with one of his best friends, a popular football player who had been voted the most handsome in his class. The stunt soured Mack on the relationship, and by the fall, he had broken things off and started going steady with a pretty redhead in Amicae. "I've never been so humiliated and torn to pieces as I am now," Betty wrote to a friend. "I feel so lonely and deserted I don't care what happens now or ever. . . . This is pure hell!"

Betty was crushed to discover that fall that Odessa High's new drama teacher did not see much promise in her and had relegated her to the role of stage manager for the spring production of

Maxwell Anderson's *Winterset,* a gloomy 1935 play based loosely on the Sacco-Vanzetti case. Worse, she learned that Mack would be playing one of *Winterset*'s lead roles, a remorseless killer named Trock Estrella. Still reeling from their breakup and depressed at the prospect of not being cast in a single play her senior year, Betty began to feel hopeless. Mack was "the one," and without him, life wasn't worth living. "She said she wanted to die if she couldn't be with Mack," remembers her cousin Shelton, who was a year her junior at Odessa's Permian High School. "She told me, 'I *have* to get him back.' " Her mood turned darker after her father rummaged through her dresser drawers, looking for evidence of her disobedience. Distraught, Betty confided in a friend that he had found her diary, in which she had detailed her experiences with boys. Though she had pleaded with her father to believe her when she swore to him that she had changed, he could not be convinced. "Betty said that the situation at home was bad," says the friend, who asked not to be named. "I wanted to help, but I didn't know what to do. I was sixteen years old."

By the winter, Betty had started telling friends that she would be better off dead. "Heaven must be a nice place," she told junior Howard Sellers. She claimed to have halfheartedly tried to kill herself by taking four aspirin. She boasted of climbing up to the auditorium rafters, intending to throw herself onto the stage below, only to find that she lacked the courage. Betty, who had always enjoyed being outrageous, talked about wanting to die to whoever would listen. But the only reaction she was able to provoke was a few eye rolls. The response was always the same: *There goes Betty again, trying to be the center of attention.* Even when she began acting more erratically during rehearsals for *Winterset,* her peers wrote off her overwrought confessions about wanting to die as nothing more than a theater girl's high school histrionics. She informed at least five students working on the play that she wanted to kill herself but didn't have the nerve. Would they be willing to do it for her, she asked? "No, I don't think I will," senior Mike Ware said, passing it off as a joke. A sophomore, Jim Mercer, also deflected the invitation. "I charge for my services," he kidded, quoting her an impossibly high price.

At a time when Betty felt marginalized by those around her and forsaken by the one boy she loved, death seemed to hold its own allure. Or was she just acting, pushing the boundaries in another bid to catch Mack's attention? One night he gave her and Howard a ride home from rehearsal, and she made the request of him: Would he be willing to kill her? She would hold the gun to her head, she said, while he pulled the trigger. Mack laughed at the absurdity of the idea, and Betty laughed with him. She even went so far as to write out a wildly melodramatic note clearing him of culpability were he to be apprehended for her murder, a note that Howard would later say had seemed like a joke. But the next afternoon during rehearsal, Betty pulled Mack into the prop room backstage. She was miserable, she told him, and she wanted to die.

It was the week before *Winterset* was scheduled to premiere, and students were busy running their lines and painting the set as they readied for the final dress rehearsal. In the middle of the chaos, Betty spotted Mike. "It's been nice knowing you," she said.

"What do you mean?" he asked.

"I finally talked Mack into killing me," she said.

Mike shrugged. "I'll send roses."

I am consumed with this burning emptiness and loneliness that has taken charge of me, body and soul. I have to fight it! If I am to live I have to fight [or] else it will pull me down, down, down into that thankless pit of fear, pain, and agonized loneliness.

TWO DAYS LATER, on March 22, 1961, the Odessa Police Department received a frantic phone call from Mary Williams, who reported that her daughter was missing. One by one, Betty's friends were called into the principal's office, where they were asked to tell what they knew. Ike Nail, a popular junior who had taken Betty home from rehearsal the previous evening, recounted a story that interested investigators. When he had dropped Betty off at ten o'clock, he said, she had suggested that he return in half an hour and meet her in the alley behind her house. As promised, at ten-thirty Betty had snuck out the back door and slipped into his car. The two teenagers had parked in the alley for a while, but they had been startled to see headlights coming toward them. Betty immediately recognized the approaching car as Mack's. "Oh, my God, I didn't think he'd come," she had exclaimed. Ike had been certain Betty was only joking when she had remarked earlier in the evening that Mack had promised to kill her—so certain that he did not try to stop her when she climbed into Mack's Jeep. As she turned to go, she said to Ike, "I've got to call his bluff, even if he kills me."

Odessa police youth officer Bobby McAlpine sat Mack down to answer a few questions. The football player told a plausible-enough story: He had dropped Betty off outside her parents' house at midnight and had not seen her since. But inconsistencies in his account led McAlpine to believe that the seventeen-year-old knew more than he was letting on. Had he left Betty at the front door or the back, McAlpine inquired? The front door, Mack answered. And no, he hadn't waited to see that she'd gotten inside safely. His answer struck McAlpine as peculiar; the officer knew that Betty had been dressed for bed when she had slipped out of the house that night. According to Ike, she had been wearing only pale-pink shorty pajamas and a blue-and-white-striped duster—not the kind of clothes a boy would leave a girl standing in on her front porch at midnight. McAlpine also felt sure that Betty would not have wanted to sneak back into the house through the front door. Mack was brought down to the police station for further questioning, and 45 minutes later, he broke down. Betty had begged him to kill her, he told McAlpine; all he had done was carry out her wishes. He claimed to have committed the crime with a twelve-gauge shotgun that Betty herself had picked out.

Mack led officers to his father's hunting lease, 26 miles north-west of town, on a lonely piece of scrubland studded with pump jacks. They turned off the highway onto a winding dirt road and continued on until Mack directed them to stop. He showed them where his and Betty's footprints—his large, hers small—led down a steep incline to a stock tank. Beside the water, the ground was spat-tered with blood. In a flat monotone, Mack told investigators that he had shot Betty next to the stock tank, weighted her down, and submerged her body. Unsure of the exact location of the body in the tank, officers asked Mack if he would retrieve it. He stripped off his red-and-white varsity letter jacket, sport shirt, loafers, blue jeans, and socks and waded into the water until it came to his chest. The assembled group of lawmen fell silent. When he reached the center, Mack oriented himself by looking at the mesquite trees on either side; then he dove under the water and came back up. He began wading back toward land, dragging an object that appeared to be very heavy; when he was near the water's edge, Odessa police detective Fred Johnson could see that he was holding a pair of human feet. Johnson advised him to leave the body, which was still clad in pale-pink pajamas, in the water. Around Betty's waist were tied two lead weights. She had been partially decapitated by a sin-gle shotgun blast to the head.

"It didn't move him when he pulled her body out of the water or when he said that he'd put a shotgun to her head," remembers retired highway patrolman E. C. Locklear. "It was as cold-blooded and premeditated as it could be. What pushed him to do it, none of us knew. Later on, when I put him in the squad car to take him to jail, I said, 'Mack, didn't you expect to get caught?' And he said, 'Not this quick.' He showed no emotion or regret or fear. It was like he was talking about shooting a dog."

Investigators called for an ambulance to be sent to the scene without sounding its siren, but reporters were not far behind. Before Mack was taken to jail, he recounted what had taken place the night before while newsmen from the *Odessa American* and the

Fort Worth Star-Telegram took down his story and six photographers jockeyed for the best angle. On the drive out to the hunting lease, "she was cheerful and chatted about how happy she was going to be when she was dead," Mack explained. He had parked his Jeep a short distance from the stock tank, and he and Betty had sat there for a while and talked. "She was happy," he recalled. "She kept saying what it was going to be like in heaven." Then they had walked down to the pond together. Shivering, Betty had hurried back to the Jeep to retrieve her duster. When she returned to the spot where Mack was waiting for her by the water, she took off her shoes. "I just stood there with the gun," Mack told reporters. "I said, 'Give me a kiss to remember you by.' She gave me a kiss and then said, 'Thank you, Mack. I will always remember you for that.' Then she said, 'Now.' I raised the gun barrel up, and she took ahold of it with the back of her hand and held it up [to her temple]. And then I pulled the trigger. She was dead—like that." He snapped his fingers for emphasis.

As word spread around Odessa that afternoon that Mack had been arrested for Betty's murder, the news was greeted with incredulity. "I just can't believe it! Not Mack!" a sixteen-year-old girl shrieked as she collapsed in tears against a wall in the police station. "We were shocked that one of our own—a popular football player who had been to our parties and had dated our friends—had committed a heinous crime," says Jean Smith Kiker. "And as more information came out, we were shocked to learn that Mack, and a lot of the other boys we knew, had been spending time with Betty after they had taken their girlfriends home." But despite the gruesomeness of the crime and the first-degree murder charges that were filed against him, Mack was not ostracized by his peers. He was still invited to parties at Carol McCutchan's house and was welcome at Tommy's Drive-In. Girls visited him at home and boasted of knowing him. Rather than seeing Mack as a killer, many classmates acted as if something tragic that was beyond his control had befallen him.

"We were all supportive, because we couldn't believe it," says a for-mer Tri-Hi-Y girl who asked not to be identified. "We figured that if Mack did it, then there had to be a good reason."

After the arrest, the gossip centered less on Mack than it did on Betty. "She was seen as a slut and a diabolical manipulator," says Shelton Williams. "My father overheard a customer at his car wash say, 'Everyone knew that girl was no good. She tricked that boy into killing her.' " Betty's classmates in *Winterset,* which was can-celed after the news of Mack's arrest, puzzled over her intentions on the last night of her life. Had she really wanted to die, or was she still hoping, somehow, to win Mack back? "I think Betty trapped herself in a real-life drama of her own making," says Dixon Bowles. "She was adlibbing all the way, and it spun out of her control. I remember a teacher taking me aside afterward and asking me, 'Was Betty pregnant?' And I said, 'No. I wish it were that simple.' It was a game of chicken, and she never backed out."

March 20, 1961

I want everyone to know that what I'm about to do in no way impli-cates anyone else. I say this to make sure that no blame falls on anyone other than myself.

I have depressing problems that concern, for the most part, myself. I'm waging a war within myself, a war to find the true me and I fear that I am losing the battle. So rather than admit defeat I'm going to beat a quick retreat into the no man's land of death. As I have only the will and not the fortitude necessary, a friend of mine, seeing how great is my tor-ment, has graciously consented to look after the details.

His name is Mack Herring and I pray that he will not have to suffer for what he is doing for my sake. I take upon myself all blame, for there it lies, on me alone!

Betty Williams

WHEN *THE STATE OF Texas v. John Mack Herring* got under way on February 20, 1962, a guilty verdict seemed to be an all but foregone conclusion. Mack's own confession painted a picture of a methodically planned murder; before driving Betty half an hour out of town and shooting her, point-blank, in the head, he had, by his own admission, procured lead weights, rope, shotgun shells, and even a miner's helmet to light his way so he could submerge her body in the stock tank. In the presence of lawmen, he had shown little emotion for his victim. (While in custody, Mack reportedly told a deputy sheriff, "I feel toward her like a cat lying in a muddy street in the rain.") "It looked, to most people, like a case that was impossible for the defendant to win," says writer Larry L. King, who had left Midland a decade earlier but still followed the case. "I mean, the defendant had admitted he kissed the girl, then blew her away, weighted her body, and buried it in the pond: What else did the state need?" So King was confounded when his good friend Warren Burnett, an Odessa defense attorney, decided to take the case. "I asked Burnett why and he said, 'Church ain't over till they sing.'"

At 34, Burnett was already considered one of the finest trial lawyers around, having earned the sobriquet "the boy wonder of the West." An ex-Marine who, at the age of 25, had been the youngest prosecutor in Texas, Burnett always brought a sense of theater to the courtroom. In his melodious baritone, he peppered his arguments with Shakespeare and Scripture and won over jurors with his down-home charisma, so much so that no jury had ever sent a client of his to prison. In the Kiss and Kill case, he hatched a plan that he hoped would prevent Mack from ever standing trial for murder, using a defense strategy that had never, to anyone's recollection, been used before. Under Texas law, if jurors found a defendant temporarily insane—that is, insane only when he committed the crime—he would walk free. Citing this statute, Burnett argued before district court judge G. C. Olsen that before any trial was to take place, jurors should first have to evaluate Mack's sanity at the time he pulled the trigger. If they determined that he had been temporarily insane, he should not have to stand trial for murder. Burnett's line of reasoning flouted legal precedent; sanity hearings are supposed to take up only the narrow question of whether a defendant is competent to stand trial. But to the astonishment of courthouse observers and over the strenuous objections of the prosecution, Judge Olsen granted Burnett's motion for the pretrial hearing. Jurors would not determine Mack's guilt or innocence; they would only render a decision as to whether he had been insane at the time of the crime. Mack, in effect, would have a chance at acquittal before his murder trial had even begun. When flummoxed prosecutors requested a 24-hour delay to prepare their case, Burnett expressed his surprise, "since insanity is the only possible explanation for this tragedy."

Because the murder had occurred just across the Ector County line, the hearing took place in Kermit, an oil-patch town 45 miles west of Odessa, where the smell of petroleum hung in the air. The jury pool was the largest that had ever been called in Winkler County; the last murder to get much attention—a stabbing at a hotel in Wink—had happened in 1947. Teenagers filled many of the 160 seats in Judge Olsen's courtroom, at times spilling over into the aisle and out the door. "It was a carnival," says former Winkler County clerk Virginia Healy. "The defendant was a good-looking boy, and all these clean-cut girls came out from Odessa to ooh and aah over him." Nicknamed "Mack's girls," they made up only a fraction of the spectators whose sympathies were with the defendant. Betty's parents, lost in their grief, were her only visible supporters; her father occasionally leaned forward so as not to miss a word of testimony, dabbing at his eyes with a white handkerchief. Mack sat behind the defense table in a dark suit, his head often bowed. The strain of the proceedings sometimes showed, as when he laid his head in his hands during jury selection; otherwise, he was impassive. Arguing for the state was 32-year-old district attorney Dan Sullivan, an earnest, if not particularly seasoned, lawyer who was out of his depth; in his sixteen months in office, he had prosecuted mostly oil-field theft cases and

DWIs. It was Burnett, with the sleeves of his suit jacket pushed up to his elbows, who commanded the courtroom.

Because the burden of proof fell on Burnett to prove that Mack was insane when he pulled the trigger, the hearing began not with witnesses for the state but for the defense. The first person Burnett called to the stand was Mack's father, O. H. Herring, who told the jury that on the day of his son's arrest, Mack had handed him a letter Betty had written. The letter, which the Texas Department of Public Safety had authenticated and which Mr. Herring read to the jury, held that Betty alone was to blame for her death. "You might say she has become a witness for the defense," Burnett quipped. Nine character witnesses—including Odessa High's head football coach, Lacy Turner—spoke on Mack's behalf; many of them concurred that Mack must have been temporarily insane at the time of the crime. Three classmates testified that Betty had also asked them to kill her. But the most compelling testimony came from Marvin Grice, an Odessa psychiatrist who had examined Mack three days after the murder. The former football player had been "dethroned of his reasoning" by Betty's pleadings, Grice said, and, in his estimation, had been temporarily insane when he put the shotgun to her head. "He became so mixed up and so sick that he felt pulling the trigger was what he should do for her," Grice testified. "He was deprived of the power of applying logic." However, the effects of this "gross stress reaction" were temporary. "He can be trusted to lead a normal life," Grice assured the jury.

Sullivan put on the best case he could given the extraordinary limitations he was working with. Judge Olsen had denied his motion to have Mack evaluated by a psychiatrist for the state, having agreed with Burnett that the defendant's current state of mind was irrelevant. Sullivan tried to establish jealousy as a motive by calling to the stand Bill Rose, the popular football player whom Betty had parked with when she was dating Mack. But Bill testified that he had spurned Betty's advances when they had parked in a secluded spot. Besides, Bill maintained, the incident had not had much of an effect on Mack. "We talked a while and agreed our friendship was more valuable than an argument about her," Bill testified. "We shook hands and forgot the whole thing." Sullivan pushed on, focusing on classmate Howard Sellers's comment that Betty's dramatic note attempting to exonerate Mack had been "conceived in a joking atmosphere." But the district attorney could not establish a motive. "The entire proceeding was a perversion of the law," says Sullivan, who is still a practicing lawyer in the nearby town of Andrews. "The jury never heard the indictment read or learned how the crime was committed. None of the facts of the case came out."

Moments after Sullivan rested his case, Burnett rose from his seat and thundered across the crowded courtroom, "Stand up, Mack Herring! Go around and take the witness chair." It appeared that Burnett was calling his client to the stand for rebuttal, but no sooner had Mack been sworn in than Burnett, for further dramatic effect, roared, "Pass the witness! Answer the questions they have for you, lad." If he had hoped to throw the prosecution off balance, he had succeeded, though Sullivan tried to make the most of the opportunity. In his cross-examination, the district attorney pressed Mack to explain at what moment, exactly, he had decided to kill Betty. "I don't know," Mack stammered. "I can't remember . . . I can't explain." He had difficulty understanding it all himself, he told the jury in a halting voice. "I have stayed awake at night trying to think so I could explain it to other people," he said. "Sometimes now I think it was a dream. Sometimes I think it was real. Sometimes I think I am watching someone else." As he sat in the witness chair, he appeared solemn and contrite. Though other classmates had believed that Betty was joking when she had asked them to kill her, Mack maintained that her pleas had had a profound effect on him. Betty had "talked about heaven a lot," he said, and had made it appear "like a place you could reach out and touch." He explained that on the night he killed her, he had believed he was doing the right thing. In retrospect, he told the jury, "I know that everything about it was wrong."

After eleven hours of deliberation, during which jurors asked that Grice's expert testimony be read back to them, they determined that Mack had, in fact, been temporarily insane on the night of the murder. Upon hearing the verdict, Mack slumped in his chair and wept, while friends and classmates rushed to his side to embrace him. Betty's parents slipped through the exuberant crowd and out of the courtroom before reporters could reach them for comment.

While Burnett had been careful not to malign Betty's character during the hearing, some details of the case, like her sneaking out of her house in her nightclothes to meet Ike Nail, had tarred her as a loose, immoral girl. "I overheard a juror talking about Betty," says Hazel Locklear, the wife of the highway patrolman who had been struck by Mack's aloofness at the crime scene. "I remember her saying, in a very ugly way, 'That girl was *nothing.*' " To some observers, it seemed as if Betty's transgressions had eclipsed those of the teenager who had killed her. "Nobody talked about how Mack could have said no," observes Sandra Scofield, who graduated from Odessa High a year before the murder. "Betty had enlisted him— this worthy young man—to do what she didn't have the courage to do herself. She had 'roped' him into doing it. So she became not the victim but the villain."

Sullivan appealed the verdict to the Texas Supreme Court, on the grounds that Judge Olsen did not have the authority to grant a hearing that only evaluated Mack's sanity at the time of the crime. On June 27, 1962, the court sided with Sullivan, vacating the judgment and ordering a new trial. But what advantage he gained in being allowed to present his evidence was negated by Burnett's skill and showmanship. Because of the intense publicity, the second trial was moved nearly six hundred miles away, to Beaumont. Burnett relied on his old playbook. He put Grice back on the stand and packed the courtroom with teammates, teachers, parents, and community leaders who took the stand to extol his client's virtues. Mack had been a stellar student, one of his teachers told the jury, and added, "I've never known a more brilliant mind." His football coach testified that

Mack had never used profanity. Howard Sellers said that Mack was his "idol" and "personified everything that was good."

In an impassioned closing argument that Burnett delivered before a standing-room-only crowd, he hammered home the fact that nearly two years after Betty's murder, the prosecution had still not established a motive. "Does the evidence show you any possible explanation?" he challenged the jury. "Until some evidence is brought to show the psychiatrists were wrong, I'd be inclined to believe them." Jurors agreed, and twelve days before Christmas, they found Mack not guilty by reason of insanity. A smattering of applause broke out in the courtroom when the verdict was announced, and once again, Mack was mobbed by jubilant supporters. A few glad observers, including the wife of a Baptist minister who sat on the jury, looked on with tears in their eyes. Mack, who had once worried aloud to a reporter that he would be sent to the electric chair, was a free man.

> *To whom it may concern,*
>
> *The time has come to leave, and as I prepare to go, I find it difficult to write the words that will explain . . .*
>
> *I love you Dick, for all that you have meant to me. You've been the greatest friend I could ever ask for. Here's to all the stories we never wrote. Maybe it's better that way—they'll never be exposed to the critics or the public. I hope our story about Jerry makes it. Think of me once in a while and know that I'm glad we met.*
>
> *Gayle . . . I'm sorry about Indiana, but I hope you'll understand. Here's hoping you'll always have the best because you're one of the best!*
>
> *I find the tears clouding my eyes as I say goodbye to those I love. May they forgive me . . .*
>
> *Mr. Herring, you're a wonderful man. So many times I've wanted to tell you how much I appreciate you. I'm sorry I have to tell you like this. . . .*
>
> *Memories, so many memories to come back and cloud my mind, memories that I'll carry through all eternity.*

———

ANYONE WHO HAD SUFFERED the unrelenting scrutiny that Mack had—the *Odessa American* alone ran nearly two dozen front-page stories on the case—might have pulled up stakes and started a new life somewhere else. But Mack chose to stay. After attending Texas Tech University, where he was once introduced to a class as "the famous Mack Herring," he returned home to the town that never turned its back on him. He made a quiet life for himself, and he steered clear of trouble with the law. He married and divorced, twice. He worked as a dock foreman at a chemical company, a carpenter, a welder, and, for at least the past 25 years, as an electrician. Few of his former classmates still see him; most have moved away or fallen out of touch. As the booms and busts of the oil patch have brought new people to Odessa and taken others away, Mack has faded into the background.

I caught sight of him one afternoon in November as he pulled up to his home, a mint-green frame house not far from where he grew up. His own neighborhood lacks the gracious lawns and spreading trees of his childhood; the house, which is a bit down at the heels, looks like the province of a man who lives alone. A meager yard of packed dirt and weeds led to the street, and an old rusted pickup sat in the driveway. Mack, who declined to be interviewed for this article, looked indistinguishable from any other working man in Odessa, right down to his beat-up truck with the toolbox in the bed. Nothing suggested that he had once been sharply handsome or held a great deal of promise. At 62, he was utterly unremarkable.

"This has not been a free ride for Mack," says his childhood friend Larry Francell. "It's ruined two lives. One's dead, one's still alive." And because many people in town would prefer never to hear the words "kiss and kill" again, the case still touches a nerve. "I suspect most of us would rather let the thing stay in the past," one Odessa High School alumna wrote me in an e-mail. "There was already enough pain in '61. Why dredge it up again?" But others refuse to forget. "I don't take well to the fact that people don't think this is an important story," says Shelton Williams, who carried a photograph of his cousin in his wallet for 35 years after her murder. "I don't believe that Betty ever wanted to die." In the Williams family, grandiose threats and melodramatic bids for attention had not been unique to Betty. "When her father lived with my parents, he used to threaten to kill himself in the middle of the night," says Shelton. "My mother would sit up with him and try to talk him out of it, until he did it one too many times. Then she told him to just go ahead and do it, which he didn't. When Betty said that life wasn't worth living without Mack, I understood it within the context of our family." Her murder and the verdicts that followed had stripped away any of his preconceptions about fairness and justice. "No other event in my life impacted me the way this did," he says. "Everything looked different to me afterward. Betty had been murdered, and everyone wanted to sweep it under the rug and make it go away."

And still, after nearly half a century's worth of other tragedies, the stories at Odessa High School live on. In October an Odessa College student named Sammie Sanchez, who was researching a paper she had to present to her speech class on the best place to spend Halloween, received permission to spend the night in the high school's auditorium. When I met Sanchez and three of her girlfriends a few weeks later, they told me, in great detail, about all the strange and unexplained things they had heard and seen: the door that had mysteriously slammed closed behind them, the eerie footsteps, the stage lights that had moved when they had called out Betty's name. After two hours in the auditorium, Sanchez and her friends were so unnerved, and so certain that they had felt Betty's presence, that they decided to leave. But first they did what they assumed any drama girl—spectral or not—would have wanted. "We let Betty know she was the star," Sanchez says. "We sat there in the theater seats, in the dark, and we applauded for her."

PAMELA COLLOFF *has been a staff writer at* Texas Monthly *since 1997. She is a graduate of Brown University and was raised in New York City. In 2001, she was a finalist for a National Magazine Award in public interest for her article on school prayer. In 2002, the* Columbia Journalism Review *profiled her in "Ten Young Writers on the Rise." She lives in Austin.*

CODA

I first heard about the "Kiss and Kill murder" from Monica Walters, a friend of friends who I met in Austin. Monica had learned of the case from a former professor of hers, Shelton Williams, and it was Shelton who made this story possible. Writing this piece was a challenge because so many of the main players were either dead or refused to talk to me. Shelton was generous enough to lend me dozens of Betty's letters, and to recount his vivid memories of his first cousin. (I was also lucky enough, using driver's license records and other public data, to track down several of Betty's former friends.) Though Betty was long dead, her letters and the memories of those who knew her gave me insight into the daring but fragile young woman she was, and allowed me to write about her with a degree of compassion and insight that would not otherwise have been possible.

After "A Kiss Before Dying" was published, I received a number of e-mails from people who had gone to high school with Mack who wondered why it was that I wanted to dredge up the past. The disgust that some of them still felt for Betty was palpable. Few of her peers seemed interested in examining why hardly anyone had cared how troubled she was, or why she had been killed, or why the community had found it easier to rally around Mack. I often wondered how Betty might have fared had she come of age just a decade later, after the sixties had played out, or in a less conformist town than Odessa.

Mack Herring still lives in Odessa, and has not publicly spoken about the case in more than forty years.

STEVE FISHMAN

THE DEVIL IN
DAVID BERKOWITZ

FROM *New York* MAGAZINE

ONE CRISP, EARLY-SUMMER MORNING, MaryAnn and Jimmy
Skubus and I are holding hands at a Starbucks—they'd extended
their hands and, taking the cue, I grabbed them. MaryAnn says
grace, blessing our scone and marble cake, then turns to the subject
that's brought us together. "David is so different from what everyone thinks," she says. "He's a special person." David is David
Berkowitz, better known as Son of Sam, and, in one sense, everyone knows that he is out of the ordinary: He's the most famous
serial killer in New York history.

But what does MaryAnn mean, David's special?

I pick at the scone. Jimmy, a big-boned, easygoing ironworker,
attacks the marble cake.

"Am I going into this, Jimmy?" MaryAnn asks. She seems on
the verge of some big emotion.

"Why not?" he says and shrugs his powerful shoulders.

As far as I can figure out, Son of Sam hasn't spoken to the press
in seven years. Yet reports filter out that he has a new outlook and a
new set of friends. And so when MaryAnn introduced herself to

me as "a good friend of David's"—we bumped into each other at the courthouse where David has a legal matter pending—I was encouraged. Perhaps MaryAnn and Jimmy can tell me about the new David.

Unfortunately, at Starbucks, MaryAnn, 48, tall and skinny, seems stalled in her tracks. She's got this intense look on her face, and an intense outfit. She wears a black motorcycle jacket, black motorcycle boots, and black motorcycle gloves. There's a pastel-colored band circling her head, a kind of homage, I learned later. The headband makes her think of Jesus' crown of thorns. She stares at Jimmy. "Oh, Jimmy, these are heavy things," she says.

Jimmy nods, encouraging her.

"It's hard to say," she begins. She leans forward, turns her electric-blue eyes on me, then announces, "I have the call of a prophet upon my life . . . It's wild because it's self-proclaimed. There's nothing I can do. I cannot escape. The Lord will defend me in it."

Then she adds, "That's how I knew about David the minute I saw him."

"What did you know about David?" I ask stupidly.

At first, MaryAnn explains, David was not a person for her but a number. "The Lord had given me, shot into my spirit and I could never shake it, the number 44," she explains. Years before she met David, she'd even named her dog 44. "Periodically I would get the number 444, which was like the perfection of the number." MaryAnn didn't understand at first, but later the meaning became crystal clear. She says, "It was the identification of David Berkowitz." Initially, the press called him the ".44-Caliber Killer," because his six murders were committed with a .44-caliber pistol. Then two years ago, she ran into a guy she knew at the local Shop Rite, a Christian like her. They started talking, and soon he invited her to visit David in prison.

"When David walked in [to the visitors' room], I knew," she tells me.

Again, I wonder, "What did you know?"

"There's nobody bigger than this guy. Oh, my God, this guy is an apostle of the Lord."

David Berkowitz, the Jewish serial killer, an apostle of Jesus?

"It would be a prophet that would know," MaryAnn assures me.

Leaving Starbucks, I hand my business card to Jimmy. Later that afternoon, I call MaryAnn. "Jesus is Lord," MaryAnn answers. She seems very excited to hear from me. There's apparently been a sign; in MaryAnn's world, there are no coincidences. Jimmy, she explains, noticed the magazine's address on my business card: 444 Madison Avenue.

"This is probably the guy we should be working with," he told MaryAnn. (If that weren't enough, the Starbucks bill came to $12.44.)

Then MaryAnn asks me if I want to meet David. "Thank you, Lord," I say aloud after I hang up.

TO MOST NEW YORKERS, Son of Sam is still the iconic figure of evil. Thirty years ago, he began a reign of terror, killing six and wounding seven over the course of a year. With the city's newspapers trumpeting each attack, he terrorized New Yorkers as no lone criminal has ever done. (NO ONE IS SAFE FROM SON OF SAM, said a *Post* headline at the time.) Sam targeted young female strangers—white, college-bound prizes of the middle class. At times, he seemed to court the city. He believed, as he later put it, that "people were rooting for me." After nearly three months without an attack, he wrote *Daily News* columnist Jimmy Breslin: "I am still here like a spirit roaming the night. Thirsty, hungry, seldom stopping to rest."

The city panicked. People turned in relatives, neighbors. Women, alerted that Sam preferred brunettes, dyed their hair or bought wigs. It didn't matter. Weeks after the letter to Breslin, Sam killed again. The victim was Stacy Moskowitz. "My daughter was blonde," the victim's mother, Neysa, lamented. Then, a couple weeks later, in August 1977, he was caught, tripped up by a traffic ticket, a pudgy, 24-year-old postal worker with a boyish face, seventies sideburns, Elvisish dark hair, and an eerie, apparently indelible half-smile.

Son of Sam was sentenced to 365 years in prison, which should have kept him out of the public consciousness for several lifetimes. But in prison, an amazing thing happened. The infamous serial killer became a holy man, holier *because* of his evil past. He's now at the center of a growing Christian mission. His humility, his piety, his charitable, Christ-like heart inspire Christians around the world—one African is even named after Son of Sam. (He's Kwaku Berkowitz.) Fellow Christians overwhelm him with letters. They pray for him and crave his advice, his spiritual insight, his fatherly guidance. He produces videotapes and journals, gives interviews to Christian radio shows. David—he hates the words "Son of Sam"—works as a pastor, walking the prison halls with a Gideons Bible and a calling from God. He's battling Satan, he says, his old friend. And David is sure Satan's afraid of him, because David knows all his tricks. The monster who terrorized New York is now apparently on the road to redemption. "I'm heaven-bound and shouting victory," he tells Christian audiences.

"HOW YA DOIN'?" calls David as he strolls toward us with a little wave. The apostle, I notice, has an accent from the Bronx. MaryAnn and I wait in the visitors' room of the Sullivan County Correctional Facility, a large tiled room that resembles a high-school cafeteria. David pulls up a chair at our assigned spot, places his aviator-style glasses on the knotty-pine table, a product, by the look of it, of the prison shop. David still has the belly, but he's middle-aged now—he just turned 53—his face rounder, softer. And he's balding. The remaining hair is nearly white. Son of Sam looks harmless, like the aging postal worker he might have become.

"I don't know how long you're planning to stay," David immediately tells me. His words are sharp but not the tone. He is wary.

MaryAnn, I know, has already pleaded my case once to David. "When she feels the Lord's hand, she won't compromise," Jimmy had explained to me. Now she intercedes again. "Tell David what's on your heart," she instructs me. Dutifully, I begin a rambling disquisition about David's changed heart, his redemption, I say, using a word MaryAnn likes.

"Oh . . . okay . . . okay," David says, pausing mysteriously between words.

To get through the metal detector, MaryAnn had removed the metal cross from around her neck. But she carried in her red-leather Bible, which she pushes toward David. She tells him to share from Scripture.

"MaryAnn is director of operations," says David good-naturedly. "I'm glad she didn't bring her bullhorn."

And so, at our little prison-made table, Son of Sam starts to lead a Bible-study group. He flips to Romans 15:13. "Now the God of hope fill you with all joy and peace in believing, that ye may abound in hope, through the power of the Holy Ghost," he reads. I extract a few sheets of paper from a pocket along with a half-pencil. David thumbs to Psalm 34:6. It's the psalm that inspired his conversion, the linchpin moment in the latter-day Son of Sam. David's conversion story opens in a prison yard twenty years ago with the protagonist in despair: "I had nothing left to lose because I lost everything. I was an utter failure," he believed.

"Hey, Dave, do you ever read the Bible?" called an inmate, his identity now lost.

"No, I never read it," David said, and the inmate gave him a Bible.

One night, alone in his cell, David fell upon Psalm 34 and began to pray: "God, you know, I can't take this anymore." He prayed and cried and then suddenly, he tells me, "the idea that I could be forgiven entered my life."

David says the proposition of forgiveness initially troubled him. "I thought, *Maybe you're not forgiven,*" he says. "An inner voice said

I've done too many bad things." Three years later, in the prison chapel, a pastor read Micah 7, the verses about a God who "delighteth in mercy."

"It was as if he was talking just to me," says David. "Right then it just hit me. Something lit up inside me. Inner chains were broken in me. I realized God had forgiven me."

Once before, shortly after his arrest, David had also declared himself a born-again Christian but soon recanted, deciding he'd been brainwashed. "Was my involvement with these Christians just out of psychological need—a love substitute?" he asked at the time. Such questions no longer trouble him. A God who delights in mercy delights him. "I knew that I knew that I had been forgiven," says David. "I know that God loves me, really loves me." For David, conversion was a supernatural event, and it changed his character, he says.

Some audiences rejoiced at the news. For a Christian, consorting with the Devil is not necessarily a liability. Instead, as David learned, it can be a mark of election. David's admirers seemed to think that the bigger the sin, the better the Christian. What, after all, demonstrates God's power better than redeeming sinners like Son of Sam?

Victims' families, law enforcement, and civil society in general tend to take a different view. Some evil is unforgivable. Once in the room where we now sit, a visitor approached David and punched him in the face, a personal attempt at payback. This summer, when David came up for parole (which happens automatically every two years), newspapers checked in with victims' families. Should Son of Sam be on the streets again? "I'll kill him," responded one father. David understands—he declined to even apply for parole this year—and didn't press charges against his assailant. He wants nothing more, he says, than to apologize to his victims' families. Several years ago, he wrote to Neysa Moskowitz, mother of his last victim, Stacy, the blonde. Neysa had rarely passed up a chance to tell the press that she loathed David.

"The Lord put it in my heart to reach out to her because Neysa's suffering a lot," David says. He wrote to her in September 2000: "I am sorry that I ruined your life and your dreams." Neysa wrote back. A relationship developed. David even sent her Mother's Day cards. Eventually David called her from the prison yard. "I started crying and began apologizing," he says. They talked about Stacy, he says, even shared a few laughs. Later, when a Christian admirer mailed David $20,000, he sent $1,000 to Neysa, which she appreciated. (He says he didn't keep any of the money.) At one time, Neysa and David even planned to meet at the prison; it was going to be filmed for TV. Neysa says she wanted information about the murder of her daughter. David backed out. "I couldn't in my heart. It would be a circus. I had personal things to share I didn't want to be used," he says. Soon thereafter, the relationship fell apart. "Neysa's forgiveness was withdrawn," David tells me glumly. "She's back to hating me."

David returned to the more reliable forgiveness of a magnanimous God. "So much has happened in my life, so much healing, so much deliverance, so much forgiveness, not from people but from God," David has explained. He doesn't really like to think about his crimes anymore. "Too painful." A grimace sweeps across his face. Plus the past is mostly "a blur." It seems to David that God has tossed the distressing details of his crimes into the sea of forgetfulness, along with his sins. For David, it's time to move on. "I can't undo what was done. It's 30 years ago. Enough already," he tells me.

THERE WAS A TIME when David could think of little besides his crimes. Shortly after his arrest in 1977, he confessed to all six murders. For an accused killer, he was unusually talkative. Effortlessly, almost proudly, he provided chilling details about each attack. ("[Stacy] and her date started to kiss passionately," he wrote. "At this time, I too, was sexually aroused . . . They went back to the car . . . I had my gun out, aimed at the middle of Stacy's head and fired . . .

I didn't even know she was shot because she didn't say anything nor did she move.") What troubled David, and what he couldn't explain, was why he committed the crimes. "I can't figure out what made me kill those poor people," said David, a surprisingly reflective monster. At times, David seemed to crave not only an explanation of his motives but a theory of himself. Soon enough, competing schools emerged to do the job, and David, like an impressionable seeker from the seventies, tried one after the other.

At first he sided with those who believed him insane. Lawrence Klausner, a novelist who wrote *Son of Sam* in 1987, partly based on David's prison diaries, proposed that he lived in a psychotic fantasy world. It was easy to believe. Months before his killing spree, David, recently back from the Army and on his own for the first time, wrote to his father in Florida: "Dad the world is getting dark now. I can feel it more and more. You wouldn't believe how much some people hate me." Another letter to his father was ebullient but also disturbing. "I feel like a saint sometimes. I guess I'm kind of one." In his prison diaries, David seems completely mad at moments. He reported that a dog spoke to him, channeling a 6,000-year-old man named Sam whom he sometimes identified with Sam Carr, a neighbor and dog owner. "He told me [to kill] through his dog, as he usually does," David wrote. He worried that his condition would worsen. "I may, one day, evolve into a humanoid or demon in a more complete state," he said. Three of four court-appointed psychiatrists didn't hesitate; they found him unfit to stand trial.

A fourth, however, took a different view. "His delusions were manufactured," wrote Dr. David Abrahamsen. ("Sometimes a dog is just a dog," quipped the doctor.) It was a view that David, too, soon found compelling. From prison, he wrote to Abrahamsen, a professor, psychiatrist, and researcher affiliated with Columbia, "I guess you see me as I really am—an animal and unhuman." Suddenly, David had only disdain for the doctors who fell for what he now called his ruse.

"All I had to do was slide 'Sam Carr' and the 'demons' into the conversation," wrote David about his relationship with another court-appointed psychiatrist. "Why he would practically be wiping the tears from my eyes and comforting me. Goodness what a nice man he was."

In Abrahamsen's view, David was sane. He was also grandiose, hysterical, and profoundly troubled. And the root of the trouble was adoption. David Richard Berkowitz was born Richard David Falco. At a few days old, he was adopted by Pearl and Nathan Berkowitz, a modest, childless Jewish couple who lived in a one-bedroom Bronx apartment. David's hardworking father, who owned a hardware store, was often absent. But Pearl was doting. "I loved her very much," David told Abrahamsen during an interview, sobbing. She died of cancer when David was 14. "After Mother's death," he said, "I lost the capacity to love."

In his 1985 book *Confessions of Son of Sam,* Abrahamsen argues that adoption was the initial wound. "He'd lost the love that should have been given him," he concluded. The death of his mother was a second, again by a woman. In 1975, the year before the shootings began, David's feelings of abandonment intensified. He launched a "personal hunt" for his real mother. He found Betty Falco in Queens and slipped a Mother's Day card in her mailbox. Betty, once an aspiring Broadway dancer, was ecstatic at the reunion and welcomed "Richie," as she insisted on calling David, into her life. David, too, had high hopes. Soon, though, they collapsed. He met his half-sister, the child Betty hadn't given away. "I first realized I was an accident, a mistake, never meant to be born—unwanted," he wrote to Abrahamsen. David learned he was the by-product of Betty's longtime affair with a married man.

He continued to visit Betty every couple months, acting the part, as he put it, of "Richie nice guy." Inside, though, something else stirred. "I was filled with anger and rage toward Betty," he told Abrahamsen. "I was getting a very powerful urge to kill most of my 'natural' family." A few months later, Son of Sam began hunting young women. "I want to be a lover to women, but I want to destroy them too," David wrote. "Especially women who dance. Them I hate. I hate their sensuality, their moral laxity. I'm no saint myself but I blame them for everything." In Abrahamsen's view, David's spree was revenge against women, especially Betty. The dogs, the demons, were metaphors for the violence within. It was no coincidence that he hunted in lover's lanes, targeting young women making out in parked cars. David wrote, "My mother Betty was sitting in those parked cars with [my father]."

David liked communicating with Abrahamsen, which he sometimes thought of as talking to God. Eventually, though, he soured on Abrahamsen and on the good doctor's interpretation. "He had a mold that he wanted to fit me in and would do what he could to make me fit that mold," David decided. David shifted his interpretive allegiance to Maury Terry, who minced few words when it came to Abrahamsen. "Yeah, everything's the fault of the mother," Terry says. "You know, it's just bullshit. Abrahamsen was so full of himself he got right to the brink of getting the truth and then stopped."

In his 1987 book *The Ultimate Evil,* Terry, a former business journalist for IBM, proposed a bold new theory of David's crimes, and also of his character. In Terry's view, David's fundamental flaw wasn't insanity or emotional instability but an abiding gullibility. "Berkowitz was susceptible to any line of shit," says Terry. His failing, the one that underpinned all others, was an intense loneliness, a vulnerability. David had once inventoried his problems: "A series of rotten jobs, to a rotten social life and a horrifying feeling of becoming an old bachelor or a dirty old man. I had no woman in my life . . . I felt like worthless shit." He "thirsted," as he put it, for normal relationships with people. One night, outside his Bronx building, he ran into Michael Carr, son of Sam Carr, the neighbor whose dog did or didn't speak to David. Michael Carr invited David to a nearby park, which Terry says was a meeting place for a Westchester affiliate of a satanic network called the Process Church of the Final Judgment.

David began attending meetings in the woods. "Before long he was cutting prints in his finger and pledging to Lucifer," says Terry. Or to Samhain, the Druid devil, and a source of the name Son of Sam. The group got into small-time arson and animal sacrifices, and then it escalated. Terry says the cult was behind the Son of Sam killings. There's long been circumstantial evidence that David didn't act alone. Six police sketches based on eyewitness accounts look dramatically dissimilar (and one closely resembles Michael Carr's brother, John). The most compelling corroboration, though, comes, as usual, from David. In 1993, Terry interviewed him in prison for *Inside Edition*. On camera, a nodding, penitent David explains, "The killings were another sacrifice to our gods, bunch of scumbags that they were." Later, he explained, "We made a pact, maybe with the devil, but also with each other . . . We were going to go all the way with this thing. We're soldiers of Satan now. I was just too far in, too loyal, too much playing the role of the soldier and trying to please people." The killings, he told Terry, were a group effort. "I did not pull the trigger on every single one of them," David said. He didn't pull the trigger on Stacy, he told Terry. He killed three people, though he was always at the scene. Others dispute the conspiracy theory. Abrahamsen, for one, considered it hogwash. And Neysa, whatever forgiveness she may have once expressed, blames David alone. She has a letter from him that settles the matter for her. "I hope that one day you will forgive me for taking your daughter's life," he wrote.

And yet, enough suspicious coincidence swirls around the case to give pause. Soon after David's arrest, John and Michael Carr both died mysterious deaths, one an unsolved murder, the other possibly a suicide. Even the Queens district attorney at the time believed David didn't act alone. In talking with me, David doesn't deny his involvement with the Carr brothers. Officially, a police investigation is still open, says Terry.

"I was expecting to go to hell," David said later about his spree. That didn't put him off. "I'll be with my friends," he thought. But then, after his arrest, he learned that their friendship only went so far. "They completely abandoned me," he said.

IN THE PRISON VISITING ROOM, David, MaryAnn, and I huddle over the Bible. David and his Christian friends, I know by now, are no ordinary churchgoers. They're right-thinking, intolerant prayer warriors for whom churches are too tame; MaryAnn left hers a decade ago. "I'm not some dorky bake-sale Christian," she let me know. "I don't quote the Scripture, I live it." For them, the world described in the Bible is vibrant and alive, as real as the world they live in. "You're like the early disciples," I once said to MaryAnn, which pleased her.

David locates a passage. A chubby finger pokes at each word as he reads it. It's a tale of demon possession from Mark.

MaryAnn prods him, "Go further."

"When I read this a long time ago, the Lord said to me, 'This is you,' and I saw that this could be the story of my life," he says.

For David, it seems the Bible is the ultimate explanatory adventure, a last attempt to name the demon. David doesn't take these verses from Mark as a parable of how people get caught in a web of sin. For David, the Bible is a detailed, precise, almost journalistic account of the struggle between fierce combatants, God and the Devil.

Reading the Bible, David finally discovers why he killed those poor people.

"There is no doubt in my mind that a demon has been living in me since birth," he says. "As a child, I was fascinated with suicide. I thought about throwing myself in front of cars. I was out of control."

As a child, David pulled apart and burned his toy soldiers, sometimes throwing them out the window at people in the street below. "I was obsessed with *Rosemary's Baby*," he says. "I felt like it was speaking directly to me. I stayed in my closet. I 'ran from the light into darkness,' as the Bible says."

Everything now makes sense. His longings, his isolation, and his serial disappointments with girls were real. They were also, he once described, "a spell to turn people away from me and create a situation of isolation, loneliness, and personal frustration, as part of [the Devil's] master plan." The speaking dog was real, too, David tells me. He believed that dogs really did communicate with him, though now he knows it was another satanic trick.

I set down my pencil. I'm not sure what to make of the return of demons and talking dogs. David, always attuned to his interlocutor, is sensitive to my secular doubts. "If people don't have a clue about spiritual things, they'll say, 'Well, this guy is nuts,' " is how David explains it.

David fixes me with blue eyes, close-set in a big oval head. "The Devil can manifest psychologically," he says serenely. "Looking at someone controlled by an evil spirit, you'd think that person's crazy . . . It's all hard to explain." There's a shrug to his tone, as if to say, make of it what you will.

"The demons are real. I saw them, felt their presence, and I heard them. You get into a state that is so far gone your own personality is dissolved," he'd once earnestly explained, "and you take on these demonic entities . . . It was like another person was in me . . . doing a lot of directing. I struggled, but things became overwhelming. I lost my sense of myself. I was taken over by something else, another personality."

To David's Christian circle, this is not incredible; it's heartening. David's dark past ushers them into the thick of a miracle, God's mercy. To them, it's as if he's a figure out of the Bible, a familiar to its intense moral struggles, its miracles, its direct, communicative God. And right here in the Catskills, a short drive away.

In turn, his Christian friends celebrate David, elevate him. MaryAnn tells me that he is a modern-day Paul, the murderer who became an apostle. "That's David," says MaryAnn. "He lives by the Scripture," says one Christian former law-enforcement officer. "He's Jesus-like," says another Christian friend, a former Jew, referring to David's pared-down lifestyle. "He has an advantage," I was told. "He's away from all the distractions." Incarceration, in this view, is a symbol: It stands for Christian suffering. "The walk of a Christian is to the cross," MaryAnn tells me. "That's the spirit of David."

David has a long scar on his neck where an inmate at Attica slit his throat. MaryAnn reaches a hand to lift his collar. She wants to show me the scar, evidence of his trials. David flinches. He doesn't want to draw attention to his past. Instead, he returns to the leather-covered Bible—MaryAnn covers her Bibles, the only books in her house, with old motorcycle jackets. He pages through, arriving at Acts 9. It is about the conversion of Saul—who, like David, was a Jew—to Paul the Christian. Saul was the persecutor of Christians; Paul the apostle of Christ. Next to this passage, I notice that MaryAnn has written, "DB's testimony."

"Paul . . . had to forget those past things and press on to the glorious future with God," David believes, "and I have to do the same."

In the visitors' room, MaryAnn begins to quietly sing a hymn. She's a musician with a beautiful voice and writes her own Christian songs. (She wrote one about David, rhyming "Son of Sam" with "the Great I Am.") David sings along for a minute, then stops, perhaps embarrassed in front of me. He blushes. There's a silence, and then MaryAnn says to David, "There are men that God raises up, and you're one of them." To me, she says, "God will build a church on David's back."

David rapidly blinks his eyes. "Okay . . . okay," he says. It's difficult to know what he's thinking. Then he raises his palms, flapping them as if shooting away the subject.

"I'm a servant," he says, which, MaryAnn assures me, is what an apostle would say.

"David is not going to tell you that he has the high calling of an apostle," she says.

"I see myself as a humble servant, not as a big shot," he reiterates. "People think I'm a figurehead . . . like Manson or something. He's supposed to have groupies. I would hate that. I wouldn't want that. I'm not the fanatic people have in mind."

"I really believe," MaryAnn tells me. "It's not even a belief. I know, even though David's in prison, he was sent to us. We waited on him."

In letters to me, David wants to make sure I don't misunderstand. In contrast to his mild presence, his letters are self-assured, assertive, formal. He's no longer in the confession business. "There are many things I no longer wish to discuss," he writes. "I kept telling MaryAnn no, that I wasn't ready [to be interviewed], but she was throwing a tantrum, stomping her feet and even shedding tears. I just moved into a different cell the day before and I was so tired that I capitulated to her request." He wants me to know that MaryAnn has him wrong. "I am not in agreement with MaryAnn's assessment that I am some kind of 'apostle,' " he writes in a bureaucratic tone. "I wish to be a servant to others, to help whosoever I can and give people encouragement and hope."

IN PRISON, David tells me he's engaged in active spiritual warfare. I'd like to hear more, but with me, he will only go so far. Seven years ago, however, he sat down with a 22-year-old Columbia journalism student named Lisa Singh, who had written him a letter. David sensed the hand of God in her interest and invited her to prison. Lisa included portions of their conversations in a *Penthouse* article, but most of the twenty hours of interviews remain unpublished; she provided tapes to *New York*. With Lisa, David seemed to feel freer to express himself, or perhaps he was simply more optimistic at the time. "I personally feel that God is calling me today to fulfill some kind of purpose," he told Lisa, "that he has some job that he wants done. God is calling me to be a prophetic voice to this nation, to people in general." God, he senses, counts on him to combat the Devil. David is sure he's up to the task. "I feel that Satan is very afraid of me because he knows I know so much about him from my own experiences," he told Lisa. David is quick to sniff out Satan's influence. The Devil lures kids down dangerous paths and also (still) targets David personally. "Strangers who lash out against me, 'Oh, he hasn't changed,' " said David. "That's all part of the battle." So was Spike Lee's 1999 movie, *Summer of Sam,* which spotlighted David's past. "I feel that the movie is purposely being designed to damage my Christian testimony," David told Lisa.

Fortunately for David, he lately has means at his disposal to counterattack. He has, by now, access to a modest media empire to spread his message. The key to his reach is his Christian celebrity, which piggybacks on his criminal celebrity which began about a decade ago. In 1997 Pat Robertson's *700 Club,* which appears on the Christian Broadcasting Network, interviewed David. Robertson praised him, citing David as proof that the Devil is real. The word was out; fundamentalist churches found David. A tiny Evangelical church out of San Diego—it calls itself House Upon the Rock, though it doesn't have a physical location—hosted "The Official Home Page of David Berkowitz." That site became forgivenforlife.com and was transferred to Morningstar Communications, a small New York literary agency, which posted David's near-daily journals back to 1998.

The journals, Christian reflections on everything from 9/11 to prayer in prison, were a turning point in his life, David says. Suddenly he was in communication with an audience. One reader was Darrell Scott, a Christian, whose daughter Rachel, also a Christian, was murdered at Columbine. Scott read in the journals how Rachel's story encouraged David. Scott traveled to Sullivan County Correctional—"David Berkowitz radiated the life of love of Jesus Christ," Scott writes—and they became friends.

With the help of another friend, Chuck Cohen, a fellow Jew who is now a fellow Christian, David soon made a Christian video—"Society wrote him off as hopeless . . . but God had other plans . . ." David passed me Chuck's phone number, and I left a message. Chuck called back almost immediately. "My answering machine," Chuck informed me, "hasn't worked in months," which he saw as a powerful sign. (I'd become accustomed to signs. MaryAnn mentioned shopping for an amplifier. The brand name, she said, was Fishman.) At his compact East Side apartment, Chuck reviewed his sinful past, though in his case, the principal sin appears to have been failure to succeed. Chuck, an Ivy Leaguer, was a stockbroker who couldn't earn a living. (These days, he delivers lost luggage and invests on the side along biblical guidelines. Chuck, sure the end of time is fast approaching, is into gold.) One day, a Christian friend laid his hands on Chuck and his wife. The Holy Spirit entered them, though it took faster for his wife. "She's already talking in tongues," he complained to the friend. (Later, talking in tongues came to Chuck too. It's not difficult, he told me, and gave a little demonstration.) Once converted, Chuck set out to bring other Jews to Jesus. He set up a table outside Zabar's, and prayed for a celebrity Jew to convert. Woody Allen, he hoped.

"Instead," says Chuck's wife, "God chose David to be that famous person."

The video Chuck helped produce in 1998, *Son of Hope,* was another turning point for David. In it, he preaches, jabbing a finger in the air and shouting, "I was the Son of Sam, now I'm the son of hope." Ministers write David "praise reports," thanking him for his testimony, which they assure him impresses their troubled teens.

David's Christian fame crossed over in 1999. That was the year David's past, repurposed as part of God's plan, attracted Larry King, who did an hour-long interview from prison. The attention snowballed. Other big Christian groups lined up: Trinity Broadcasting Network and, in 2004, Focus on the Family, which sells a CD of its interview with David.

As word of David's testimony spread, he was also working with African ministers, sending Bibles. And ordinary Christians increasingly sought him out.

The letters pour in. David receives five, ten, sometimes more, a day. People write that they're praying for unforgiving victims' families to get over their bitterness. And they write of their own troubles, as if this serial killer were the one person in the world who could understand their loneliness, their disappointments. Some identify with David. "I wanted and planned to kill my ex-boyfriend," wrote one young woman, whose letter from David apparently pulled her from the brink. David grew especially close to one troubled 17-year-old from Long Island. "Hey Berkoman!" he wrote, then told David that he was "insanely depressed . . . I can't stand life any longer." He wanted David to pray for him. "I don't care what you've done in your past," he wrote, "I think of you as a dad . . . you are like the best role model ever! . . . When I pray for you, I feel loved . . . I want a life like you are living today."

IT'S MID-AFTERNOON, the fourth hour of our visit, and the visitors' room at Sullivan Correctional is nearly empty. In the center of our little table, MaryAnn has stacked eighteen single dollar bills. "Make sure David gets fed," Jimmy had instructed. He had in mind the vending machines lined up in the back of the room. Food has always been a way to David's heart. Prisoners aren't permitted to touch money, so MaryAnn urges me to buy David some lunch.

We walk shoulder to shoulder toward the thicket of vending machines. David, paunchy and bald, wears a not-quite-clean white polo shirt tucked into bright-green, elastic-waist pants, and spotless white sneakers. He looks like a middle-aged civil servant ready for retirement, the uneventful future he sometimes imagines for himself if, as he puts it, "all this hadn't happened." I slip money in a machine. David delights in all the choices. There's a machine with flavored waters. "They didn't have this before," he says. He selects a Nathan's hot dog, and breaks into a smile. I don't know how many times I've seen his perp-walk photo by now, the one with that

unnerving smile. I wonder how it could have escaped me: Son of
Sam has dimples.

At our table, David eats his hot dog, gripping it with those murderous hands (the thought never disappears). Is the new version the
sincere one, as his religious friends insist? "A Christian can tell,"
Chuck assures me. Or does Sam's appetite for the spree lurk inside?
Is Richie still controlling the grudge within? There is, in David's
life, this disturbing symmetry: Once he was Satan's devoted soldier,
and now he's a celebrated man of God. Who is he, really, beneath
the goofy postman's grin? When I raise the topic, David nods indif-
ferently, and, as a holy man should, offers a Bible verse. "And some
believed the things which were spoken, and some believed not," he
reads.

David says that sometimes he imagines a life outside of prison.
"Everyone does," he says. If he ever gets out, David's Christian
friends see him running a church. "He has the ability to pastor,"
says Rich Delfino of New Jersey, an ex-sheriff's deputy and ex-
drug addict who is David's Bible-study partner. ("There's never a
time I haven't learned something scripturally from David," he says.)

David, though, can't see himself at the head of a church. He's
already MaryAnn and Jimmy's pastor. And he's the inmate pastor,
which he finds exhausting. "Guys are very needy in here," David
says. Plus, he sometimes works as a peer counselor in the mental-
health unit, a $2-a-day job that he also thinks of as part of his min-
istry. "I'm gentle with guys," he says. "I'm a big brother, a helper. I
see myself as a caregiver."

When he imagines life on the outside, David tells me he thinks
of becoming an Evangelist, a minister traveling to schools and prisons. He could reach out to kids, though the thought of traveling
freely must be an enticement, too.

"But God had another plan for me," David says softly, cutting off
the thought.

To leave prison, he tells me, "God will have to do a miracle."

Perhaps the Lord himself will preside over David's release. "Suppose the Old and New Testaments, and all that is written therein is true?" David asked me. If so, then there is the Rapture to think about, the foretold moment when God will take his chosen home. David sometimes imagines the day that God plucks him from his elastic-waist prison greens. "Jesus is going to come and take his people out of the world," David told Lisa. "One day, that trumpet is going to sound and we're going to be gone."

In the meantime, and perhaps for the rest of his life, God's special servant experiences little beyond prison life, which David lets me know is depressing. Jesus may have improved David's character, but a stable mood is still a struggle. He's not on medication or in therapy, he says. Yet bouts of sadness, crying spells, and hopelessness sometimes beset him. "Prison is crushing, oppressive. There's anger and disappointment, broken lives," he tells me. "Every day is a challenge. To get up in the morning and see the bars . . . Sometimes I can't get out of bed."

It's striking, after a few hours, to hear David speak this way. Christian talk usually conforms to set themes: pitched battles, God's warming love, triumphal futures. Despair is preamble. Then comes Christ, and worlds, and moods, are remade. Yet sitting here, his hot dog gone, David sounds sad. I ask about his daily satisfactions.

David thinks a moment. "I love nature," he offers.

It seems a strange thing to say. I look around. It's the view from inside a concrete mixer. "I am an avid birdwatcher," he persists in a quiet tone. From his cell window, David says, he watches sparrows and crows splashing in puddles in the prison yard. Sometimes, geese fly overhead. He likes that. "I saw a deer," he says.

Nature may break the monotony, but for David, happiness, earthly happiness, is a thing of the past. The very thought of it takes him back. As a prison guard looks on, David's mind drifts into the past, to racing with the neighborhood kids to a Yankees game. "My mom packed a bag lunch," he tells me. He had a three-speed

English Racer on which he sometimes spent entire days. "I miss my dad," David says abruptly. "I'd love to be leading a normal life."

David is lonely, though not as lonely as he was. With Jesus, everything is possible, a new future, a different past, even the admiration of others. Once he'd prayed, "Please give me a reason for living." The Lord came through. "Without Jesus," he tells me, "I wouldn't have survived. Because of Jesus, my life is not a waste."

Our time is up. Visiting hours are over. David spots a guard approaching and, ever attentive to the rules, rises preemptively. He offers me a brotherly hug. MaryAnn and I turn to go. An indulgent guard allows David to linger a moment longer.

"Where do you go now?" I call.

"To hell," David says, and smiles. That smile.

STEVE FISHMAN *is an award-winning journalist and a contributing editor at* New York *magazine. He is the author of two books,* A Bomb in the Brain: A Heroic Tale of Science, Surgery, and Survival *and* Karaoke Nation, or How I Spent a Year in Search of Glamour, Fulfillment, and a Million Dollars.

Coda

David Berkowitz continues to preach and pray in prison. The number of his admirers seems constantly to grow, and most pray that he soon will be released to continue his work for God in society.

ALLISON HOOVER BARTLETT

THE MAN WHO LOVES BOOKS TOO MUCH

FROM *San Francisco* MAGAZINE

ON FEBRUARY 7, 2003, opening day of the San Francisco antiquarian book fair, Ken Sanders warily paced his booth. He was surrounded by some of his treasures, including *The Strategy of Peace* inscribed by John F. Kennedy and a first edition of the *Book of Mormon*. With his long black-and-white beard, thinning ponytail, and ample paunch, Sanders didn't resemble the many bow-tied, blue-blazered dealers at the fair, and he didn't share their anticipatory excitement. Instead, as security chief of the Antiquarian Booksellers' Association of America (ABAA), he was haunted by the fear that John Charles Gilkey, the elusive book thief he'd pursued for three years, the rogue collector who'd just posted bail, might be brazen enough to show up.

Sanders, now 54, watched as collectors drifted from one book dealer to the next, gazed into glass cases, and asked to hold in their hands venerable volumes like William Wordsworth's *The Prelude* ($65,000). They consulted maps of the fair floor, squinted through spectacles across booths, and stooped to better run their eyes down the spines of books, eager to locate, say, a signed first edition of *Harry*

Potter and the Sorcerer's Stone or Lewis Carroll's copy of the 1482 edition of Euclid's *Elements,* one of the great mathematical texts (both of which were for sale that day for $30,000 and $175,000, respectively). They also roamed the aisles hoping to be surprised, because that's what rare book collectors live for, to stumble upon a book whose scarcity or beauty or history or provenance is more seductive than the story printed between its covers. It was in the midst of this literary sleuthing that Sanders locked eyes with a man he didn't recognize. "I had the weirdest goddamn feeling," he remembers, "but I couldn't place the guy." So he turned to his daughter, Melissa, to ask if she recalled whether this stranger was perhaps a customer they'd met before, and not Gilkey, as he suspected. But by the time Sanders turned back, the man had vanished.

Gilkey did stop by Sanders's booth that day, but after strolling up and down the aisles for about 45 minutes, he started to feel as though he was being watched. "As I passed one booth, I heard a woman say, 'He could go to jail for that,'" says Gilkey, "and I thought she might be talking about me." So he slipped out of the fair, carrying under his arm a book he had been hoping to sell to an unsuspecting dealer. It was a copy of H. G. Wells's *The Invisible Man*.

PEOPLE HAVE BEEN COLLECTING—and stealing—books ever since they were made available to secular society in ancient times. These days, the Bay Area is among the hottest places in the country for book collecting (the San Francisco antiquarian book fair, for example, is larger and more diverse than those in Los Angeles, Boston, and New York). Shops may be elegant, old-world havens, like John Windle Antiquarian Bookseller near Union Square, or the offbeat and slightly disheveled Argonaut Book Shop on Sutter Street, which specializes in books on California and the American West. Many used bookstores also have small rare-book offerings.

Book collectors—the most ardent referred to as bibliomaniacs—are a passionate, determined breed. As A.S.W. Rosenbach, the most famous 20th-century rare book dealer, said, "I have known men to hazard their fortunes, go long journeys halfway about the world, forget friendships, even lie, cheat, and steal, all for the gain of a book." Fortunately for the trade (and collectors' friends), most of them simply go prospecting at fairs and stores. They read bibliographies of authors and devour any material they can find on genres of interest: medical texts, children's books, California history, WWII, incunabula (books printed before 1501), Pulitzer Prize winners, erotica (although, according to one dealer I spoke with, most ABAA dealers "leave that to the Europeans"), and more. There is probably no subject, author, illustrator, or specialty printer whose books are not collected, and no potential venue—Goodwill, yard sale, estate sale—that goes unscoured. You never know when someone may have tossed dear, departed Grandpa's first edition of Fitzgerald's *Tender Is the Night* into the Salvation Army trailer, unaware of its value (with a first-issue dust jacket, about $45,000).

As much as such prices might set a gold digger's heart racing, they are not usually what motivates book collectors, whose relationship to their objects of desire is varied and complex. At a Boston fair in October, I heard a dealer with an impressive selection of dust jacket art say, "Don't judge a book by its content." However tongue-in-cheek, this twisted aphorism exposes the curious fact that many collectors don't actually read their books. Yet many have a scholarly interest in a particular subject, amassing copious quantities of books—on the Vietnam War, for example, or cookbooks from Colonial times—which they may one day bequeath to a library or other institution. For some, possession of the book provides a physical link to a period in time, often their own childhood, or to an author who may have touched the very same pages. For others, it is the book as talisman of knowledge and affluence that both satisfies and spikes their lust for more—and, in a very few cases, lures them to what Sanders calls "the mythical dark side."

Case in point: John Gilkey. Like most collectors, he's not in it for the money. Nor does he read the books he's acquired. But his interest in books has gone from being a pastime to a full-blown obsession. In the Bay Area, no one book thief has been as prolific. And no one has been as determined to catch him as Ken Sanders.

One of Gilkey's earliest known thefts in the city happened on March 14, 2001, at the Brick Row Book Shop on Geary Street. At the time, owner John Crichton didn't know it was Gilkey—that wouldn't become clear until much later. He says a man who identified himself as Dan Weaver called the store and asked if they had a first edition of Thomas Hardy's *The Mayor of Casterbridge*. They did, for $2,500. Later that day, an older man whom Crichton describes as "in his late 70s, not looking real sharp" came into the store and said he was there to pick up a book for his son. He was abrupt and seemed rushed. "I'm in a hurry," he scowled, "double-parked. I gotta get the book." Crichton checked to make sure the credit card charge had gone through. It had, so he handed over the book.

A month later, Crichton discovered that the charge was fraudulent, made to a stolen credit card number. He notified Sanders in Salt Lake City, who had begun hearing similar reports. Dealers always recounted the same scenario: a man would call and inquire about a book or two, chat for a while, settle on a price, sometimes ask about where to have a clamshell box (a protective case) made for it, and pay by credit card. The charges would be in the hundreds or thousands of dollars, but never more than $10,000. The caller would say that either he, his father, son, nephew, or brother would pick the books up. The question in Sanders's mind at that point was why dealers sometimes described the thief as a man in his 30s, other times as a man in his 50s, and still other times as a man in his 70s. Was this an individual or a gang? Even more perplexing was that neither *The Mayor of Casterbridge* nor any of the other books that had gone missing in the same way were showing up for sale anywhere—not at dealers' shops, not at book fairs, not on the Internet.

————

SANDERS, who jokingly calls himself "the book cop," has been collecting and dealing in books for most of his life. His father likes to say he was born clutching a book. As a child, he braved the glare of the neighborhood's irascible junk store owner in order to reach, on tiptoe, into a lard barrel full of old comic books. He started selling books as a teenager. His current store is Ken Sanders Rare Books, which his friend "Captain Eddie" (artist Ed Bateman) says is the nexus of Salt Lake City's counterculture. It's a 4,000-square-foot, sun-filled former tire shop, with over 100,000 books and old paintings, maps, photographs, postcards, posters—and a seemingly endless supply of impassioned conversation that revs up around 5 p.m., when Sanders offers drinks from a small fridge next to the counter. More than one friend of Sanders describes him as a man of extremes. When he is not reading books or selling books or going after people who steal books, he is white-water rafting or exploring Utah's deserts or planning his annual "burning cow festival," which his friend and ABAA past president Ken Lopez has heard described as "about four notches weirder than Burning Man and three notches less commercial."

Like many book dealers, Sanders is also a spinner of yarns. But the difference between him and most of the dealers I've met is the force of his narratives: like tornadoes. In a style that gathers its momentum from equal measures of rage (toward the thieves) and protectiveness (toward his colleagues), he has told me about various thieves he's caught or helped to catch or still hopes to catch. There's the Red Jaguar Guy, who stole valuable copies of the *Book of Mormon* from him and several other dealers; the Irish Gas Station Gang, which routinely places fraudulent orders with dealers through the Internet and has the items shipped to a gas station in Northern Ireland; and the Venezuelan, a dapper con artist who's pilfered from several high-end dealers. There are countless others, but the story Sanders has probably told most often is that of Gilkey, whose criminal ingenuity and tenacity matched his own ardor for catching him. With characteristic fervor, Sanders wanted to stop the scoundrel who had been robbing his friends.

When Sanders started working as security chief in 1999, he had no idea how fully his pursuit of thieves, especially Gilkey, would consume him. But soon after he received word of the theft from Crichton's shop, he began getting fraud reports from a number of dealers in Northern California. *The Patchwork Girl of Oz* by L. Frank Baum ($1,800) and a signed two-volume *Joseph in Egypt* by Thomas Mann ($850) were stolen from Heldfond Book Gallery in San Anselmo, and a *Lord Jim* by Joseph Conrad ($3,000) was stolen from Robert Dagg Rare Books in San Francisco. These dealers had been swindled by someone using the same MO as in the Brick Row case: payment was made with a stolen credit card number, it was weeks or months before the cardholder was notified, and the dealers had to eat the cost of the book.

In 2002, theft reports from Northern California slowed down, but other regions began reporting losses. Ed Smith Books in Washington State, for example, reported losing a first edition of Joseph Heller's *Catch 22* ($3,500) and a signed limited edition of Samuel Beckett's *No's Knife* ($850). Kevin Johnson of Royal Books in Maryland reported losing Jack Kerouac's *On the Road* ($4,500). In both cases, one detail in the thief's method had changed: rather than telling dealers that he or a relative would pick up the books, he requested that the books be mailed overnight. The addresses he gave were later discovered to be hotels in the Bay Area. With this new twist, Sanders started referring to the perpetrator as the Nor Cal Hotel-Motel Credit Card Thief. He also started to believe that the thief was a collector who in fact had gone to the dark side, because the books were not being offered for sale anywhere. If this person was a collector, Sanders knew that catching him, or her, would be very difficult.

I FIRST MET JOHN GILKEY in the spring of 2005 while he was an inmate at Deuel Vocational Institution in Tracy. A native of Modesto, he is 37, about five feet, eight inches, with long, nail-bitten fingers and thinning dark brown hair that he takes a black plastic comb to whenever he removes his baseball cap. He is soft-spoken, calm, and almost courtly, and he is forthcoming about how he built his book collection, yet averse to using words like *steal* or *prison* or *theft*. Instead, he "got" books and has been "away" for "doing that."

During our interview, Gilkey smiled politely and nodded in a deferential sort of way. His voice sounded hesitant, which I attributed to the awkwardness and poor acoustics of the prison-booth phones. Later, I would come to view his hesitation as a kind of watchfulness, as though he were playing a role he's not entirely comfortable with: that of a cultured, revered man he has encountered often in books and movies, but hasn't had occasion to study much in person.

One of the only books in his collection that he has read is *Lolita,* because of its history of controversy. "It was disgusting," he says. Most of what he has collected is fiction, but most of what he reads is nonfiction, either histories or bibliographies or books about collecting books. As a child, his objects of desire, like Sanders's, were comic books, and his favorite was *Richie Rich.* "But you can never get a sense of completion with that one," he says. "I had 1,500, but there are 2,500 total." He says he was a sensitive boy who asked his mother to walk him to school until the sixth grade. He stole only once back then, a baseball glove from Montgomery Ward, but when he got it home, he realized it was a lefty.

Most of his time was spent at home, playing on his own or hanging around with his father. He occasionally spent time with one or two of his seven siblings, but he didn't play with children in the neighborhood. Instead, he made up his own games. He would line up his comic books on the floor, *Richie Rich Cash* on one side and *Richie Rich Money World* on the other, and make them do battle, smashing one comic book against the other. "But then the comics were ruined," he says, "and I wondered why I was doing it. I realized they wouldn't be worth anything."

I had heard that in the past, Gilkey had denied having stolen books, so I assumed he would reiterate his denial. When I picked up the phone to begin our conversation, however, the first thing he said after we introduced ourselves was, "Do you want to know how I got my first book?"

Gilkey explained that he "got" Ira Levin's *Rosemary's Baby,* Isak Dinesen's *Seven Gothic Tales,* and an H.P. Lovecraft at the Burbank book fair in 1997 by writing checks from a closed account. The next year, he says he found a receipt on the floor of a hotel and decided to use the credit card number to call in orders for a few things he wanted: a watch, a pizza, and a poster for the movie *Psycho.* He describes these fraudulent purchases as though they were larks, why-the-hell-not pranks, but the ease with which he pulled them off stuck with him. "It was that easy" is something he says often.

In 1999, Gilkey applied for a job at Saks Fifth Avenue in San Francisco in order to have access to the credit card numbers of wealthy people. He was hired and methodically went about harvesting receipts. "I'd try to get 5 a week, occasionally 10," he says. "Sometimes, they'd put me in a room with a phone and a computer. I wasn't that busy, so I'd research books, then I'd go outside to make calls from a pay phone." He selected his victims from a free ABAA directory he picked up at the Burbank book fair. But it wasn't until 2001 that he says he started collecting seriously.

While Gilkey dabbles in the acquisition of collectibles like crystal, stamps, snuff bottles, and autographs, it is books—or what they signify—that captivate him. He dreams of building a "grand estate." He says he wants to "feel like royalty, rich, cultured." He would like to be a Victorian gentleman. "I keep visualizing a Sherlock Holmes with a smoking jacket and an old library. I'd have a big antique globe and read next to it." He describes the allure books have for him. "It's a visual thing, the way they look, all lined up on the shelf." The challenge, according to Gilkey, who's spent much of his life alone, is finding people to show the books to. "If you could somehow get visitors over, the first thing you're going to show them is the books. I could say, 'See, look, these are all first editions: this one, this one, this one.' "

One of the most infamous book thieves in recent history is Stephen Blumberg, who stole about 24,000 books from 268 libraries across the country in the '70s and '80s, until he was caught in 1990. When I ask Gilkey if he had ever been tempted to take a book from the library, he says, "That would be stealing." Gilkey says that when he orders books using stolen credit card numbers, "nobody loses really. The cardholder gets paid back, the bookseller gets paid. Course, I'm the big winner 'cause I get the merchandise for free." When I tell Gilkey that some dealers don't carry insurance, and that even when they do, by the time they've paid their deductible, they've still lost money, he says, "If you want to open up a business, you gotta be prepared for stuff like that. Take a liquor store, for example. You're probably gonna get robbed once a month."

Gilkey also doesn't like spending his own money on rare books. "I have a degree in economics," he says. "I figure, the more books I get for free, if I need to sell them, I get 100 percent profit." He is not joking. Gilkey is one of the most diffident, polite people I've met—always early for meetings, always taking care at restaurants to order less expensive items than I have, always remembering to say thank you. So statements like these are particularly jolting, bringing into sharp and unnerving focus his skewed sense of what is fair and right and reasonable, at least in the world of rare books.

IN JANUARY 2003, a man identifying himself as Heath Hawkins called Ken Lopez's bookstore in Hadley, Massachusetts. He chatted, decided to order a first edition of Steinbeck's *Grapes of Wrath*

($7,500), and asked if they could recommend a good place in California to have a clamshell box made for the book. Lopez recognized the content of the conversation more than the voice. Gilkey had called him six months earlier, attempting to order Kesey's *One Flew Over the Cuckoo's Nest* ($6,500), but the charge had not been approved, and the order was dropped. Lopez had a hunch that this caller just might be the Nor Cal Hotel-Motel Credit Card Thief.

This was the chance Sanders and Lopez had been waiting for. While the caller was still on the phone, Lopez Googled the shipping address. It came up as the Westin hotel in Palo Alto.

After agreeing to send *The Grapes of Wrath* (a first edition library facsimile—"Our little joke on him," says Sanders) overnight to the hotel, Ken Lopez called Ken Sanders, who called San Jose Police Department detective Ken Munson. The "trilogy of Kens," as Sanders calls them, got to work. Munson, a detective in the high-tech crimes unit, had never worked on a case like this but was eager to give it a shot. He set up surveillance in the hotel parking lot and put two undercover detectives in the lobby, one female, one male, posing as a couple. "We had no idea what we were looking for," Munson said later. "We assumed it was a guy, but it could have been a guy and a gal, two guys—we didn't know. We had arranged everything the night before, to have somebody behind the desk signal us if anyone asked for the package."

Gilkey showed up, asked for the package, and was handcuffed. He told the detectives he was on his way from San Francisco to a Stanford library to do some research, and that a man on Caltrain had offered to pay him $20 to pick up the book at the hotel. Munson told Gilkey they were going to take the handcuffs off, escort him to the Caltrain station, and hand him the package. "You go meet the guy and point him out to us," he said. On the platform, Gilkey wandered back and forth, walking up to people and making conversation. "I don't know what he was up to," says Munson. Gilkey later told me that one thing he was up to was chewing up a credit card receipt he had in his pocket and, he says, "thinking about running."

When questioned, Gilkey gave the police his name but wouldn't say where he lived. "At the hotel, he'd said he was there to pick up a book for Heather Hawkins, which is the name on the credit card," says Munson. "Later, he said the guy on the train told him to pick up a book for Heath Hawkins. When I asked him about it, I could see the wheels turning. 'Oh yeah,' Gilkey says, 'maybe the guy told me Heather and Heath Hawkins.' I knew he was lying. Later, it was easy to prove. He had a prepaid phone card in his pocket with only three calls on it. They were all to Ken Lopez."

When the police ran Gilkey's fingerprints, they discovered he was already in the California state penal system; he had been arrested three times for passing bad checks. Munson called Sanders, told him they'd caught the thief, and gave him Gilkey's name. Lane Heldfond, of Heldfond Book Gallery in San Anselmo, was able to correctly identify Gilkey in an online photo lineup, which enabled them to charge him. Shortly thereafter, Gilkey met his $15,000 bail and was released.

For the next couple of months, he went from bookstore to bookstore, first in Los Angeles, and then in the Bay Area, trying to sell a number of books, including several first editions of *Winnie-the-Pooh,* to raise money for his attorney's fees. The dealers kept in contact with Sanders as Gilkey stopped by their stores. At Gilkey's hearing, when the judge heard what he'd been up to, she set the new bail at $200,000.

While in Los Angeles, Gilkey had left his home address with William Dailey Rare Books. It was for an apartment on Treasure Island, and Sanders assumed it was bogus but notified Munson anyway. On April 22, he got a call from Munson, who said, "I'm in Gilkey's apartment on Treasure Island." The address turned out to be the home Gilkey shared with his father, Walter Gilkey. "There were books on every surface," says Munson. "On counters, in closets, in the bedrooms, on the dining table, the dining chairs, the floor." Some were covered in bubble wrap. "It was haphazard, but it looked like he took care of them," says Munson. "You could tell he had a love for these things."

Munson asked Sanders to give him the names of any books he was sure were stolen.

"Is there an *On the Road* by Jack Kerouac?" Sanders asked.

"Yes," said Munson.

"Grab it!" said Sanders. "What about a *Mayor of Casterbridge?*"

"Yes."

"And *Lord Jim?*"

"Yes."

And so it went. With Sanders's help, Munson was able to identify 26 stolen books in Gilkey's apartment. But with no further proof of theft, the majority of books were left behind. Sanders says that to this day he's plagued by the thought that if he had been able to provide Munson with more information, more books could have been saved.

Some of Sanders's fellow dealers have told him he is exaggerating when he estimates that Gilkey stole $80,000 to $100,000 worth of books before he was put behind bars. But Gilkey told me that during one four-month period in 2001, he "spent" around $200,000, mostly on books. But perhaps as significant as the still-unknown number of books he stole or their value is the way his deceptions helped to change the trade. Dealers are now far more vigilant when taking orders, securing more information from buyers and confirming with credit card companies that the shipping address matches the cardholder's billing address. They are now warier, less trusting.

Gilkey served about half of his three-year sentence and was released from Deuel Vocational Institution in July 2005. He was paroled in San Francisco and carries a notepad with a list of what to do each day. These lists almost always include rare book research at the library and visits to legal advisers to check on the feasibility of one of the many lawsuits he is interested in filing.

He is a curious man with an energetic mind, and he is full of ideas. He would like to collect a first edition of each of the Modern Library's 100 Best Novels, although he realizes that the prices near the top are astronomical, so he's starting at number 100, *The Magnificent Ambersons* by Booth Tarkington. He wants to make a documentary film about how he searches for famous people's autographs in unexpected places, such as school yearbooks. He has written a 100-page homage to John Kendrick Bangs, an obscure late-19th-century American writer whose signature work involves fantasies set in the afterlife. He also plans to write a book about "a guy who gets recruited by the government to be a spy to look for missing rare books."

Gilkey spends his days visiting bookstores, doing research at the library, and walking around Union Square, where he likes looking in the shops. When I ask if I can tag along with him on a trip to a bookstore, Gilkey agrees and, to my disbelief, suggests that we visit Brick Row. Then he hesitates. "Maybe they'll recognize me," he says. But he reconsiders, thinking it won't be a problem.

It is.

ON SEPTEMBER 12, 2005, Gilkey and I walk into Brick Row. Located near Union Square, it is on the second floor of a building that houses several art galleries. I can see why he favors this shop. If you were to ignore the computer and phone on Crichton's heavy wooden desk, you could imagine yourself in a 19th-century book-shop or in the opening scene of a *Masterpiece Theatre* episode. Majestic-looking, leather-bound books sit in cases along every wall and on a graceful arc of shelves that runs through the middle of the shop. It smells of history and knowledge and privilege, an intoxi-cating blend for someone like Gilkey.

As soon as Crichton looks up from his desk, he suspects who is standing before him. The tension is as thick as an *Oxford English Dictionary,* yet it seems not to bother Gilkey in the least. (When I met with Crichton later, he told me he had decided not to make a scene or throw Gilkey out because he did not know who I was or if I knew about Gilkey's past.) Gilkey asks Crichton if we can look around. Crichton mumbles something, turns his back to us for a moment, and then turns to face Gilkey. "What's your name?"

"John."

"John what?"

"Gilkey."

Crichton pauses a moment and walks toward his desk. He turns back around and watches intently as Gilkey points to various books and whispers, instructing me about the authors he might be interested in: Nabokov, D.H. Lawrence, Willa Cather. He tells me he stays away from bibles. Pointing to his list of the Modern Library's 100 Best Novels, he further explains how he goes about looking for books. He asks Crichton if they have anything by Nathaniel Hawthorne. Crichton answers firmly, "No."

Then, in a show of astounding hubris, Gilkey tells me, in a slightly louder voice, an improbable story about how at age 8 or 9 he bought his first rare book, a first edition of William Saroyan's *The Human Comedy*, published in 1943, for $60. Given the circumstances, it is excruciating to listen to. "And what happened was, they actually cheated me. I found out six or seven years ago that it wasn't a first edition, first printing, which is how they sold it." He tells other tales, one about buying a $3,500 book that was supposed to have been sent with a dust jacket but wasn't, dropping its value by 50 percent. In an even louder voice, he describes buying books at book fairs, only to discover later that he'd been ripped off.

Later, I ask Gilkey if he had told those stories for Crichton's benefit, and he admits that he had. "Those book dealers have more fraud in their business than I ever committed," he says. "What goes around comes around. I was just evening things out."

After that, each time I spoke with Gilkey, he was more incensed at the inequities between the haves (rare book dealers) and the have-nots (collectors, like himself, "who are not multimillionaires"), and more strident in his justification of what he has done. "I could have got much more," Gilkey has said numerous times, as though in defense of what he sees as a collection that's not big enough. "I could have, if I hadn't been working."

He won't say where his unrecovered books are stashed, but fondly recounts what it is like to hold one of these ill-gotten treasures. "Strangely enough, it's like a bottle of wine. I kinda smell the newness of the book, and I feel the crispness of it, see how it is, make sure there's nothing wrong with it, open it up very gently, thumb through a few things. I think about whether I want it signed. Then I put it in a plastic container. I'm thinking that maybe 30 years later, this book could be worth something. I don't want to make any mistakes. That's what I think. Preserve the book."

Late last September, Gilkey walked into Acorn Books on Polk Street and was recognized. The man at the store asked him to leave, which Gilkey found absurd. "It's hard for them to figure what's in my mind," he says. "I was just going in there looking for a bibliography. I was actually going to pay for something." He also thinks that ordering him out of the store may have been a civil rights violation, and he intends to add that bookseller to the list of people he may sue. For the first time since I started meeting with Gilkey, he seems dispirited and speaks in a resigned tone of voice.

"I probably won't be able to go into any bookstores around here anymore," he says. "Not in San Francisco."

POSTSCRIPT: After this story was written, Gilkey was arrested for violating parole after he attempted to sell stolen items on eBay, and was sentenced to three and a half months in prison. He is expected to be released this month.

ALLISON HOOVER BARTLETT *has written for the* New York Times, *the* Washington Post, Salon, *and other publications. She is a*

*member of the San Francisco Grotto, a collective writers' studio shared
with about thirty authors, and a founding member of North 24th Writers,
a group of nonfiction writers. She lives in San Francisco with her husband
and two children and is currently at work on a book about Gilkey,
Sanders, and the dark side of the rare book trade.*

Coda

I discovered this story when a friend of mine came across a beautiful, nearly four-hundred-year-old German book that he had reason
to believe was stolen. For days, the book haunted me. With the help
of a German-speaking friend, I learned that it was a *Kreuterbuch,* a
book of botanical medicine by Hieronymus Bock, but I couldn't
determine where it was from. I searched the Internet for information, but while nothing turned up about the *Kreuterbuch*—even a
lead I had about a library in Southern California was fruitless; they
had no record of it—I stumbled upon something even more
intriguing: story after riveting story of book theft. I contacted rare
book dealer and ABAA security chief Ken Sanders, and in our first
conversation he regaled me with stories, from his first encounters
with run-of-the-mill robbers to his *pièce de resistance,* the story of
John Gilkey. For three years Gilkey had been the most successful
book thief to infiltrate the trade in many years, and during that
time, his capture had been a driving force in Sanders's life. His theory, "but no one believes me," he said, was that Gilkey was a collector who steals for the love of books. I knew then that I had to find
him. When I did, we began meeting in prison and out for almost
two years, during which time he shared with me his extraordinary
story—criminal chapters of which unfolded even as we spoke.

From the start, I was fascinated by the mix of genteel book collectors and devious criminals in this story, and the more I learned about
both, the more questions I had. I understand a simple love of books,
but why are some people obsessed with acquiring hundreds, thou-

sands? What is it about the book as a physical object that elicits such passion? Why would anyone risk his personal freedom for them?

I learned that for centuries, refined book lovers and greedy con men have brushed up against each other in the rare book world, so in some ways this story is an ancient one. It's also a cautionary tale for those who plan to deal in rare books in the future. While researching this story and, subsequently, the book I'm now writing, I began to see myself as a collector, not of books, but of pieces of this story, and like the collectors I met, who become increasingly rabid and determined as they draw near to completing their collections, the more information I came across, the more I craved. I couldn't be satisfied until I had gathered every scrap of detail, of which there were volumes. When I had, I realized this story is not only about a series of crimes, but about people's intimate and complex relationship to books.

Ariel Levy

DIRTY OLD WOMEN

FROM *New York* MAGAZINE

THE OLDER WOMAN. Knowledgeable, seasoned, experienced. Hot! The fantasy creature who embodies full-blown female sexuality in all its mysterious glory. Of course, she's out of reach; it will never happen. She inhabits her own complicated realm of emotions and responsibilities and lingerie, and you are just . . . a kid. But imagine the initiation! The possibilities! (Sexually, sure, but also for bragging.) It would be awesome.

Or would it? What if the impossible happened and she started paying unmistakably romantic attention to you. What if "she told me that she had feeling for me. She told me that she was thinking about me a lot and had feeling for me [and] she didn't know what to do with them," as 24-year-old Debra Lafave told one of her 14-year-old pupils, according to his statement to the police. What if you had sex in the classroom? What if she fell in love with you? What if she wanted to *marry* you? If it stopped being a fantasy and started being your actual sex life, your actual life, would it be thrilling or upsetting? Or both? Would you be scarred for life or psyched for months?

These are questions we've had plenty of opportunities to contemplate lately. A few months ago, 37-year-old Lisa Lynette Clark pleaded guilty to statutory rape of her son's 15-year-old close friend, whom Clark married and whose child she recently gave birth to. In January, a 26-year-old math teacher from Kentucky named Angela Comer was arrested in Mexico with one of her eighth-grade male students (who had allegedly stolen $800 from his grandmother for trip money). They had been trying to get married.

Dirty old(er) women do not reside exclusively in states with alligator problems; we have our fair share in the New York area. In August, Sandra Beth Geisel, a former Catholic-school teacher and the wife of a prominent banker in Albany, was sentenced to six months in jail for having sex with a 16-year-old, and she has admitted to sleeping with two of her 17-year-old pupils. (The presiding judge in the case infuriated the youngest boy's parents when he told Geisel her actions were illegal but that her youngest sexual partner "was certainly not victimized by you in any other sense of the word.") In October, Lina Sinha, an administrator and a former teacher at Manhattan Montessori on East 55th Street, was charged with second- and third-degree sodomy and third-degree rape for allegedly having sex with a former student—who is now a cop—for four years starting when he was 13 and she was 29 (she denies the charges). And last May, Christina Gallagher, a 25-year-old Spanish teacher from Jersey City, pleaded guilty to second-degree sexual assault of a 17-year-old male student.

The story that probably set the most imaginations in motion is Lafave's. Debra Lafave, a 24-year-old middle-school teacher who looks like a Miss America contestant, is currently serving three years under house arrest for having sex repeatedly with one of her 14-year-old male students. After a hearing, Lafave's lawyer, John Fitzgibbons, notoriously said that his client, a former model, was too pretty for jail: "[T]o place an attractive young woman in that kind of hellhole is like putting a piece of raw meat in with the lions." As in several of the other cases, Lafave's beauty and youth blurred the lines of her narrative. What were these stories about? We couldn't tell if they were instances of abuse by adults in positions of power who were badly harming children or if they were *American Pie / Maxim* magazine-style farces about lucky little dudes.

When I was growing up, my father used to say as a joke (sort of), "Teenage boys: the lowest form of life on earth." He was probably imagining some combination of his adolescent self and Philip Roth's Alexander Portnoy, a character who revolved around a tight coil of urge and surge and shame, whose repertoire of obsessions ranged from onanism to defilement and whose actions seemed almost piteously in thrall to his loins rather than his head (which was too busy processing anxiety and guilt to offer much guidance). *Portnoy's Complaint* was a best seller in 1967, but to this day its protagonist is for many people besides my father the epitome of adolescent-male sexuality: desperate, reckless, insatiable. The horny little devil.

If you conceive of teenage boys as walking heaps of lust, you probably conceive of attractive adult teachers who hit on them as public servants in more ways than one.

Media representations of grown women who pursue teenage boys have hardly been scary in recent years. Phoebe's brother on *Friends* married his home-ec teacher and proceeded to live happily ever after. Jennifer Aniston's affair with little love-struck Jake Gyllenhaal in *The Good Girl* would be difficult to describe as abuse. He pined for her, he worshipped her, and if he ended up destroyed, we couldn't blame her . . . a lost little girl who happened to be in her thirties.

The most famous older woman is, of course, Mrs. Robinson: sinister as well as smoldering, coolly and mercilessly manipulating Benjamin to get what she wants and keep what he wants out of reach. But the fictional figure who is really more representative of our stereotypes is Blanche DuBois in *A Streetcar Named Desire.* Tennessee Williams made her a skittering, simpering hysteric. Where Mrs. Robinson unfurls her silk stocking with utter confidence in her own allure and smoky erotic power, Blanche rushes to cover the lightbulb with a paper lantern so nobody will see the years creeping over her face. (For the record, her advanced age was *30.*) She is desperate for attention and dependent upon the "kindness of strangers," and, it is suggested, she hit on her 17-year-old male student because her own maturity was stunted and only a young boy would make an appropriate companion for the young girl still living within her withering skin. By the end of that play, she is raped by Stanley Kowalski, then carted off to the loony bin: a victim.

It's jarring, however, to think of a teenage boy—say, a 16-year-old—who's been seduced by a female teacher as a victim. It clashes with our assumptions. A teenage boy who gets to live his fantasy? What can be the harm?

As it happens, that is a very dangerous question. In 1998, Bruce Rind, Philip Tromovitch, and Robert Bauserman (professors at Temple University, the University of Pennsylvania, and the University of Michigan, respectively) published a study that has resounded through the psychological Establishment ever since. The article, published in the American Psychological Association's *Psychological Bulletin,* was what's known as a meta-analysis, an overview of the existing science, in this case on the long-term effects of childhood sexual abuse. The authors concluded that "negative effects were neither pervasive nor typically intense" and that men who'd been abused "reacted much less negatively than women."

Though Rind and his colleagues bent over backward to emphasize the difference between something's being wrong and something's being harmful (it's wrong, for instance, to shoot a gun at someone, even if you miss), the study was spectacularly demonized. Dr. Laura Schlessinger had three psychologists on her show who declared it "junk science." One of them compared its authors to Nazi doctors. The Alaska State Legislature passed a resolution condemning the study's conclusions and methodologies. In May 1999, the Family Research Council along with Tom DeLay held a press conference in Washington demanding the APA retract the Rind study. (Schlessinger was teleconferenced in.)

About a year after the study's publication, Congress passed a formal resolution condemning Rind in an uncontested vote. The president of the APA initially defended the paper and pointed out that it had been peer-reviewed and determined to be scientifically sound, but as the resolution was being debated, he sent a clarification to DeLay saying that child sexual abuse was always harmful and—though the study has never been scientifically discredited—the organization has been trying to distance itself from Rind ever since.

Although it is tempting to assume that the finding that childhood sexual abuse is not as damaging for boys as for girls confirms various widely held beliefs about gender—that boys are tougher and hornier than girls, that males enjoy sex in any form—the issue is more complicated. For one thing, when men seek out sex with underage girls, they are more likely than their female counterparts to have more than one victim and to utilize methods like coercion and threats to secure complicity and secrecy. Women who seek sex with underage boys are more likely to focus on one person and to proffer love and loyalty and a sense of a particular and profound bond. In many of these cases, the woman has floated the idea of marriage.

WE (STILL) LIKE TO KEEP our understanding of masculinity connected to our understanding of maturity. We'd never had a female anchorwoman deliver our news until recently, we don't often let female columnists explain the news, and we've never had a female president to make the news. For many Americans, being a real grown-up requires a penis. And if you've got that, even if you're only 15, you must have the maturity and the manliness to know what you want to do with it—even if that involves intercourse with a 42-year-old. Who among us would say the same thing about a 15-year-old girl?

"For guys, the different issue than for young women is that it's supposed to be the best thing anybody could want in terms of what society is saying or their friends," says Lonnie Barbach, a clinical psychologist and the author of *The Erotic Edge*. "But they don't necessarily feel okay about it, so then they're acting against their feelings. I see a lot of guys with sexual problems who've had that experience. Problems with erections are pretty common, as is anxiety around sex in general." But then, she points out, she only sees the ones who have problems.

It's extremely common for boys who have been molested to be drawn exclusively to much older women from then on. "There is something about early experience with sexuality that tends to stay with you," Barbach says. "A lot of it is by chance. If you are a child who stumbled upon a magazine with women who have very large breasts, you may eroticize women who look like that in adulthood. It's funny, I don't know why it is, but as a child you are just more susceptible." Anything sexual that happens in childhood has a better chance of making a kind of imprint on your erotic consciousness.

EVEN IF WE TAKE as a given that it's always wrong for a grown woman to have sex with her teenage students, or her son's friend, or whatever other 15-year-old she gets her hands on, a question still remains: Why would she want to in the first place?

Teenage boys are not, as a rule, the world's most expert lovers. They are not known for their emotional sophistication or sensitivity. And they do not excel at the tests of masculine status women are supposed to be fixated upon. "If Debra had had an affair with a man who was richer than me, or more successful, that I could have understood," as Debra Lafave's estranged husband, Owen, put it. "But this was a boy. What could he offer her that I couldn't?"

Power, for one thing. Compared with a teenage boy, a woman will almost always make more money. She will always know more about sex. She will generally be more competent and experienced and more able to assert her will on him than vice versa.

If you spend a little time going over stories of grown women who pursue boys, they start to blur together. Often, the woman was a victim of sexual abuse in her own childhood. So in some cases adults having sex with children is familiar, reiterative. Psychologists say one reason women engage in this is to create a new narrative: If they as adults can have sex with a child in the context of a loving romance (imaginary or real) rather than as an obvious enactment of exploitation, they can then more easily conceive of their own abuse as a love story. To them, the experience of being a gentle perpetrator can be redemptive.

"Sometimes, the woman is not much older psychologically than the boy is in her developmental stage," says clinical psychologist Judy Kuriansky. "She has arrested development. So she's having sex with a 14-year-old, and in her head, she's 14, too. She's getting the attention she never got." She's Blanche DuBois. And, Kuriansky says, "there's nothing more erotic than being adored, for women."

Consider the poster couple for pedophilia or true love, depending on your point of view: Mary Kay Letourneau and Vili Fualaau. A review: Letourneau was Fualaau's second-grade teacher, then she taught him again—and had sex with him—when he was a 12-year-old in her sixth-grade class. She gave birth to their first child shortly before she went to jail. She became pregnant with their second child when she was out on parole. She went back to jail for seven years. After her release, they got back together. Letourneau and Fualaau were married in a televised ceremony last May and registered for china at Macy's. They have been together ten years.

You could clearly hear Letourneau imbuing her student with power; trying to convince the public as she'd convinced herself that Fualaau—her lover, her hero—was on more than equal footing with her: "He dominated me in the most masculine way that any man, any leader, could do."

He was 12. She was 34.

WHEN DIANE DEMARTINI-SCULLY first started going for walks with her daughter's 15-year-old boyfriend on the North Fork of Long Island, it made him feel special. "She would just talk to me about life situations and shit," he says now, a year and a half later. "It was pretty cool." This is something DeMartini-Scully, a 45-year-old blonde who vaguely resembles Erica Jong, would have been good at. She was, until recently, a school psychologist at East Hampton Middle School. She knew how to draw a kid out.

And the boy, let's call him Jason, had some things on his mind. "I was making a lot of money in New York," he says, and when I ask him how, he gives a nervous laugh. "I was doing a lot of things." I ask if the things he was doing and the company he was keeping (mostly in Jamaica, Queens, he says) were part of the reason his family left Mattituck, Long Island, where they lived just down the road from DeMartini-Scully, for Jacksonville, North Carolina, where they currently reside. He says yes, but the reason his mother has given the press for the move was to escape the escalating cost of living on the North Fork. Detective Steven L. Harned of the local Southold Police Department says, "We were already aware of [Jason]. He has had some court cases here on other matters."

When Jason's family was ready to relocate to Jacksonville, he still had a few months of school remaining. It was decided that Jason would finish off the year living at DeMartini-Scully's house on Donna Drive. "We would go to Blockbuster and rent movies, and when we watched them, she would put her hand on my lap," Jason says. "I didn't think much of it at the time."

One night, when DeMartini-Scully's daughter, with whom Jason was still involved, was at a friend's house, and after DeMartini-Scully's son had gone to sleep, she asked Jason if he wanted to watch television with her in her bed. "Then she kissed me."

That night, Jason and DeMartini-Scully "basically did everything." He remembers the experience as "okay . . . I wouldn't say it was upsetting. I wouldn't say I didn't want to, but . . . I figured she was letting me stay at her house, I'd just do what she wanted."

This was not an isolated incident. For the next three and a half months, Jason estimates, the two continued having sex at the house and in her car. "Nobody suspected anything," he says. "And I didn't want nobody to know because I was messing around with her daughter. I found it funny that Diane was letting me stay at her house when she knew about that, but I never asked her why: I figured she was doing it because she wanted something."

I ask Jason what he wanted: whether he was having sex with DeMartini-Scully because he enjoyed it or because he felt obliged to. "When I wasn't drunk, I felt pressured to, but when I was drunk, I wanted to . . . you know what I mean?" He claimed he got alcohol, and sometimes pot, from DeMartini-Scully.

When summer came, DeMartini-Scully took her son and daughter and Jason down to Florida, where they met up with Jason's family for a vacation en route to Jacksonville. What was supposed to be a quick stop to see Jason's family's new house became an extended stay when DeMartini-Scully was injured in an accident. "She hurt her leg pretty bad when I was teaching her how to ride the dirt bike," Jason says. "You could see her bone and shit." She stayed in North Carolina for a month.

When she finally left, Jason's mother was glad to be rid of DeMartini-Scully. She had become suspicious when she found out that Jason and DeMartini-Scully had been in a room with the door locked. But on Columbus Day weekend, unbeknownst to Jason's mother, DeMartini-Scully returned to a hotel in Jacksonville to visit Jason. "So I want to know, what's so special about me?" Jason says. I ask him what he thinks. He laughs. "I'm not gonna say."

He spent three days at the hotel. His mother found out about the visit, and "that's when all the drama started." She contacted the police, who charged DeMartini-Scully with kidnapping and providing marijuana to a minor but not with sexual assault, because

Jason had, at this point, already turned 16 and passed the legal age of consent in North Carolina. She was subsequently charged with third-degree rape and performing a criminal sexual act in Suffolk County, where the age of consent is 17.

Jason stayed in school for just three weeks in Jacksonville before he dropped out. He says he will join the Marines after he gets his GED, "but just for the money." He doesn't miss DeMartini-Scully, he says, who by the end was suggesting she wanted to marry him. But he also says he doesn't feel raped. "I just, I don't know, I feel weird. She was 30 years older than me, so I feel a little bit taken advantage of. If I was a girl, I probably wouldn't talk to you about it, but a female can't really rape a guy, you know?"

Jason says he would not have given a statement to the Long Island police incriminating DeMartini-Scully if he hadn't been under pressure. "They said if I didn't they were gonna press charges on me because I was with Diane's daughter," who is only 14, and now Jason is 17, thus making him guilty of "sexual misconduct" himself. As of his last birthday, Jason's relationships switched status in the eyes of the law: Sex with the then-44-year-old school psychologist who had been after him since he was 16 became okay; sex with her teenage daughter became a crime.

("It is a strange law," says Harned. "I didn't write them, I just enforce them." Harned says that it is still likely that the Southold Police Department will press charges against Jason for his relationship with the daughter and that Jason was not pushed into giving a statement about the mother.)

"I just think about how Diane's daughter must feel now," Jason says. "I was pretty close to her; I still am. I'm talking to her on the computer right now."

I ask Jason if this is an experience he will try to avoid in the future, getting involved with much older women. He thinks about it for a minute. "Depends how old," he concludes. "How old are you?"

Ariel Levy *is the author of* Female Chauvinist Pigs: Women and the Rise of Raunch Culture. *She is a contributing editor at* New York *magazine, where she has been writing for the past ten years.*

CODA

I tend to think the differences between men and women are vastly exaggerated. But every once in a while, a story comes along that makes me question my own stubbornly egalitarian assumptions. This was one of those.

There had been a spate of high-profile stories about women (often teachers) having sex or sometimes running off with boys, usually between the ages of 12 and 17, just before I wrote this, and though statistically this wasn't happening any more frequently than usual, because the women involved were attractive and photogenic, these stories had a potent media presence. Mostly, they were fodder for jokes about how the boys had gotten lucky. Certainly this was the opinion of many of the guys at my office.

When I started looking into the surprisingly small body of comparative clinical research on the way male and female lives are affected by early adolescent sexual abuse, I was surprised to learn that there really are significant differences. It's complicated, though, because the ways and reasons grown women tend to target boys for sex are pretty different from the ways grown men go after girls. So while I started out thinking about different experiences of victim-hood, I ended up more interested in the different methods and pathologies of male and female perpetrators.

Dan P. Lee

WHO KILLED ELLEN ANDROS?

FROM *Philadelphia* MAGAZINE

HERE'S ELLIOT GROSS. Sixty-six years old, short barrel-shaped body, big mostly bald head. A tiny, odd-looking man. Hunched over, dressed in a blood-splattered plastic apron and blue scrubs, white surgical gloves gone crimson, a clear plastic shield covering the huge glasses on his large face.

And there, on the metal table in front of him, her body splayed from skull to hips, lies 31-year-old Ellen Andros. It is—it will prove—a somewhat difficult case. But from the start, from the moment a few hours ago when he first approached her still-warm corpse at her home outside Atlantic City, Elliot Gross, the former chief medical examiner for New York City, a man who autopsied Tennessee Williams and John Lennon and many other noteworthies during a 40-year career, thought he was on to something.

What's going on here isn't just science. It's something deeper, something stranger, something at the same time both terrifying and fascinating. With Ellen's body reduced to parts—organs and tissues and arteries and veins, each one removed and given careful attention—Gross is attempting to communicate with her. He's asking questions, asking each part of her body a question. And so far, this is all he's hearing back:

Someone did this to me.

The cops think this, too. Really, they've already begun writing this, in investigators' notebooks and reports. Prosecuting crime depends to a great extent on The Story. And crime stories are the product of many hands and minds. Despite what TV shows suggest, no one in the criminal justice system operates in a vacuum, in separate scenes, separate frames. Not even the medical examiner. Because, unlike on TV, the ME does not walk up to a table cold, in a blue-lit morgue, charged with determining what happened based purely on the body. No, earlier this morning Elliot Gross got a call, a call that summoned him to the scene and provided him with information and the beginnings of a story, of this story:

On Saturday, March 31, 2001, Ellen's husband, 32-year-old Jim Andros III, an Atlantic City cop, dialed 911 at 4:27 a.m. When authorities arrived at the unimpressive home in Pleasantville, a small, downtrodden city across the bay from the lights of A.C., they were immediately suspicious. The victim had no medical problems. Standing beside her body in their young daughters' bedroom, Jim Andros, according to police, was clearly drunk. He behaved erratically, admitting he was "fucked up," relinquishing the handgun he was wearing at his ankle—though he was off duty. He said he feared he'd hurt himself. He cursed the officers. When his in-laws arrived a little while later, they accused him outright of murder.

"What did you do to her?" Ellen's mother shouted at her son-in-law, racing across the front lawn to confront him. "Did you kill her?"

Now it's all up to Elliot Gross. Earlier this morning, the investigators, at the scene, apprised him of their suspicions; it's part of the subplot he's been pulled into. Chief ME for neighboring Cape May and Cumberland counties, and a part-time assistant ME here in Atlantic County, Gross stands over the emptied body, the organs dissected and set aside. His focus once again returns to Ellen Andros's face. It is young-looking, beautiful.

And it is dotted with countless tiny red spots called "petechiae"—pinpoints of bleeding into the skin. In his mind, he's certain.

More than 7,000 times, Elliot Gross has sliced open a body in pursuit of the facts behind how and why a human life has abruptly ended. When murder is the possible cause, getting it right is, of course, fundamental. At stake at this moment is not only solving what happened to Ellen Andros. For the fate of Jim Andros—the sole suspect—hangs in the balance of the answer Gross comes up with as well.

The word "autopsy" comes from the Greek *autopsia,* meaning to see with one's own eyes. For the next five years, determining precisely how Ellen Andros died will consume the lives of Elliot Gross and Jim Andros. Along the way, a bright light has been shined into the dark, mostly hidden world of death's doctors.

At this moment, though, Elliot Gross is certain. A call goes out to Sergeant Bruce DeShields of the Atlantic County Prosecutor's Major Crime Unit.

PART ONE: THE PROSECUTION

SERGEANT DESHIELDS heads back to the room where Jim Andros has been repeatedly interviewed since agreeing earlier this morning—still Saturday—to come in for questioning. Andros has now been awake for 24 hours. His head is pounding, his eyes are bloodshot, his shirt is crusty from the dried tears and snot he's wiped there.

Andros—a tall, muscular man with close-cropped reddish hair—has stuck to his story. He last saw his wife alive Friday morning, when he got home from working the overnight shift. It was his understanding that she was taking the girls to her parents' house in Pennsauken, where she and the kids typically spent Friday nights. By the time he woke in the late afternoon, they were gone. Around 8:30 p.m., he drove to Brigantine, to the Beach Bar, a legendary old wood-paneled haunt opened by an ex-prizefighter at the base of the dunes, and met up with his dad and some old friends. He left around 4 a.m. Arriving home, he was surprised to see Ellen's car. He unlocked the front door and walked down the hallway and into his daughters' bedroom, where he found his wife, unresponsive, at the computer.

DeShields doesn't buy it, and goes at Andros: *You were drunk. You came home drunk. You and Ellen began fighting. You got angry. In the heat of the moment, you put your hands over her nose and mouth. . . .*

I did not kill my wife.

Finally, around 6 p.m., a relative calls the office and says Andros should be permitted to go home and get some rest. Without sufficient evidence to charge him, DeShields lets him go.

In the ensuing days, Andros hires two attorneys, who advise him to stop speaking with the investigators. Andros's in-laws, aware Jim is a suspect, petition for custody of their granddaughters.

On April 9th—a day when the weather is lurching violently into the new season, the temperature rising to a record 84 degrees before furious storms move in—Ellen Andros is laid to rest. The atmosphere inside the Merchantville church is poisonous. By now, the two families aren't speaking to each other. Ellen's friends and family stare at Jim. There is muttering: *"Murderer."*

DeShields and the investigators continue crafting their version of The Story. While Jim's supporters portray him as a loving and devoted police officer and family man—who in fact had just returned two days before his wife's death from a week of skiing with her and their kids in Vermont—Ellen's friends and family offer an image of a relationship, and a husband, on the edge.

In sworn statements, they tell investigators that Ellen's six-and-a-half-year marriage was in tatters, that Jim drank excessively, that he'd been violent, that Ellen suspected he'd been unfaithful. Jim had for some time been sleeping in a separate bedroom, no longer welcome in Ellen's bed. Ellen and the girls had left before. At the time of her death, her friends say, she was planning to leave again.

And then there's this: Ellen Andros was seriously involved with another man.

He is Calvin Gadd, a former neighbor she met while walking her daughters past his house one day; he was outside playing with his son. He's a cop, too. She had been successful in keeping him from Jim, though their relationship appeared to have been intensifying recently. She spoke with Gadd from her parents' house just hours before her death, discussing her plans to leave Jim and move in with her mom and dad. He waited anxiously for an e-mail from her after she got home. When it never came, he drove by her house the next day. The coroner's van was parked in the street.

Gadd tells investigators, according to DeShields's report, that Ellen feared her husband. He says that Jim threatened her repeatedly. He recounts a conversation in which Ellen told him that Jim put a gun to her head, threatening to pull the trigger. She told him that while she and Jim were in the car together, Jim would sometimes drift onto the shoulder of the road, warning he'd keep going and crash, make it look like an accident. According to Deshields's report, Gadd says Ellen told him that Jim would sometimes come home drunk and force himself on her sexually.

She struggled with what *she'd* become. "I feel like such a failure," she e-mailed a friend late one night in 1999. "I have these beautiful little girls and they can't even have a nice happy childhood because their Mommy can't marry a nice guy. . . . I've seen TV shows about people like myself and I would always be like man . . . what a loser."

Another friend, Mary Ann Bakogiannis, tells investigators that Ellen said Jim had put his hand over her nose and mouth one night while they were being intimate, according to a police report. Ellen said his eyes locked in a terrifying stare, that she fought to get away, and that she was no longer going to have sex with him.

———

INSIDE SHORE MEMORIAL HOSPITAL in Somers Point, in a basement morgue covered in yellow tile and saturated in fluorescence, Elliot Gross, whose height does not place him so much above the metal table he's standing beside, peers over the thin, naked body.

From the outset, Gross finds the presence of petechiael hemorrhages highly suspicious. He notes these red dots scattered over Ellen Andros's face and on her eyelids. While petechiae can form in a variety of deaths, they are classic in strangulation; as blood continues pumping upward through the back of the neck, it becomes trapped in the head, causing the tiny capillaries in the face to burst. He also notes pallor on the tip of the nose and chin, and an indentation in the skin corresponding with the top button and seam of her shirt. The result of pressure, he suspects.

The body is lifted, and plastic blocks are positioned beneath the shoulders, exposing the neck and causing the chest to rise and spread. He raises the large scalpel.

Elliot Gross is indisputably one of the world's most experienced and lauded medical examiners. That he should find himself, at 66, working in a basement morgue in Somers Point, New Jersey, of all places, must be as surprising to him as it is to anyone who knew him when.

In 1985, the *New York Times* accused Gross, then that city's chief medical examiner, of serious improprieties. By then, the city ME's office—the most prestigious in the country—had been rocked by a series of mini-scandals and controversies. Gross had started his career there in the 1960s before becoming chief ME for Connecticut, and had been named top ME in New York by Mayor Ed Koch in 1979, after Koch demoted Gross's former friend and colleague, Michael Baden. Baden would eventually assume the role of *the* most famous medical examiner in the world—consulting on behalf of celebrity defendants, including Claus Von Bülow and O.J. Simpson; publishing a well-received memoir; and becoming the star of his own recurring special on HBO. But Gross and Baden—who were classmates in med school at NYU in the 1950s—had been feuding ever since they had adjacent offices in New York as young MEs, and now Gross was sure Baden and his loyalists were behind the *Times* assault. The paper claimed Gross had produced inaccurate or misleading autopsy reports as part of an extraordinary pattern of solicitousness to police and the D.A.'s office. One allegation—that he covered up for police when suspects died in their custody—was transparently criminal. Gross fought back, blaming Baden.

The *Times* assault would prove deleterious. Even though four separate investigations cleared Gross of any wrongdoing, his reputation and that of his office had been badly damaged. Koch fired him in 1987. He moved to the Midwest, where he worked in relative obscurity in coroners' offices in Indiana and Ohio.

But in 1995, he became chief ME for Cumberland and Cape May counties. He also takes part-time work as an assistant ME for Atlantic County, home to Atlantic City, a magic dateline. It's proved a hard slog back, but he's well-respected here, and he's already had some big cases. Though he doesn't know it yet, he's in the midst of the biggest of his career.

With his scalpel, Gross presses down hard and swift, slicing a deep Y shape across the shoulders and down the chest and abdomen of Ellen Andros's body.

The tissue separates, revealing a thin layer of yellow fat; with the heart still, virtually no blood seeps from the incision. He separates the skin and fat from the muscle and bone, and pulls the tissue back in wide flaps on either side, revealing the rib cage, protecting vital organs, and the open abdominal cavity. He separates the rib cage and sternum from the body.

Visible now is practically the entirety of her body's contents. Popular opinion has it that MEs are freakish ghouls, that autopsies are graceless and macabre. But to observe an autopsy—to watch a pathologist peel open the body's exterior and enter into its core—is to witness more art than butchery. It is a disturbing and beautiful image.

The organs fit together perfectly, like a jigsaw puzzle. They are still and silent and glistening, seemingly ready to recommence their operations at any moment. Positioned on either side of the chest cavity, like an angel's wings, the lungs are large and the color of bubble gum. The heart is tucked between and slightly behind them, hidden inside the yellow pericardial sac. Below the thin diaphragm, a portion of purple liver is visible, resting atop the pink stomach. The intestines coil into one astonishingly dense piece. The smell initially is faint; some MEs compare it to raw lamb meat.

Gross cuts opens the pericardium, and slices the major arteries and veins, including the massive aortal opening at the top, to release Ellen's heart. He pulls it out and holds it in his hand. Covered in a thin layer of yellow fat, dripping blood, it is the shape of a lopsided softball. He draws back a long, sharp blade called a bread knife and begins cutting into it, exposing a deep burgundy interior. He slices open lengthwise the large pulmonary artery running down the middle, searching for clots; he finds none. He crosscuts the coronary arteries running like branches around the exterior of the heart—the primary site of blockages—creating small sections through which he can look. He finds nothing unusual.

He removes each lung. They appear healthy. He removes Ellen Andros's liver, and it spills over his hands. He cuts it into thin slices. Once again, nothing remarkable.

He moves on to the digestive system, and the odors from this part of the autopsy are overwhelming—a mix of bad breath, vomit and feces. He removes and opens the pink J-shaped stomach. Inside, he finds pieces of broccoli, asparagus, potato and white meat. He removes the massive collection of intestines, like a huge bundle of uncooked sausage. Once again, they are unremarkable.

The pancreas, bladder and kidneys all appear normal as well, as do the sex organs.

Gross dissects the neck, and removes the contents, including the tongue, all together. Jim Andros has already told the authorities that his wife suffered from chronic tonsillitis, and Gross finds intense congestion in both tonsils, which were significantly enlarged; he dismisses the tonsils, however, as a contributing factor. Curiously, though, there is no hemorrhaging in the throat, and the bones and cartilage of the neck have no fractures. In other words, there is no evidence of strangulation.

The autopsy assistant makes an incision across the back of the head, from ear to ear. She works to reflect the scalp down over the face. There is the sudden whine of the power saw, which she uses to delicately cut around the circumference. She pulls the skulltop slowly away, and it makes a sucking sound.

The human brain is pinkish-gray, with purple blood vessels swirling along its surface. Gently cradling it, Gross lays it on a table, and it shifts easily, like Jell-O. He makes slow slices through it. The interior is gray and white, solid, and utterly plain. He scrutinizes the vessels; there are no signs of aneurysm or clotting.

It's late afternoon, three and a half grueling hours since he began. With the exception of the microscopic analysis and toxicity studies—which won't be ready for some time, and which Gross has determined he won't need to make his ruling—the autopsy is essentially complete. Bright red blood coats the table, the floor, the weighing scales, Elliot Gross. The body lies open and empty down to the spine, literally a shell of its former self.

A call goes out from the morgue to Sergeant DeShields at the Major Crime Unit.

Through what amounts essentially to a long and sophisticated process of elimination, Gross has arrived at his conclusion. Her face dotted with those countless petechiae, pinpoints of bleeding into the skin, Ellen Andros, Gross rules, died from suffocation. Ellen Andros, Gross is certain, was the victim of homicide.

And there it is: *corpus delicti*—the fact of a crime. The proof the investigators have been anxiously awaiting.

In a few weeks, Jim Andros will be arrested and charged with killing his wife. ACPD immediately suspends him without pay. A judge awards his in-laws custody of his daughters. In jail, he's sequestered, and officers wake him every 15 minutes, on suicide watch. A week later, he posts $170,000 bail—representing his every asset, and then some—and, with no money or income, moves in with his sister and brother-in-law. For almost two years, the case against him—The Story—will grow and coalesce on its way toward trial, surviving repeated attempts by his lawyers to squash it. It will seem unimpeachable, obvious, open and shut.

But never what it really is.

PART TWO: THE DEFENSE

OVER THE COURSE of 20 months, as *New Jersey v. James Andros III* slowly moves toward trial, the prosecution continues building its case. This is The Story the state is prepared to present to a jury:

Jim Andros demonstrated a pattern of alcohol abuse and violent behavior toward his wife. In the early morning hours of March 31, 2001, he arrived home after a night of heavy drinking. He confronted his wife, possibly soliciting her for sex. When she rebuffed him, he grew angry. He pulled her onto the floor, and in a homicidal process called "burking" sat on her chest and put his hand over her nose and mouth. Asphyxia occurred quickly, leaving virtually no physical evidence. He moved her to their daughters' bedroom, and sometime thereafter, he dialed 911.

Now it's the defense's turn. During strategy sessions in their office atop Lefty's piano bar in Atlantic City, Jim Andros's lawyers have been writing their own version of The Story.

They believe their client's profession made him a particularly delicious target—that the Atlantic County prosecutor, like many prosecutors, views convictions of "rogue cops" as trophies. On top of that, the Andros family—particularly its patriarch, Jim Andros Jr., a longtime Atlantic City cop himself—has developed a certain notoriety over the years. In and around Brigantine, where Jim III and his seven siblings grew up, their father's drinking and hair-trigger temper are well-known. In one much-publicized incident back in 1981, he was off-duty, riding his bike near the family's home, when an eight-month-old retriever mutt began chasing him. The pup allegedly snarled. Still riding his bike, the elder Andros unholstered a .45-caliber pistol and shot it in the head.

In an attempt to build an alibi, Andros's lawyers go to work on establishing his whereabouts the night of his wife's death. Several fellow patrons corroborate Andros's account that he arrived at the Beach Bar about 9 p.m. and stayed until around 4 a.m. While these witnesses' recollections don't mesh perfectly—and some were obviously drinking heavily (including Andros's father, who was so drunk that he spent the rest of the night in his pickup in the parking lot)—the earliest anyone places him leaving is 3:30. The drive home averages about 20 minutes. He dialed 911 at 4:27.

Next, they try to establish the time of Ellen's death. America Online records show Ellen sent her last e-mail at 1:48 a.m.; her account logged off automatically due to inactivity at about 2:30. According to the autopsy, her last meal, eaten at her parents' house at about 10 p.m., was still in her stomach. Healthy individuals' stomachs typically empty within four to six hours. EMTs at the scene noted cold extremities and early lividity. Lividity, or reddening of the skin due to blood sinking after circulation ceases, isn't usually seen until 30 minutes after death. This proves to Andros's lawyers that Ellen must have died well before 4.

Still, the lawyers know that establishing time of death is more art than science, and they're reluctant to pin their client's fate on this alone. They have from the outset resisted suggesting another suspect, acknowledging that the prosecution's storyline leaves Andros the most viable target. Instead, in an unusual and risky move, they decide to attack the assertion—so far accepted as fact—that Ellen Andros was murdered in the first place.

They brainstorm an alternative explanation: During his autopsy, Gross saw Ellen's enlarged tonsils. A local doctor Ellen had visited confirms Ellen's existing tonsil condition and says this swelling could have obstructed her airways. But a specialist at Jefferson

Hospital who'd seen Ellen recently rejects the tonsil problem as a possible cause of her death.

Of course, this "alternative cause of death" theory has one significant caveat—that the medical examiner erred in his autopsy. Andros's lawyers begin doing a little research into Elliot Gross's recent cases, and stumble onto the story of Tracy Thomas.

Very early one snowy morning in 1997, a driver on a deserted Cape May County roadway happened upon a Ford Explorer that had sheared a telephone pole. Tracy Thomas, six months pregnant, sat belted in the driver's seat, the airbag deployed, dead. Her husband, Eric Thomas, sitting in the passenger seat, was unconscious but otherwise relatively unscathed; their young daughter, strapped in her car seat, was uninjured. Eric, a well-respected dentist, said the family was en route to the ER to have their daughter evaluated for a high fever when a deer ran into the road; Tracy swerved, and his memory blacked out there.

Elliot Gross listed the cause of death as blunt-force trauma with asphyxia, sustained in the accident and apparently the result of the airbag's force. In 1999, however, when Eric Thomas filed a wrongful-death suit against Ford, the company investigated Thomas, and uncovered unsavory details. He had increased Tracy's life insurance policy one month before the accident, and by the time of his suit, he'd married his high-school sweetheart, whom he'd secretly flown to meet repeatedly prior to Tracy's death, and whom he spoke with on the phone at least seven times on the day she died. Though he passed a lie-detector test, and a federal investigation blamed the airbag, Thomas, citing legal bills, eventually dropped his suit.

Critical to Ford's success in muddying Thomas's claim was the opinion of the forensic pathologist the company hired, who, focusing on the hemorrhaging in the neck and eyes, determined that Tracy had been strangled. The pathologist did more than that, however, advising the lawyers in the deposing of Gross, who stuck by his findings but conceded that strangulation was possible.

Ford's pathologist was Dr. Michael Baden.

IT'S A GRAY DAY in mid–October 2002, a few weeks before the expected start of Andros's trial, and his lawyers are feeling butterflies. Today, Michael Baden comes to town. One of the defense lawyers and Baden arrive at Shore Memorial Hospital early in the afternoon, ride the elevator down to the basement, and are led into the fluorescent-lit morgue.

The metal tables are empty. Standing there waiting are an assistant Atlantic County prosecutor, an investigator, an ME assistant, and Elliot Gross. It has been at least 15 years since Gross and Baden have seen each other.

The two men—wrinkled, hair gone gray and thinning, both almost 70, a 45-year history between them—exchange greetings.

"You're balder than I remember," Baden tells Gross, towering over him.

"You're fatter than I remember," Gross says.

To those in the morgue watching, who are familiar with their long history, it is an extraordinary, surreal reunion.

They gather around one of the tables, Gross on one side, Baden directly across from him, the others filling in the spaces in between. Baden asks the defense lawyer to take notes; the man stands beside him, pad in hand.

Small pieces of Ellen Andros's remains are preserved in formalin, in a plastic lidded container like one that might hold a large order of coleslaw. Baden and Gross snap on gloves, and Baden begins by picking up the pieces one at a time, staring at them. There is no conversation, and everyone's eyes are on Baden's hands.

The pieces, which have gone white in the formalin and resemble small bits of boiled chicken, are samples from all the major organs of the body. Baden examines the tonsils; they are certainly enlarged, but since they've been removed from the throat, it's impossible to tell the degree of obstruction. He picks up a tiny piece of liver, finds nothing remarkable. A tiny piece of brain; unremarkable. A tiny piece of kidney; unremarkable. Piece of spinal cord; unremarkable. And then he picks up a tiny chunk of heart muscle, about the size of a nickel, containing a cross section of the left anterior descending coronary artery.

The coronary arteries, which supply the heart with oxygenated blood, are embedded on the surface of the muscle, stretching down its length; it is by chance that Gross chose to preserve this particular portion and not another. During the autopsy, Gross crosscut the artery. Baden stares through the tiny section in his hands. He's shocked by what he sees.

A RARE CONDITION CALLED "spontaneous coronary artery dissection" killed Ellen Andros; only about 150 cases have been reported since 1931. It occurs when a microscopic tear forms within the three layers that make up the wall of the artery, leading the layer beside the tear to bulge from the bleeding and obstruct the artery. It was visible within the section of artery as a tiny occlusion of unknown origin, millimeters large, and then on one of the microscopic slides Gross reviewed after the autopsy.

On December 4, 2002, the Atlantic County prosecutor, hugely embarrassed, moves to have *New Jersey v. James Andros III* dismissed.

Stunned, Jim Andros stands outside the courthouse, a horde of media around him. "How could I be any happier?" he tells them. "Now we can do what we should have been able to do from day one, which is mourn the passing of my wife. . . . The people who did this to me, may God forgive them. I'm going to do everything in my power to make sure these people are exposed for what they've done."

He is reunited with his daughters. ACPD reinstates him with back pay. For the next few days, he sleeps with the court's paperwork, waking up to check it, making sure he's not dreaming.

Government agencies immediately move to distance themselves from Elliot Gross. Atlantic County fires him at once. The New Jersey chief medical examiner declares him professionally incompetent. The state attorney general, on the advice of the state medical examiner, bans him from performing autopsies. Gross claims he's being railroaded by the state medical examiner, and a state administrative law judge later twice agrees with him, determining that the error in the Ellen Andros case cannot, on its own, constitute professional incompetence. Gross nevertheless is essentially forced to resign from Cape May and Cumberland counties, though he vows to fight the state's actions.

On April 22, 2003, Jim Andros files a 37-count federal lawsuit against Gross, Atlantic County, the prosecutor's office and the investigators, alleging that they conspired to recklessly prosecute him in spite of the overwhelming evidence that he was innocent. The suit, unsurprisingly, focuses on Gross. It seeks unspecified damages understood to be in the millions of dollars.

As of this writing, Andros's suit is still working toward trial. How much Gross's past will figure into the trial's outcome isn't clear. It seems a safe bet that Andros's lawyers plan to dredge up every controversy over his long career in an effort to portray him as, essentially, a buffoon whom Atlantic County officials should not have hired.

But is that fair?

Donald Jason, the former chief ME of Atlantic County, is now director of the forensic pathology program at Wake Forest University Medical School and a forensic pathologist for North Carolina. Following Baden's trip to South Jersey, it was Jason whom the prosecution flew in to review the official diagnosis in the Ellen Andros case. (Baden knew only that there was an arterial occlusion of some sort.) There are only about 450 full-time MEs in the nation, and in a beautiful bit of irony, Jason did his training in the New York City ME's office, where he worked with both Baden and Gross.

Jason says that before he arrived in Atlantic County and saw the artery and slides himself, he agreed that asphyxia seemed probable and was disinclined to trust Baden, whom he calls a "pain-in-the-neck dilettante" to work with. (Despite Baden's mostly sterling reputation in the medico-legal community, others have raised questions about his tactics. When Baden's 38-year marriage to Judianne Densen-Gerber—the New York City psychiatrist, socialite and heiress—dissolved sensationally in 1997, her accusations made tabloid headlines: Not only was Baden serially unfaithful and a certifiable slob, she said, but he had also conducted autopsies on the dining room table of their multimillion-dollar townhouse, and kept AIDS-infected tissue in their basement.)

When asked what he thinks of Baden's skills as a forensic pathologist, Jason's answer is succinct: "Not much."

"He shoots from the hip," Jason continues. "He says whatever first thought comes to mind, whether it makes sense or not. He's not a great pathologist. Gross was the better pathologist." But Jason says that Gross's odd physicality, strange affect and public reticence hindered him, hampering his ability to play his role as a principal character, as an actor, in The Story behind every criminal case. "Gross," he says, "didn't know how to play the part of medical examiner at all."

But what about the Ellen Andros error? How could Gross have made such a mistake?

"He was set to see asphyxia as soon as he heard about the bad family environment and [saw] the petechiae," Jason says. "And don't let the facts get in the way."

During an interview at his spacious high-rise condo just off Fifth Avenue, Michael Baden himself calls his feud with Gross an invention of the media. Baden remains the international ME of choice, having participated in the re-autopsy of the teen apparently killed in boot camp in Florida, fielding calls from Greece requesting that he re-autopsy a victim in that country's worst-ever espionage case, and making regular appearances on Fox News.

But when asked whether he's ever made a serious mistake, Baden is surprisingly forthcoming with a story.

In the mid-1970s, he autopsied a woman found dead in a flophouse, and cited alcoholism as the cause. Later, a man confessed to having strangled several women in the same flophouse. Baden had the body exhumed, re-autopsied it, and, sure enough, found evidence of strangulation. He changed his report and admitted his mistake. Not long after, the chief of homicide at the New York City D.A.'s office was appointed to the House Select Committee reinvestigating JFK's and MLK's assassinations. He'd admired Baden's honesty in the flophouse case, and recommended him to head the inquiry's forensic pathology portion, a major break in Baden's career. And then Baden abruptly says this:

"Look, to say that [Gross] is not competent to do autopsies is a stretch, I think. Because clearly he's competent. He was chief medical examiner of New York. You can make mistakes, but it's not lack of competence."

That leaves this possible outcome for Jim Andros's lawsuit—that the jury will find in favor of Gross. Such a ruling would say, in effect, that the system worked, that honest mistakes were made and caught and an innocent man was proven innocent. And, implicitly, that Gross should gain back something of his lost reputation and career.

But where would that leave Jim Andros? He lost his wife in a sudden, unexpected death. For almost two years, the state accused him of her murder. He was vilified publicly, branded an abusive drunk. He went hundreds of thousands of dollars into debt proving that the case—The Story—against him all along was wrong. If not for a tiny piece of tissue preserved by chance, all parties involved in the case concede, he'd likely have been convicted and spent the rest of his life behind bars. And the people who did it to him—the system that prosecuted him—would owe him nothing.

EPILOGUE

IT'S SOMETIME BEFORE 2:30 A.M. on March 31, 2001, and despite the many versions of The Story that will emerge over the next five years, this is what happened. This is the objective truth, as much as we can believe in one:

Elliot Gross is asleep in his modest house near the marshes in Ocean City. Michael Baden is asleep in his apartment in midtown Manhattan. Jim Andros is drinking yet another 7&7 at the Beach Bar in Brigantine. And Ellen Andros, at her home outside Atlantic City, her 31-year-old body fully intact, begins dying.

In the bedroom, she sits in front of the computer, the room aglow with the blue light of the screen. As she types an e-mail to a friend, inside her body, beneath her breasts, her skin and fat and muscle and sternum, a microscopic tear begins in one layer of the wall of the left anterior descending coronary artery.

Like a run in a pair of pantyhose, the tear begins small, and spreads. The bleeding quickly fills the tiny space between the layers. The pressure of the bleeding causes a bulge across the channel of the artery, which is smaller in diameter than a pencil. Within seconds, the bulge overwhelms the artery.

There is crushing chest pain.

The flow of blood to the heart backs up in the artery. The muscle begins starving for oxygen. Ellen's heart, which for 31 years has pumped in the same perfect rhythm, 100,000 times a day, suddenly begins beating chaotically, racing, trying in vain to bring in fresh blood. The rhythm soon falls apart completely, the chambers of the heart contracting randomly against each other, an image heart surgeons liken to a writhing bag of worms.

The blood flow within the body's miles of arteries, veins and capillaries ceases. The brain quickly sucks up the remaining oxygen within its vessels. Brain cells begin dying. Ellen Andros's sight and consciousness fade to black, as if by the turning of a dimmer switch. As more brain cells die, her arms and legs begin contracting and spasming in terrible jerks.

Until, suddenly, she's slumped forward, still.

Moments—perhaps minutes—have passed.

This is how The Story begins.

DAN P. LEE *is a staff writer at* Philadelphia *magazine. He was formerly a newspaper reporter, including for his hometown paper, the* Atlantic City Press. *He graduated from the University of North Carolina at Chapel Hill in 2001. This story is the first magazine piece he ever wrote.*

Coda

Even as the civil suit against Elliot Gross remained unresolved, the state of New Jersey late last year reinstated his autopsy privileges. The move came after a state administrative law judge ruled twice that the error in the Ellen Andros examination did not, in and of itself, constitute "professional incompetence," and that the actions of the state against him were not justified.

Gross had lost his privileges in the first place based primarily on the testimony of the state's then-chief medical examiner, Dr. Faruk Presswalla, who claimed that Gross had overlooked an "obvious" abnormality and demonstrated gross negligence. As it turned out, in another example of how small, incestuous, and ruthlessly competitive the field of forensic pathology can be, Presswalla and Gross had, as the judge in the case noted, "an acrimonious past history together." (Years earlier, Presswalla had competed unsuccessfully with Gross for the position of chief medical examiner of New York

City, and Gross filed suit against Presswalla for statements he had made in the *New York Times* series attacking Gross's performance and leadership.) After first appealing the judge's decision, the state ultimately accepted that Gross's mistake in the Andros matter was legitimate; that Presswalla's testimony was "equivocating, inconsistent and somewhat confusing"; and that his "so-called investigation" into the error never included interviewing Gross and consisted primarily of reading newspaper accounts and other pathologists' reports after the fact.

That Gross will ever again hold a public position nevertheless seems doubtful. He continues to work as a forensic consultant, and divides his time between his homes in New York City and Ocean City, New Jersey.

Jim Andros is a patrolman with the Atlantic City Police Department. He retained custody of his children, and his relationship with his former in-laws has apparently improved. In April 2007, Atlanta County officials agreed to settle Andros's federal lawsuit for $2.7 million.

For his part, Michael Baden remains a ubiquitous presence in the small world of forensic pathology. In addition to his consulting practice, lecturing, and work with the New York State Police, he is Fox News's forensic analyst, and continues to weigh in on the most high-profile cases of the day, including the deaths of Terri Schiavo, Saddam Hussein, and Anna Nicole Smith. He is remarried, to Linda Kenney, a lawyer whom he met in the morgue, and with whom he recently wrote and published a crime novel.

David Bernstein
_____

FATAL CONNECTION

FROM *Chicago* MAGAZINE

SHE CALLED HERSELF CHERYL OF CHICAGO, and she was a high-priced escort. Her booking sheets listed the names of hundreds of lovelorn and lusty clients—doctors, lawyers, accountants, CEOs, traders, bankers, pro athletes, mobsters, even police officers. "It was the whole spectrum," says Chicago police detective Mike Landando of Cheryl's roster of customers. "A cross section of Chicago."

So the potential suspects ranged far and wide when Cheryl of Chicago, whose real name was Kathryn Hogue, turned up dead in November 2004 inside her Wicker Park condominium. She was 45. Her roommate discovered her lying naked and face-down on a bed in the subterranean cathouse where she entertained clients, a space Hogue dubbed the "Gypsy Love Room." An autopsy showed ligature marks around Hogue's neck, indicating to investigators that she had been strangled.

The murder sent investigators into the new cyberworld of vice—where prostitutes, often working alone, manage their careers through the Internet; where johns browse Web sites to find their "escorts," then rate their skills online. That world is a far cry from the seedy underground of streetwalking, but sex arranged through the Internet is still isolating and virtually lawless, and those who engage in it—as the case of Cheryl of Chicago suggests—are still at risk of violence.

AS A YOUNG GIRL growing up in Ann Arbor, Michigan, Kathryn Hogue dreamed of being a professional ballerina, but by 17, she was lap dancing at strip clubs. (The limited information on her background, as well as events leading up to her death, comes from police investigators and from friends in Chicago. Members of her family could not be located.) After several years on the exotic dancing circuit, she turned to the sex business. Before long, Hogue became a recognizable fixture in Chicago's escort-for-hire scene, marketing herself over the Internet and on her own Web site, CherylofChicago.com.

Friends and former clients who agreed to be interviewed for this story recall Hogue's "heart of gold" and her "million-dollar smile." But for as much as $400 an hour, with a two-hour mini-mum, the five or so johns she saw each week could buy more than her seven-figure smile.

Hogue promised the ultimate "GFE," an abbreviation used in the escort business to mean the "girl-friend experience," or paid sex, plus paid companionship and affection. And Hogue typically delivered, judging by her reviews on TheEroticReview.com and BigDoggie.net—two popular online clearinghouses for the paid-sex trade.

Rated by customers on a scale of 1 to 10 for both appearance and performance, she consistently piled up 8s and 9s, and every so often a perfect 10 (defined as "one in a lifetime"). *Chicago* posted interview requests on BigDoggie's online message board, and one former client who responded said he first booked a "date" with Hogue after reading the glowing reports on the Internet. "If you read the boards awhile, names come up," says the man, a business owner in his mid-50s from the north suburbs, who spoke on the condition that his name not be used. "She was well reviewed and had a reputation in the community. She had a very, very upscale side to her, and that appeals to me."

Police say some of her relationships with customers, particularly with older ones, didn't even involve sexual intercourse; men in midlife crises would pay top dollar for her to be a trophy wife of sorts. And sometimes she just kept friendly company with lonely men, boosting their morale with cheerful conversation.

One of Hogue's best friends, another escort whose professional name is Kelly Shannon, says several of Hogue's clients fell in love with her. "She knew how to make you feel special," says Shannon. "It was instinctive."

After Hogue's death, detectives discovered documents from one of her regulars, a businessman who promised to give her 100,000 shares of stock in Lucent Technologies to start a retirement fund. (At press time, Lucent was trading at $2.75 per share.)

Standing five feet eight inches, with sharp facial features, sexy locks of blond hair, and a 125-pound, toned dancer's body, Hogue recalled Nicollette Sheridan of *Desperate Housewives*. And inwardly, she was as desperate as the housewives of Wisteria Lane.

Another friend, Jim Delorta of Matteson, says Hogue badly wanted to get out of the escort business. "She wanted to find a job and have a normal life," he says. "But you get trapped in your way of living; you're stuck until you find a way out."

Thomas Kolman, one of the Chicago police detectives who worked on the case, says Hogue's unhappiness in the sex trade led her to drink heavily. "She always would have to drink, like, a bottle of wine—be drunk just to be with these guys," Kolman says. "This was a business to her."

GIVEN THE HIDDEN and anonymous nature of the business, it's impossible to know exactly how much buying and selling of sex

exists in Chicago. Still, David Sobczyk, commander of the Chicago
Police Department's vice control section, argues that the sex business here is "ubiquitous." "It's in all four corners of the city," he says.

Not to mention in the phone book and, most prevalently today,
on the Internet. (With "escort services" and "Chicago" as search
terms, Google clocks 2.2 million matches in 0.11 seconds.) Every
year in Chicago, some 4,000 men and women are arrested on prostitution charges—a number that typically leads the country, beating
even New York City, Los Angeles, and Las Vegas, according to a
Scripps Howard News Service survey published last February.
Thomas Hargrove, the Scripps Howard investigative reporter who
analyzed the figures, says Chicago's high number of arrests probably
has more to do with the city's aggressive law enforcement than the
sheer number of prostitutes living here. "They have a vice squad,"
he says of Chicago. "Most big city police departments don't have
vice squads anymore, or they're diminished. If you have fewer vice
squads and fewer vice detectives there'll be fewer arrests."

As part of the city's efforts to crack down on prostitution, the
vice squad impounds the cars of the johns who are caught soliciting prostitutes. And in June police also set up a controversial Web
site (www.chicagopolice.org/ps/list.aspx), which posts the names
and mug shots of arrested suspects as a way to humiliate them publicly. (The site has tallied about 800,000 hits.)

Arrests are only a small part of the prostitution picture, however.
The Center for Impact Research, a Chicago-based non-profit that
studies poverty and social justice issues, estimates that—based on
arrest and court data, police interviews, advertisements, and statis-
tics from various social service providers—"a minimum" of 16,000
women and girls are involved in the sex trade in the Chicago area.
"That's just the tip of the iceberg, though," says Jody Raphael, a
senior research fellow at the DePaul University College of Law.
"It's believed to be an ever-growing industry."

And while the image of streetwalkers cruising up and down the
city's seediest streets is a common perception, most prostitution—

80 percent, according to the Impact Research Center—is not
solicited on the streets. Raphael maintains that the Internet is the
perfect place for selling sex: it's virtually anonymous, cheap, far-
reaching, and safer than the streets. Ads for sexual services flourish
on Web sites like TheEroticReview.com and BigDoggie.net, and
even on Craigslist.org, the popular site that posts wide-ranging
classified ads. On the sex sites, "hobbyists," as those with the
"hobby" of patronizing escorts are called, can pay monthly mem-
bership fees for access to immense databases of escort reviews.

Most online escorts don't think of themselves as prostitutes,
Kelly Shannon and others say. Instead, they call themselves, more
respectably, "service providers." And to many customers who pay
for female companionship, the Internet hookup helps launder the
stigma that sticks to street-level prostitution.

Although vice officers try to reel in the business, online sex
workers are unlikely to be arrested. Typically, they work under a
guise, such as exotic dancer or erotic masseuse, making it difficult
for police and prosecutors to build criminal cases. Also, because
escorts don't stand on street corners, fewer people complain about
them. Sobczyk concedes that the "vast majority" of prostitution
arrests are for street-level action.

AT FIRST GLANCE, the tidy, red-and-gray-brick three-flat at
1261 North Bosworth Avenue appears an unlikely place for a one-
woman red-light district. The quiet, visibly gentrified street is lined
with trees and dotted with a mixture of vintage row houses and
newer-looking condominiums. But for Hogue it was the perfect
spot for entertaining clients: "Two blocks from the Kennedy, two
blocks from a cabstand and right across the street from an ATM
machine," she noted on her Web site.

Upstairs in her tastefully decorated three-bedroom condominium, there were no signs of its business use. She even had a
roommate—a woman who had been tutoring Hogue in French

and who had moved in recently. But down the spiral staircase, on the basement level of the duplex, the Gypsy Love Room beckoned. Depending on your tastes, the place was racy and seductive or just tacky. Black and red velvet covered the walls, and the room was amply stocked with sex toys, condoms (protected sex was always the rule), and X-rated videos. Sexy lingerie, S & M paraphernalia, slinky dresses, and stilettos filled the closet. And Hogue had even put in a tiny dancing stage, equipped with a floor-to-ceiling stripper's pole. "It was the kind of room you'd expect to find in a house of ill repute," recalls a former client.

Apart from her work, though, Hogue led a relatively quiet life, according to people who knew her. She loved the arts: photography, theatre, the opera and ballet. Especially ballet. She was a committed dancer, taking ballet classes three times a week for 15-plus years. She liked to cook, and had a penchant for gourmet foods and expensive Champagne, as well as for the fresh corn she would buy from the Mexican street vendors on Ashland Avenue in her Wicker Park neighborhood. She frequented the boutiques and thrift stores along Division Street, often walking with Prieta, the mutt she had adopted from a local animal shelter.

Kelly Shannon says Hogue didn't socialize much with other escorts and never got romantically involved with clients. "She tried to keep her personal life and professional life separate," says Shannon. "When she was up making soup and taking care of Prieta, she was Kathryn. When she entered the Gypsy Love Room, that's when she became Cheryl."

Hogue talked seriously of pursuing a photography career once she quit the escort business, or starting an adult Web site for various sexual fetishes. Police say she was thinking about taking a job offer as a madam at a suburban strip club—a kind of den mother among the dancers. It wasn't a full break from the flesh trade, but at least it wouldn't be her body for sale anymore, she figured. "Cheryl knew she needed to get out," says Shannon. "She wanted to find Mr. Right. She wanted to start a life. She wanted a family. She wanted the fairy tale."

SOMETIME IN LATE 2001 or early 2002, Hogue met a
named Daniel Rallo, a man in his mid-30s who lived
Streamwood and who called himself a mortgage broker. She wa,
having trouble refinancing the mortgage on her condominium,
and police believe she turned to Rallo for help in October 2002.

When she had bought the condo for $295,500 two years earlier,
she listed her mother as a co-owner. But in February 2002,
Hogue's mother turned over the title to her daughter in a quit-
claim deed. When Hogue tried to take advantage of low interest
rates to refinance, she was stymied, police say, because she had no
proof of employment.

Rallo told Hogue he could help by laundering her money.
According to police, he connived a few business associates into creating phony office jobs for Hogue, so she could have W2s, which
show wages. (Forms listed her as a "general office manager" with a
yearly salary of $56,100.) She gave Rallo $20,000, and he arranged
to refinance her mortgage and pay part of it down through the
mortgage firm in Roselle where he worked.

In Hogue's underground world, the smooth-talking Rallo
seemed like the perfect type to handle her money discreetly.
"Because she earned her money illegally she thought she could
trust him," says Robert Cordaro, another Chicago police detective
who worked on the case.

Rallo fancied himself a Chicago gangster, and he often bragged
to Hogue and others that he was "connected." He wore flashy,
expensive suits over his beefy, five-foot six-inch, 180-pound frame.
He drove a black Cadillac. "He gave the persona that he was a wise
guy," adds Cordaro. "He'd want to be the big shot, the guy who'd
walk into a restaurant and always have to buy."

Around January 2004, authorities say, Rallo was fired from his job in
Roselle for stealing commissions. He then opened D.A.R. Financial
Corp., a supposed mortgage brokerage firm, in his Streamwood home.

Sometime in April 2004, Hogue gave Rallo more money, this time $56,000 in cash: $50,000 to pay down and refinance her mortgage again, and $6,000 for Rallo for brokering the arrangement. But the deal never went through. Friends and police say Rallo strung Hogue along, making excuse after excuse for the delays. When Hogue received a notice of delinquent payment, he told her he had cancer and was receiving treatment at the Mayo Clinic. Another time when Hogue pressed him he told her his mother was dying. In fact, she was already dead.

Hogue "was extremely savvy when it came to her business and dealing with clients," Cordaro says. "But outside of that—in the business world, she was a 17-year-old kid who started stripping. What kind of knowledge is she going to have about the mortgage business? She got sucked into trusting Danny Rallo."

By June 2004, after many calls to Rallo, Hogue began to suspect that he had kept the money. Police say she asked a friend who was a bouncer at a strip club to phone Rallo and demand that he either complete the mortgage deal or return her money. Rallo, furious, warned Hogue the next day that he would kill her if she ever again had any heavies threaten him. "That's when she went off the deep end," recalls Delorta.

Police believe that by then Rallo had spent Hogue's money. Detectives learned he had bet large sums on the online gambling site Poker.com, and they later found scores of receipts from riverboat casinos. What's more, police suspect Rallo used most of the money to woo Kimberly Damato, a mortgage lender from Elk Grove Village. He wined and dined Damato, then 37, and bought her an engagement ring that, police say, cost around $10,000. They were married in August 2004 at St. Paul of the Cross church in Park Ridge.

Police say things for Damato changed swiftly and drastically once she became Mrs. Rallo. Her new husband started borrowing large sums of money from her to pay off credit card debts. "She was writing checks for, like, $10,000, $15,000," says Cordaro, and when she would question him about his finances, he became abusive. "She thought he had all kinds of money," says police detective Mike Landando. "He scammed her, too, hook, line, and sinker." (She later moved out, and could not be located for this story.)

By September, Hogue was deeply distraught. "She would be fine one minute and bursting into tears the next," recalls Delorta. By then, friends and police say, she was taking prescription pills for anxiety and drinking more heavily than usual. "Cheryl was so consumed by this money being gone," recalls Shannon. "It was a lot of money. She worked on her back for that money."

Hogue posted a plea for help on the Big Doggie Web site, and she spoke about her problems with Rallo to anyone who would listen—from her mother and close friends to her housekeeper, her ballet instructor and masseuse, even to some of her clients. "There was not one person in her life that didn't know that this guy had $56,000 of her money," Landando says. Police records show she told one friend a few weeks before her murder, "This guy's probably going to kill me, you know. I'm bugging him so much."

A panicked call on November 16th to the bank that held her mortgage finally confirmed her worst fears: there never was a refinancing agreement. "The jig was up," says Kolman. "She knew she was being ripped."

When she phoned Rallo, he angrily insisted that the mortgage company was mistaken and that the deal had, indeed, gone through. He would come over the next day with all the paperwork. Remarkably, Hogue was relieved. She jubilantly told her friends the good news, though why she believed Rallo then, after nearly eight agonizing months of lies and excuses, is still a mystery.

A ONE-MINUTE-AND-12-SECOND cell phone call placed at 11:18 a.m. on November 17th from Rallo to Hogue is the last known record of her alive. Sometime later that day, police say, Rallo came over, fell into a violent rage, and strangled her, possibly with a cord.

That night, police say, when Hogue's roommate—her name has not been released—arrived home around eight, she found Prieta locked up, a sign Hogue didn't want to be bothered. The door to the Gypsy Love Room was closed, so the roommate assumed Hogue was entertaining a client. By the next morning, with no sign of Hogue, the worried roommate peered into the Gypsy Love Room and saw Hogue lying face-down on the bed, her naked body covered with a sheet. She thought Hogue was sleeping off a bender. Hours later, she saw that Hogue hadn't moved. She sat on the bed and gently stroked Hogue's hair. Then she touched Hogue's shoulder. It was ice cold.

Word of Hogue's death traveled quickly around escort circles. Web sites registered an outpouring of grief, shock, and anger. And then fear. The murder of a call girl in Atlanta just days after Hogue's slaying further alarmed many escorts. The anxiety escalated when someone on the online message boards posted a newspaper story about a string of three violent homicides on the South Side that had prompted police to issue a citywide warning to women of "high-risk lifestyles" (a euphemism for prostitution).

One escort calling herself New Orleans Natalie announced on the message boards that she had abruptly canceled her scheduled liaisons "[i]n light of recent incidents of violence against providers." Another jittery observer with the invented name Frankenstein posted a chilling question to the rest of the city's escorts: "Do we have a Jack the Ripper out there?"

Fortunately, Daniel Rallo was no criminal mastermind. His slip-ups led investigators to settle on him early on as the prime suspect after they saw his name on a truth-in-lending statement they found at Hogue's home. For starters, police say, he initially consented to be interviewed, then never showed up. While it's fair to say that at least a few men in this city of three million were nervous when detectives contacted them about Hogue's murder, the worried johns—except for Rallo—all complied with police interviews. By the time detectives contacted him again, he had hired an attorney, who told investigators that his client was invoking the Fifth Amendment right not to talk. Rallo's refusal to cooperate, says Landando, "wasn't a red flag—it was a target."

The team of detectives working on the case fanned out across Chicago and the northwest suburbs, gathering information on the suspect. They subpoenaed records and interviewed dozens of Rallo's friends, family members and business associates, about 70 in all. "Our plan was to be all over his life," says Landando.

Detectives say they also started receiving anonymous tips from people who knew Rallo and who said he had been behaving erratically—talking about committing murders and carrying guns. "He was asking guys, What kind of mistakes would you make if you did a murder?" says Detective Cordaro. "How would you cover it up? It looked as though Danny was fishing to out-think us, try to be a step ahead of the police."

But although investigators were "backing Rallo up like a rat in the corner," as Thomas Kolman, the Chicago police detective, puts it, they weren't able to amass enough evidence—other than the circumstantial—for an arrest. Still, the detectives were relentless. "There was no way this guy was going to kill this woman and just walk away because he's hiding behind his *Miranda* warnings," says Landando. "It ain't gonna happen, not with us."

With the case lagging, homicide detectives turned to the police department's Asset Forfeiture Unit, which cracks financial crimes, for help. Investigators knew that Rallo had forged employee tax documents for Hogue and helped launder her money. They figured if they couldn't nab him for murder, then they could follow this shady paper trail to uncover proof of possible financial crimes.

On January 27th, a Cook County judge granted detectives a warrant to search Rallo's home. Police say they wanted, at the very least, to gather enough evidence for money laundering charges. And maybe they could fool Rallo into thinking that they were coming to arrest him for murder, not simply to rummage through his file cabinets. They hoped, under pressure, he might even confess to foul play. "We knew if we could just talk to him—get him in a room—he'd crack," says Landando. "The more he tried to be a tough guy, the more it showed through that he was just a little weasel."

The next morning, around 8:45, the detectives drove to Rallo's home in suburban Streamwood. They arrived at 223 Monarch Drive, a three-story white townhouse indistinguishable from the others in the large ring-shaped subdivision. They knocked on the door and yelled, "Police! Police! Police!" No answer. Kolman, a burly Paul Bunyan type, swung a battering hammer, crushing the steel door. As they stormed inside the tiny entry foyer, Rallo stood just a few feet away—six steps up a stairwell at the entrance to the living room—out of their sight and with a snub-nosed revolver in his hand.

The detectives suspect Rallo was set for a shootout, but at the last second he put his gun to his temple and pulled the trigger. They found him sprawled in a pool of blood on the living room floor, the .38-caliber Taurus and a cell phone by his side.

Upstairs in his home office they discovered garbage bags filled with shredded documents and financial records, not to mention books on the mobsters John Gotti, Tony "The Ant" Spilotro, and Henry Hill. In his bedroom, they also found a packed suitcase and tickets for a "Freestyle Caribbean" vacation on the Norwegian Sun cruise line.

"CHERYL'S [MURDERER] HAS BEEN FOUND!" The news, posted on the BigDoggie Web site by an escort named Gemini, set off an online celebration. "The monster is dead," wrote an observer calling himself Admiral Dewey. Many escorts heaped praise on the police, normally their archenemy.

Police and friends still aren't completely sure how a scam about "a lousy 50 grand," as Delorta puts it, turned to murder. Landando guesses that Rallo was probably just "playing a game, being a wise guy wannabe." He probably spent Hogue's money, "and when she starts pressuring him, I think Danny felt like his back was up against the wall."

Kelly Shannon has a slightly different theory: Rallo, she says, simply figured, " 'What's one dead hooker?' " She sighs, and then adds, wistfully, "She wasn't just some hooker. She was someone's daughter. She was someone's sister. She was someone's niece. She was someone's best friend."

DAVID BERNSTEIN *is a senior editor at* Chicago *magazine. Previously he was a freelance writer, frequently contributing to the* New York Times, Chicago, *and* Crain's Chicago Business. *His work has also appeared in* The Best of Technology Writing 2006 *(Digital Culture Books). He lives in Chicago.*

Coda

Until this story, I had never seen a dead body. A real one, that is. Actually, make that, *photographs* of a real dead body. I was at the Grand Central Area police station on Chicago's Northwest Side, perusing evidence photos of a man sprawled in a pool of blood on his living room floor—picture after picture of his lifeless body and, most unforgettably, close-ups of the blood and brain matter oozing from a gunshot wound to his head. They weren't the kind of images that I was accustomed to seeing on my usual beats, mainly politics and culture.

The photographs were of Daniel Rallo, a suburban Chicago financial broker who had fancied himself an Al Capone–style gangster and who was the primary suspect in the killing of Kathryn Hogue, a high-priced escort. I first learned about Rallo from a short article in the *Chicago Sun-Times* published the day after Rallo shot himself as police attempted to serve him with a search warrant. The story mentioned Hogue and how Rallo was suspected of stealing thousands of dollars from her—money she was counting on to quit the sex trade. It just seemed rife with tragicomic characters and unanswered questions. I was intrigued, if for no other reason that a prostitute would have a financial adviser. Also, I was convinced that the story offered a window into the city's underworld of online prostitution.

The trickiest part of writing "Fatal Connection" was to preserve the climate of a whodunit, even though most readers had probably unraveled the mystery as soon as I introduced Rallo as a leading figure about midway through the story. Some credit, of course, goes to my editor, Richard Babcock, for helping me frame the story in a way that maintained the mystery. Another big challenge was to penetrate Hogue's secretive life as "Cheryl of Chicago," the online escort for hire. For that, I did things that would get me fired in most workplaces: I surfed local pornography Web sites for escorts who had known Hogue and posted messages on TheEroticReview.com and BigDoggie.net, the popular clearinghouses for the paid-sex trade. Because the escort business is so secretive (and illegal), many of the escorts and johns who responded to my interview-request posts on the message boards resented my poking my nose around their lives. Even before the piece was written, they accused me of writing a trashy, exploitive, and judgmental story about Hogue. One person wrote that I deserved to be killed, too. Luckily, the homicide detectives working on the case were more helpful, providing me virtually unhindered access to police reports and steering me to potential sources.

A quick postscript to the story: Trouble followed Daniel Rallo, even after his death. Not long after he killed himself, con artists used the identity of Rallo's financial lending firm, D.A.R. Financial, to scam people out of thousands of dollars.

Mark Fass

Last Seen on September 10th

FROM *New York* MAGAZINE

On Monday, September 10, 2001, Sneha Anne Philip had the day off. After her husband, Ron Lieberman, left for work at about eleven, she had their sunny, one-bedroom Battery Park City apartment to herself. Just her and the kittens, Figa and Kali. She planned to spend the day tidying up—the apartment was a mess, and her cousin Annu was coming over for dinner on Wednesday. She repotted four purple-and-white orchids that had arrived from Hawaii and placed them in the bathtub to dry out. At about 2 P.M., she sent her mother an instant message that mushroomed into a two-hour electronic conversation: "You should have seen Ron play guitar this weekend!" On Saturday, they had gone to a party where Ron, an emergency-room intern at the Jacobi Medical Center, jammed until midnight with his co-workers. Sneha also wrote about her plans for the week. She'd been wanting to check out Windows on the World, where an old friend was getting married in the spring. Finally, about 4 P.M., Sneha signed off so she could run some errands.

The 31-year-old internal-medicine intern changed into a

brown short-sleeved dress and sandals, her black hair pulled back in a ponytail. After dropping off some dry-cleaning, Sneha headed to Century 21, the discount department store a few blocks from their apartment, just past the Twin Towers. Just after 6 P.M., she used Ron's American Express card to buy lingerie, a dress, panty hose, and linens. Then she headed next door to the shoe annex and bought three pairs of shoes.

Ron came home from work that night to an empty apartment. Although it was almost midnight, he wasn't all that surprised. Sneha was supposed to call when she stayed out late, and she hadn't. Again. He petted Figa and Kali and went to bed. He had to leave for work by 6:30 A.M.

When his alarm clock went off Tuesday morning, Sneha still wasn't home. Ron was irritated, though still not particularly worried. Perhaps she'd spent the night at Annu's place a few blocks away or ended up in the West Village with her brother John—she did that sometimes. Resolving to talk to Sneha once more about her habit of staying out all night without checking in, he sleepily made his way to the Bowling Green subway station, where he caught an uptown 5 train in time for his 8 A.M. meeting at Jacobi in the Bronx.

When the meeting ended at nine, Ron saw his co-workers gathered around a television. A plane had just struck the north tower of the World Trade Center, about two blocks from his apartment. He called home immediately—Sneha didn't have a cell phone—and got the machine. He left a number of messages that morning, but Sneha never called back. He called her mother and brother—neither of them had heard from her, either.

Now Ron was worried. The city was in chaos, and he had not spoken to his wife since he kissed her good-bye the previous morning. Where was she? Because Sneha had no reason to be in the Trade Center, the possibility that she was trapped in the towers barely crossed his mind. But other horrifying images ran through his head: Had she been kidnapped off the street while running errands Monday afternoon? Had she been hit by a car and sent to a hospital, unidentifiable without her I.D.? Had she stopped for a drink on the way home and sidled up to the bar next to the wrong stranger?

At 3 P.M., Ron decided to stop wasting time waiting at Jacobi for the Twin Tower casualties that never materialized and to hitch a ride downtown with an ambulance to look for Sneha. The ambulance ride, against the stream of frantic people fleeing lower Manhattan, took six hours. When he finally reached Tribeca about 9 P.M., the NYPD had cordoned off the area. Still wearing his scrubs, he talked his way past the police line, then raced past burning cars and overturned fire trucks toward their Rector Place apartment. Without electricity, the front doors to the 23-story building wouldn't open. Eventually, he gave up and walked to a friend's place in the West Village, where he spent a sleepless night on a couch before heading home early the next morning. This time, he got inside. Gray soot from the fallen towers had poured in through an open window. Paw-print trails from the kittens crisscrossed the floors, but there was no sign of Sneha. No one has seen or heard from her since.

More than 9,000 people were reported missing on September 11, though the NYPD quickly whittled down the list. Officials discovered names that had been listed more than once. People called to say they had heard from "missing" loved ones. Investigators uncovered numerous cases of fraud. But years later, a few stragglers remained, people whose fates had never been resolved. Did they die on September 11? If not, what happened to them? In January 2004, the medical examiner's office announced that it was removing the last three names from the list of 9/11 victims, leaving the total at 2,749, where it still stands. Sneha's was one of those three names.

For the Philips, the loss was almost as painful as the first. Every young person who dies becomes an angel in memory. Soon after Sneha disappeared and presumably died in September 2001, her family began the beatification process: She must have run into the burning towers to use her medical expertise to try to save lives. She must have died a hero. But something got in the way of their efforts to shape their memories, to simplify the complexities of a life. City officials believe that Sneha led a secret double life. According to court records, her struggles with her dark side had cost her a job and damaged her marriage and may have led to her death the night before the terror attacks. But as the fifth anniversary of 9/11 approaches, Sneha's family is still trying to shape her legacy. They are still trying to prove that she died virtuously, one of the glorified 9/11 victims.

SNEHA AND RON met in 1995 at Chicago Medical School. She was a pretty and gregarious Indian girl who had grown up in Albany. He was a Jewish boy from L.A. with shoulder-length hair and a goatee. She was an artist, he played guitar—they stood out among their medical-school classmates and before long started dating. Sneha was a year ahead of Ron in school, so when things got serious, she took a year off, traveling around Italy, to let him catch up.

The couple graduated in 1999 and landed internships in New York—Ron at Jacobi, Sneha at the Cabrini Medical Center in Manhattan. They found a roomy, dark one-bedroom apartment on East 19th Street and began to build a life together. They worked interns' hours but still found time to spend with each other. They favored the jazz clubs of Greenwich Village and hole-in-the-wall sushi joints near Gramercy Park. Their life suited Sneha. She was near her brother, who lived on Greenwich Street, and only an hour-long train trip from her parents, who now lived in Dutchess County.

In May 2000, the couple got married in a Jewish-Indian celebration before 250 guests at a Dutchess County inn. At the end of the ceremony, Ron placed around Sneha's neck a gift from her mother: a teardrop-shaped gold *minnu,* the traditional Indian wedding pendant. At the reception, he had the band play a jazz tune he composed for the evening titled "Wow! She's So Great."

Less than a year and a half later, Ron was walking the streets with photocopies of his wife's picture. The day after the attacks, he went to the 9/11 help center at the Lexington Avenue Armory to drop off flyers. When he saw the television cameras, he thought he might be able to get Sneha's picture out all over the country. He hoped someone would recognize her and provide clues about her disappearance. But when reporters learned that Sneha had not been heard from since the 10th, they lost interest. They wanted real 9/11 stories. Though Ron still did not believe his wife had been in the towers, he was desperate. He called Sneha's brother and suggested he come down to talk with reporters, leaving out a few details.

John took it one step further. Although he had been fighting with Sneha and had not spoken with her in two weeks, he concocted a scenario of her final moments, live on WABC. Staring mournfully into the camera, he said, "I was on the phone with her, and she told me she couldn't leave because people were hurt. She said, 'I have to help this person,' and that's the last thing I heard from her."

The lie worked, and WABC ran a picture of the flyer. But no leads were uncovered, no witnesses found. As time passed, John began to worry that he had led investigators down the wrong path, preventing her from being found. "Maybe if I didn't do it . . . maybe it would have gone another way," he told me. "It became a hero story."

The hero story notwithstanding, the family's initial search focused on the 10th, which at the time seemed more hopeful than the alternative. Ron, who spent much of 9/11 waiting in vain to treat the injured, knew as well as anyone that survivors were unlikely to emerge from ground zero. Whatever may have occurred on the 10th, at least Sneha might still be alive.

Ron approached the crisis methodically, like a physician. His first clue came from Sneha's instant messages on Monday to her mother: She left the house in the late afternoon to run errands. Then Ron called American Express and learned of the Century 21 purchases. (Hoping it may yet provide a lead, Ron has kept his AmEx account open.) The downtown Century 21 had temporarily closed, so he dispatched friends to drop off flyers at its other branches. Later that week, he received a phone call from Sonia Mora, a shoe-department salesclerk who had been relocated to Brooklyn. Mora said that she recognized Sneha as a Century 21 regular. Sneha came to the store with a friend on the 10th, she recalled, describing the other woman as small, in her early thirties, dark-skinned, possibly Indian. The shoe department did not use security cameras, but—after spending three weeks alone in a windowless room at Century 21's offices reviewing videotape—Ron discovered a coat-department video from an hour earlier that captured Sneha browsing alone. Sneha's mystery friend—if she existed—was never found.

Ron filed two missing-persons reports, but detectives—after ruling him out as a suspect—appeared inclined to lump Sneha in with the World Trade Center victims, he says. So Ron hired a private investigator, former FBI special-operations agent Ken Gallant, who scoured Sneha's favorite hangouts, interviewed employees at bars and hotels near Century 21, and talked to Sneha's friends, family, and co-workers. Gallant brought photos of Sneha to ferry docks, looking for people who remembered her fleeing on the 11th or being dragged out on the 10th. He even recommended a psychic whom the family flew in from Pennsylvania.

Gallant also raised the possibility that Sneha might be alive and living a new life somewhere. He oversaw a forensic examination of Sneha's computer, searching for evidence of a secret lover, an upcoming tryst. But he found nothing, and the fact that Sneha left behind her glasses, passport, driver's license, and credit cards (with the exception of Ron's AmEx) seemingly ruled out the theory that she intentionally disappeared.

The search did unearth a few clues about Sneha's final hours. Although Ron was the only one home on the night of the 10th, someone made a call from their home phone to his cell at about 4

A.M. Tuesday, he discovered. He doesn't remember making the call but figures he may have sleepily checked his messages. Because Ron found neither footprints in the dust nor the Century 21 bags, he knows Sneha never came back to their apartment after the terror attacks. But the most tantalizing clue came from the apartment building's security camera: a videotape of a woman who resembled Sneha in the lobby just before the first plane struck the Trade Center. Because of the angle of the sun, the image is too bleached out for Ron to be sure. But on the tape, a woman who in silhouette looks very much like Sneha—a similar haircut, similar mannerisms, wearing a dress like the one Sneha wore the afternoon before—enters the building. She stands near the elevator, waits a minute or two, then turns around and leaves.

FACED WITH THIS DEARTH of meaningful leads, Ron and the Philips began to reevaluate their hypothesis that whatever happened to Sneha happened on the 10th. "These kinds of crimes don't happen in lower Manhattan, that somebody goes missing from a homicide, and they don't find the body," Ron says. "Killers are usually stupid, they leave clues. A body will come up. Sneha just vanished. Vanished, vanished, vanished, with no trace. The only thing that makes sense is that she burned in the World Trade Center."

A story of a heroic death—a story very much like the one John made up for the television cameras—took root. Perhaps that was Sneha on the videotape. Perhaps she went shopping, bumped into the friend whom the salesclerk remembers, went out for drinks, and, thinking that Ron would be working late, ended up spending the night at her place. Perhaps Sneha returned home the next morning, was in the lobby when the plane struck, and, as a doctor, reflexively ran toward the towers to help. The theory had flaws—the woman on the tape, for example, was not carrying shopping bags—but it fit perfectly into the family's idealized image of Sneha, the version of her they hoped to remember.

This account of Sneha's death also gained the Philips entry into the special community of grief surrounding 9/11. They no longer had to suffer alone. On the first anniversary of the attacks, Sneha's parents went with their two sons and Ron to a memorial in Poughkeepsie, where Sneha's name was read aloud as part of a tribute to local victims. Three days later, the Philips held a small ceremony at the Church of the Resurrection, near their home in Dutchess County, where they buried an urn filled with ashes from ground zero. A few months after that, a plaque went up in a grove at Dutchess Community College, where Sneha's mother, Ansu, works as a computer programmer, that reads DR. SNEHA ANNE PHILIP, OCTOBER 07, 1969–SEPTEMBER 11, 2001. By 2003, attending memorials had become a routine for the family, an opportunity to discuss their loss with others whose loved ones were heroes and martyrs. That October—intent on creating a memorial fund, he says—Ron filed a claim with the Victim Compensation Fund.

BUT AS THE PHILIPS were coming to the conclusion that Sneha died in the Trade Center, another investigation was going on. Although the police had initially considered Sneha a 9/11 victim, they later uncovered a very different version of her life—one that makes her family very uncomfortable.

Police reports and court records describe a life that was reeling out of control in the months leading up to Sneha's disappearance. Citing tardiness and "alcohol-related issues," Cabrini's director of residents had informed Sneha in the spring of 2001 that her contract would not be renewed—for interns, the equivalent of being fired. Shortly thereafter, Sneha got into a dispute at a bar that landed her in jail for a night. She claimed that on an evening out with co-workers, a fellow intern grabbed her inappropriately. She filed a criminal complaint, but after conducting an investigation, the Manhattan D.A.'s office dropped the charges against the alleged groper and instead charged Sneha with filing a false complaint. The prosecutors offered to drop the charge if Sneha recanted, but she refused. She was arrested and spent a night behind bars, where she meditated with a cellmate.

Sneha was also experiencing "marital problems" in the months after she was fired from Cabrini, according to court papers, and "often stayed out all night with individuals (not known to her husband) whom she met at various bars." She favored the loungy midtown lesbian bar Julie's, the rocker-dyke bar Henrietta Hudson's, and the divey gay rock club Meow Mix. According to the investigations, Sneha's indiscretions appear to have reached a low point in the month prior to her disappearance. A police report says that her brother John walked in on her and his girlfriend—now the mother of his son—having sex. Her alleged struggles with depression, alcohol, and her sexuality spilled over into her new job as well. Staten Island's St. Vincent's Medical Center suspended her for failing to meet with her substance-abuse counselor.

Apparently these problems reared up again on the day she disappeared. Sneha had a court date on the morning of September 10, 2001, where she pleaded not guilty to the charge of filing a false complaint. Ron went with her before he left for work. According to the police report, the couple got into a "big fight" at the courthouse because Ron was upset that Sneha "was abusing drugs and alcohol and was conducting bisexual acts." In this account, Sneha stormed out of court, leaving Ron behind.

Unable to tie Sneha's death to the attacks, the medical examiner's office removed Sneha's name from the official list of 9/11 victims in January 2004. "This particular lady was known to be missing the day before," explains Ellen Borakove, the medical examiner's spokesperson. "They had no evidence to show that she was alive on 9/11." And in November 2005, a Manhattan judge denied Ron's petition to set Sneha's date of death on September 11, 2001. Judge Renee Roth ruled that Sneha officially died on September 10, 2004—as set forth by state law, three years to the day after her "unexplained absence commenced." Because Ron could not produce a 9/11 death certificate, the Compensation Fund denied his claim. Based on Sneha's age and potential earnings, the claim would have been worth about $3 million to $4 million, according to an attorney who represented numerous other families who sought compensation.

The police still don't know what happened to Sneha, but the implication of the court decision is obvious: Sneha was just as likely to have left her husband, committed suicide, or even been the victim of a violent crime as to have rushed into the World Trade Center on 9/11.

SNEHA'S FAMILY—Ron, John, and her parents, Ansu and Philip—dispute essentially everything in the police and court accounts. The event that precipitated Sneha's decline—being let go by Cabrini—had nothing to do with alcohol, they contend. Instead, they claim Sneha was the victim of persistent racial and sexual bias at Cabrini and was dismissed because she was a whistleblower. (A spokesperson for Cabrini says they have "no knowledge of any sexual harassment allegations made by Dr. Philip.")

Ron admits that Sneha had gone home with women she met at bars but claims that her actions were innocent of the obvious implication. Sneha liked to see live bands and to have an occasional drink, and she preferred to do so at lesbian bars, where men would not hit on her—particularly after the groping incident, Ron says. She spent a few nights with women she met out on the town, but they talked or made art or listened to music until they fell asleep, he insists. One night, he recalls, Sneha met an artist at a bar and the next morning she came home covered in paint. "These allegations of her being bisexual are ridiculous," Ron protests. "Because we don't live a conservative lifestyle doesn't mean that anything abnormal is going on. I'm a musician. I've been going out to bars and clubs my whole life. It doesn't mean these things are dangerous activities."

John claims that the missing-persons report, which states that he told Richard Stark, the detective assigned to the case, that he walked in on his sister and his girlfriend having "sexual relations," is simply untrue, a product of cops sitting around playing Mad Libs. He maintains that he never even spoke with Stark, who has since retired and could not be reached for comment. Ron also says the report is riddled with fabrications. The fight at the courthouse, for example, never took place, he says. "Either I'm a liar or they're lying, because I'm 100 percent positive about this," he says. Ron and John offer little to explain what would motivate the police to lie. Mainly they suggest that investigators needed to compensate for their ineffectual police work by wildly extrapolating from the few facts they uncovered. (An NYPD spokesperson said that he was reviewing the case but could not comment at press time.)

In the family's version of Sneha's final days, little had changed from the halcyon times of just a year or two earlier. Her drinking was merely a short stint of self-medication during a hard time. The depression was temporary and on the mend. The career was back on track, her recent suspension notwithstanding. The nights spent at the homes of random strangers were not illicit, just inconsiderate. And then, just when she was putting her life back together, she disappeared.

Perhaps Sneha's family is trying to protect her, and themselves, from a truth that would taint her name and their memory. Perhaps they simply do not know about her other life, the one detailed by investigators after she went missing. Perhaps, though it seems unlikely, the police conjured up a wild story out of thin air. Ron refused to allow me access to the private investigator's report, which might have corroborated or refuted the police account.

But as Ron puts it, "even if she did all these things, it doesn't explain what happened." No matter how Sneha spent the last months of her life, her family might be right about how she spent her last moments. At any given time there are approximately 3,000 active cases of missing adults in New York State, so people do, it seems, sometimes just disappear. But a murderer pulling off a perfect crime on the same day that 1,151 people (the number of 9/11 victims whose remains have never been discovered) also disappeared without a trace seems an extraordinarily unlikely coincidence. Even Detective Stark eventually testified in the death-certificate proceedings that he thought Sneha *probably* died in the towers.

Under New York law, establishing that a person died as a result of 9/11 requires clear and convincing evidence of the person's "exposure" to the attack. But application of this law has been uneven at best. A Manhattan judge rejected a petition filed on behalf of Fernando Molinar, even though Molinar called his mother on September 8, 2001, told her he was starting a new job at a pizzeria near the World Trade Center, and was never heard from again. A Dutchess County judge, on the other hand, ruled that Juan Lafuente, who worked eight blocks north of the towers, did in fact die in the attack. During Lafuente's death-certificate proceedings, his wife, Colette, the mayor of Poughkeepsie, presented no direct proof of her husband's whereabouts on 9/11. Her circumstantial evidence included the testimony of a witness who frequented the same deli as Lafuente and claimed he overheard Lafuente tell a brown-haired man about an upcoming meeting at the Trade Center.

Sneha's case contains a number of parallels to Lafuente's. Both stories have red flags: Sneha and Lafuente each lost a job, suffered from depression, and spent a night or two away from home each month, according to their spouses. Both victims also might have been tempted to rush into the burning buildings: Sneha was a doctor and Lafuente a volunteer fire marshal. One factor, however, distinguishes Colette Lafuente's successfully expedited death-certificate application and Ron's four-and-a-half-year mission, Sneha's parents believe. "Ron's not the mayor," says Ansu.

The other difference: Sneha was a woman who allegedly engaged in an illicit lifestyle. The family's attorney, Marc Bogatin, calls her death-certificate ruling moralistic and illogical. The decision implies that Sneha was "partially at fault for her own death for participating in this high-risk and immoral behavior," he says. "It's like she walked into a courtroom in the fifties."

For Sneha's family, the 9/11 death certificate would represent proof of what, disturbingly, has become the best-case scenario. "All her parents and I really want is for her name to be on the list," Ron says. "End this family's suffering right now. Her mother's crying all the time. Is it going to hurt anybody to do it? But for some reason they're not going to do it."

AT THE PHILIPS' quiet, spacious home on top of one of the highest hills in Hopewell Junction, there are pictures of Sneha everywhere. In the den hangs her portrait, on the living-room wall a picture of Ron and Sneha at their wedding. On the mantelpiece above the fireplace sit another half dozen pictures of her—Sneha in her wedding gown, Sneha receiving a diploma, Sneha and Ron standing in the kitchen—and one of Jesus.

Sitting at the kitchen table while Philip listens quietly, Ansu talks about how close she was to her only daughter. "She tells me everything," she says, slipping into the present tense more than four years after Sneha's disappearance. "She can go on in detail. That's one of the things I really love about her." Ansu spent the Friday night before September 11 visiting Sneha in the city. They ate Chinese food, walked around Battery Park, and watched *Portrait of a Lady* on video. When Ansu left the next morning, Sneha said to her, "Mom, can we do this more often?"

The family has finally stopped looking for clues to Sneha's whereabouts. "I don't have even a grain of hope that she's alive or that anything else happened to her," Ansu says. "It's more peaceful for me to think she died in the World Trade Center than . . . I cannot bear to think that somebody killed her."

What they're looking for now is official recognition, if not proof, of what they've come to believe. Or, as Ansu calls it, "closure," a word the family repeats like a mantra.

"There is no final closure for me," says Philip, breaking his silence in frustration. "She cannot just disappear in the air. There should be a body, an accident report, there should be something. How can they say she died on the 10th?"

Although they've been counseled that the odds are exceedingly slim, they intend to appeal Judge Roth's death-certificate decision. It's not about money, Ansu says; with the Victim Compensation Fund closed, Ron's claim is worthless no matter what the decision. It's about getting Sneha's name added to the coming memorial. It's about proving wrong the insinuations that alcohol and adultery might have led to her death.

"They're trying to fabricate a picture," says Ansu, "making Sneha look so bad. It looks like she's some kind of confused, mixed-up, horrible person. She's far from it. So kind, compassionate, beautiful inside, beautiful outside."

If the mystery is to be solved, it will likely be through DNA evidence. As recently as a few months ago, it appeared that the city would not be able to identify any additional victims via DNA. But a recent advance in forensic technology—the use of a reagent that helps retrieve a higher percentage of purified DNA from bone fragments—has convinced city officials to send samples of the 9,069 still-unidentified remains back to a laboratory in Virginia for a new round of testing. In January, the process made its first 9/11 identification.

Sneha's family, however, has pinned its hopes on her jewelry: her wedding band, engagement ring, diamond earrings, and the *minnu* she always wore. The melting point of diamonds is more than four times higher than that of bone, which turns to ash in just a few hours at 1,500 degrees Fahrenheit. A body trapped in the depths of ground zero (where the fires burned at 2,000 degrees) would leave virtually nothing behind, but a diamond could survive essentially unscathed. The city property clerk has recovered 1,350 pieces of jewelry from the ruins, only about two thirds of which have been returned to victims' families. For the Philips, the remaining jewelry represents more than 400 chances to prove that Sneha was a hero.

They cling to a reply from the property clerk's office like a life preserver. It says that they may have Sneha's jewelry and requests photographs for confirmation. "When I got the letter," Ansu says. "I was just so, like, hopeful that there was something."

But, more than a year after she and Philip sent the clerk photos of Sneha's jewelry, they have received no answer and have become increasingly frustrated by the delay. When I called to find out the status of the match, a spokesperson for the property clerk's office said that the letter the Philips received was essentially meaningless. "If you sent in a letter about a plain piece of jewelry, a Timex watch, if there was one of them, we sent you back a letter that there's a possibility," he told me. "We had no idea if there could even be a match. But everybody got those letters."

I ask Ansu what she would do if, hypothetically speaking, they didn't find a match to Sneha's jewelry. "I'd be very disappointed," she says. "I know in my mind, part of her is in the ashes. There's some kind of peace in that."

I didn't have the heart to tell her.

MARK FASS *is a staff writer for the* New York Law Journal *and a frequent contributor to* New York *magazine. He is a graduate of Hastings Law School and the Columbia School of Journalism and lives with his wife, Monica, and daughter, Clara, in Brooklyn.*

Coda

Like any good mystery, Sneha's story revealed itself page by page. For me, it started off with Judge Roth's decision denying Ron's petition to set the official date of Sneha's death on September 11, 2001. From there, a quick Lexis-Nexis search uncovered that the story the family presented to the press was very different from the one that unfolded in the courtroom. The major themes were immediately obvious: What would you do if your loved one disappeared the day before 9/11? How far would you go to find her? What happens when you uncover her secrets?

I struggled with a number of obstacles, most notably that the family continued to tell me a very different story than the one contained in the police and private-investigator reports. As sympathetic as their story and situation were, I had to tell both sides, much to their dismay.

For a long time, I thought I might actually solve the mystery, or at least be able to prove that Sneha died in the towers: The police clerk's office still has a mountain of recovered jewelry that may contain Sneha's wedding pendant. I thought that, with my reporter skills, I might be able to do a better job negotiating the city's cold bureaucracy than Sneha's parents had done. I was wrong. After dozens and dozens of inquiries, as far as I know, the city still hasn't looked for Sneha's jewelry.

Brian Boucher

MY ROOMMATE, THE DIAMOND THIEF

FROM *New York* MAGAZINE

Seeking roommate for one-bedroom in Washington Heights. It's a bit small for two but I have to catch up on some bills. Two friendly cats, but we keep clean because I'm a little allergic myself. A little more than half of the $950 rent gets you the privacy of the bedroom.

IT WAS AUGUST 2003. I'd only recently found work, nearly a year after losing my job organizing school tours at an art museum, and my fiancée had just moved out of our apartment. It was a small, sunny place on the fourth floor of an old building, high enough on a hill that you could even see a little of New Jersey from the right angle.

We'd moved up there when she landed a medical residency at Columbia University Medical Center, but we'd split six months before the wedding. Without a job, I'd run up a ton of debt, and I urgently needed extra income to make rent, so I figured I'd lease out my bedroom and crash in the living room. I tried to pretend it was darkly funny, but really it just felt pathetic.

I got a flood of responses. A panicking female college student from the Midwest offered three months' rent sight unseen, but she couldn't meet me in person. An asshole with the e-mail handle of "elitist1" got impatient when I didn't answer his questions fast enough. I fell for a blue-eyed, tongue-pierced vegan the moment I opened the door to her, but she wasn't interested in the room, or me.

John "Don" Williams was enthusiastic about the apartment, at least. A middle-aged ghostwriter from California who'd lived all over, he turned up at my door in cargo pants and long sleeves despite the summer heat and talked with a slight southern drawl. He was punctual, which I liked. And he greeted my two cats warmly, which I also liked. "I've looked at a lot of apartments, and this is definitely the best arrangement I've seen," he said. I was flattered, though he must have seen some real squalor. We played with the cats and chatted about pets. The two of us—a ghostwriter and an aspiring art critic—could compare notes on the writing life, we agreed. He moved in on August 21.

At first Don struck me as the perfect roommate. He was uncommonly neat and clean. To keep cat hair from coming into his room, he rolled up a towel and push-pinned it to the bottom of the door. He was often out, and when home, he stayed in his room without a peep for hours on end. Sometimes he would emerge from his room when I had imagined myself alone in the apartment and had been blasting music, talking on the phone, or listening to public radio while cooking dinner. He hardly ever had guests and was frequently gone for days at a time. I wasn't thrilled with his unannounced comings and goings, but I let it go.

If anything, Don seemed boring, either putting his head down or making dull small talk as he passed through the living room. When he did speak, it was mainly to praise the beautiful women of New York. He had female guests a couple of times and alluded to several girlfriends. Despite a ring on his finger, he wasn't married, and in fact, "the ring doesn't seem to discourage women who are interested," he said. I hadn't dated in a while, I mentioned, but there were some situations I hoped might develop into something. "But it's like film," he advised. "It isn't going to develop unless you bring it into the store to get developed."

Four months into Don's stay, with cash coming in on time each month, all was going smoothly enough, until the morning of December 13, when I got home after a long night out to find his room in total chaos. It had been ransacked. His clothes, toiletries, and magazines were strewn about the bed and floors. The closet door hung from one hinge off a busted frame. His locked red Swiss Army luggage lay slashed open on the floor, the cats sleeping happily among the jumbled contents. My stuff was untouched, but I was horrified.

I called 911, but the cops were useless. "Talk to your roommate about it when you see him," they said.

Who knew when that might be? At this point, I hadn't seen Don for well over a month. In mid-November, I'd e-mailed to ask whether he'd be back anytime soon. Had he taken the business trip to London that he'd mentioned? No, he replied. His younger sister had been in a car accident, and he was in Seattle visiting her. I hadn't heard from him since. I e-mailed him repeatedly and got no answer.

I started to wonder about my lodger and what he might be hiding in his room. The break-in seemed too calculated and selective to be the work of a common thief, who might have simply stolen Don's luggage or my computer. Even the cash I'd stowed in my sock drawer was untouched. My fantasies turned paranoid. Was Don a spy—or an Al Qaeda operative who'd turned my apartment into his base? Had the injured-sister story been a ploy to gain my sympathy? Or maybe the accident was real but had been caused by some other agent to distract Don long enough to retrieve something from his suitcases.

Unable to reach Don and thoroughly spooked, I changed the locks, packed his few things into a closet, and moved back into the bedroom, convinced he'd never return.

He did. On Christmas Eve, he called when I was in the middle of tree-trimming at my parents' home in New Jersey. He told me that his ailing sister had died and he was back in New York but couldn't get into the apartment. At first I was petrified just to hear his voice, but as we spoke, I started to relax. Maybe I was insane and he was a normal guy—a possibility I'd consider over and over in the ensuing months. I told him about the break-in and said I'd meet him at the apartment at three the following afternoon.

I got there two hours early. Mortified at having assumed he skipped town when he'd actually had a family tragedy, I wanted to make it seem as though I had never moved back in. Back out of the closet came his luggage, and I scattered things around to make it look convincingly ransacked. Back on the windowsill went the action figures he had kept there. His plastic storage containers, just about his only furniture, went back against the wall where I'd found them. I reset the clock. I held my breath.

The doorbell rang at three o'clock, and there he was. He seemed tired and sad, as you might expect, and at the same time he seemed obsessed with trying to solve the crime. He searched through the room, sat among the wreckage looking closely at his scattered belongings, and even joked about the perpetrator's clumsy closet break-in. Strangely, despite the damage, little had been stolen—old cell phones, a little cash, a printer, and some marijuana, according to Don. (The drugs surprised me. I'd only seen him drink a beer once, and he'd said one was his limit.)

I imagined the invasion as retaliation for his womanizing. One of Don's lady visitors had an on-again-off-again ex-con boyfriend—was he the culprit? "It doesn't make sense," Don said. "That guy, I've seen him around, and if he did this, he would have made it worth his while."

Don advanced his own theory: "Three people had the keys," he said. "I didn't do it, my sixth sense tells me you weren't involved, and that leaves one person." He suspected our eccentric next-door neighbor, Lev, a deeply indebted Lithuanian jazz pianist and self-published science-fiction novelist who fed the cats whenever I went away. "You know, he grew up in the Soviet Union," Don said, "so you don't know who he might have been involved with." I just listened. It was ridiculous, but his explanation did have a certain Occam's-razor appeal.

Don proposed that we mount surveillance Webcams in the apartment (I refused) and called in the help of his family. He brought over a woman he called his sister and had me relate the story of finding the crime scene. ("I'm sorry for your loss," I told her. "It's been a hard time," she replied.) He also told me he'd sent some items to his brother-in-law in D.C., "a Fed," he said, "so if there are any fingerprints on them, we'll find out."

It occurred to me I'd touched all his stuff when I moved back into the bedroom. What if he found out? To clear my conscience, I confessed. "You handled pretty much everything in there," he said, as if asking for confirmation of something he already knew. "I found your prints, too."

"Strong work," I said, shocked but trying to play it cool. "How did you get them in the first place?"

"Oh, well, you know, you could always just take an empty out of the recycling bin or something."

Don's familiarity with law-enforcement techniques might have alarmed me, but I was too embarrassed about my stunt to think clearly—and his anger over the incident only fueled my guilt. When I asked him for compensation after he inadvertently damaged an artwork of mine, Don retorted that it should be balanced against the losses he'd sustained in the break-in, which, as he saw it, happened on my watch. "And when you told me about it, you were just, like, 'Hey, here's what happened, sorry.' My reaction would have been, 'What can I do?' Because if I see you have a problem, I'm going to try to help you. That's just the way I was raised."

Stung by the insult, I told him he needed to move out. I didn't understand why he'd want to stay, I said hotly, "when this whole arrangement is obviously broken." But he didn't react, and in the end, I backed down. Maybe he was right. Perhaps I had been selfish and insensitive. Over my objections, he installed a lock on the bedroom door and left his radio playing WNYC around the clock to discourage intruders. I complained to friends. "He sounds crazy," they said. When I griped to Don about the lock, he made me out to be the lunatic. "You said it wasn't a good idea," he argued. "You didn't say to take it off." Once again, I gave up. I needed the money.

In June 2004, Don was missing again, and he had been gone for weeks. E-mails I sent him began to bounce back, and his cell phone was not taking calls. June 21, rent day, came and went. I let two more weeks pass before changing the locks. I then broke into my own bedroom, turned off the radio, and, for the second time, angrily set about packing up the possessions he had left behind.

In his bed, I discovered a laptop and a bulging manila folder that seemed innocuous enough, though I couldn't help but look inside. There, to my total shock, were scraps of torn-up preapproved credit-card offers I'd received in the mail and tossed in the trash. That wasn't all. On a sheet of notebook paper, he'd scribbled the names, addresses, and phone numbers of my family members; my mother's maiden name; the date my parents had married; and the name and address of a contractor I was working for, apparently copied from a pay stub. He even had the name and number of a woman I'd met at a party. Equally alarming were notes on my credit-card information, along with my sign-in names and passwords to various Websites.

In an instant, I felt like an idiot, a sucker, the Jersey boy I am. Why had I trusted this stranger? I burned with shame and anger as I pictured him listening for me to leave for work in the morning so he could methodically search my trash and boot up my computer. A ghostwriter? What a moron I'd been. I'd never seen him write a word. But who was he? I searched everything in the room. A letter from JetBlue addressed to a Brandall Platt confirmed a flight to Oakland, California, in November 2003, the time of one of his previous absences. There were photocopies of Social Security cards and California driver's licenses of a Charles Brown and an Andre Holmes and others. From the photocopies, I couldn't tell whether the pictures were of my roommate. I found nothing bearing the name "Don" had given me: John Williams.

His bike was gone, but a bunch of withered bananas suggested his absence was unplanned. Had Don been in an accident? A detective from the local precinct suggested I contact local hospitals. When that didn't work, he said he'd start checking jails. I called my banks and credit-card companies. Thank God there were no unauthorized charges and no new cards in my name.

I searched the closet, where I spotted a classic composition book that looked like a diary. Seething over how he'd invaded my privacy, I tore it open, looking for revelations amid his cramped scribblings, rife with misspellings and sentence fragments. On one page, Don had mapped out a movie of his life story: "He learned to drive at eight, he could do anything with his hands, and throughout his life, he could become invisible . . ." "Met with Spike Lee today," read one entry. "He's really interested in the story, and wants me to send him the articles." His journal said he once met Danny Glover by chance in the street and tried to sell him his story as well. He had even cast the big-screen version of his life: He was to be portrayed by Denzel Washington. Laurence Fishburne would appear as his brother. Angela Bassett would take on the role of his wife, and, of course, Halle Berry ("the sexiest woman in the world") would be his girlfriend.

The diary also contained transcriptions of text-message exchanges with real girlfriends—"u have hurt me 2 many times," one wrote—and vague laments over his kids: "I don't even know who I am anymore . . . all I know is I'm the father of three beautiful, innocent children. . . . My babies, my babies . . . your dada cries every day." Apparently, he also had reason to fear the police: "I'm only now just starting to get over being afraid every time someone looks at me twice in the street . . . every time a cop looks at me . . . thinking they know." Know what?

I was becoming frantic. Craving more answers, I turned to his laptop, handing it over to a systems-administrator friend to circumvent his password protection by installing a new operating system.

The sign-in name added yet another entry to the growing list of pseudonyms: Dino Smith. There, among various pictures of Don and his family, flyers for a business venture offering tours of the Bay Area in a Hummer, and a poster offering his services as a "personnel assistant," was the following diary entry, dated April 27, 2003:

> I'm @ location 4. It's been how many days now? Lets count from the 14th–15–16–17–18–19–20–21–22–23–24–25–26–27> 13 days today, dam, two weeks tomorrow . . . how the hell do I prove I was not there? When I truly was not there? Who the hells going to believe me. I can't even get up on the witness stand, When those fuckers are going to do everything they can not to lose this case . . . I won't sit up in jail for who knows how long and I know I've been set up by those no good fucking cops that I know don't like me.

MY HANDS STARTED TO SHAKE. Had I been harboring a fugitive? Don had struck me as creepy, but I wasn't prepared for this. My heart raced as I wondered what crime the cops could possibly want him for. I thought about the break-in, his absences, the dead sister, the fingerprinting . . . but what did it all add up to? Was he a victim of circumstance—or a serial killer? Was I his next target? I became obsessed with getting answers. Then I searched the most obvious place of all: Google. I typed in the name "Dino Smith," and a couple of clicks later, there it was. His mug shot, on the *America's Most Wanted* Website. He was a suspect in the biggest jewel heist in San Francisco history. I gaped at the screen in disbelief, then ran in circles, howling obscenities: *"Fuck fuck fucking shit fuck fucker! Holy FUCK!"*

I scanned the Web for more clues, cringing at each revelation. According to the Los Angeles *Times,* one night in April 2003, Dino, his brother Devin "Troy" Smith, and accomplices allegedly broke into a vacant restaurant adjoining Lang Antique & Estate Jewelry, burrowed through the wall, disabled the motion detectors, and hid in the bathroom overnight. When the employees arrived in the morning, the thieves forced them to empty the safes at gunpoint, then tied them up. The robbers hauled away $6 million to $10 million worth of diamonds and other jewelry in garbage bags. Four months after the heist, "Don" the ghostwriter moved in with me.

He'd been eluding the cops for fourteen months when he was captured on June 4, just a few days after I had last seen him. The police finally caught up with him outside the A subway station at Howard Beach-JFK Airport, where they had followed a girlfriend who'd flown in from the West Coast to visit him.

Dino and his brother had served time before. They were a notorious crime duo despised by cops and prosecutors for their slick arrogance and flamboyance. Known for his acrobatic robbery style, Dino reportedly escaped the police by using a handcuff key he'd hidden in the seam of his underwear. Between them, Dino and Troy had generated 20,000 pages' worth of court documents, according to the L.A. *Times.*

In 1990, the brothers were arrested, and later convicted, for a foiled plot to kidnap and rob Lawrence Lin, also known as Dr. Winkie, the eccentric owner of the San Francisco nightclub DV8. (Wearing body armor and carrying semi-automatic rifles at the time of their arrest, the two improbably told cops they were on the way to protect Lin.) They were also convicted for a 1989 robbery in which they stole $400,000 worth of jewelry from the home of Victoria Magana, the widow of a Nicaraguan drug lord. This time, they told police she staged the theft herself to avoid payment on a $500,000 drug debt.

All told, Dino had 47 years to serve, and Troy 42. But they were sprung after less than a decade when both convictions were overturned, one because of attorney misconduct, the other thanks to police misconduct.

After their 1998 release, the brothers tried—and failed—to go straight. A brief stint as seamen for merchant ships at the Port of Oakland ended badly when the Coast Guard realized they'd lied about their criminal past on the applications, the *Times* reported. Troy fell deep into debt, and his marriage was falling apart. His wife claimed he had punched her in the face and had allegedly threatened that if she tried to leave, "I'll make what O.J. did to Nicole look like a paper cut," according to the paper.

What, then, might Troy have in mind for me? After all, he was still at large. Could Dino have given him my personal information? Could Troy be living as Brian Boucher at this very moment? I was so scared I called 911, convinced that he was on his way to find me. The cops looked around the apartment, twirling their batons as I tried to explain. "If you see the brother, call the police," they said, and left.

I had better luck with the San Francisco police the following day. "We've really been hoping for a phone call like this," said Dan Gardner, a robbery inspector for the SFPD. One evening just before the Republican National Convention, four men arrived at my apartment: the towering Gardner and his partner, along with two New York detectives. "So where'd ya find da jewels?" one of them cracked.

They donned rubber gloves and went to work, tearing outlets and switch plates from the wall, fondling the futon. One mentioned a Manhattan Mini Storage locker of Dino's containing power tools and a concrete saw. I asked if they thought I'd hear from Dino again. "Look," Gardner told me, "I don't want to scare you, but they did catch him trying to escape from Rikers Island once already while he's been in custody."

IN MAY 2005, I received a call from Jerry Coleman, a San Francisco assistant district attorney who asked me to come testify in the trial. Weeks later, I sat by myself in a San Francisco court-room. The sole observer was a woman I'd seen in pictures from Dino's computer, and it struck me that she and Dino had the same features. She had to be his mother.

A door opened and in walked Dino, looking sharp in tan pants and a black polo. No orange jumpsuit, no cuffs. The room fell silent. I hadn't seen him in almost a year, and I couldn't take my eyes off him. He sat and arranged his files, then turned to me and nodded hello with a nervous look of forced ease. "Hey, roomie. How funny seeing you here," he seemed to say.

As they swore me in, I was afraid the microphone on the witness stand would pick up the sound of my heart pounding.

"Sir, in the events you've described, would you say you were acting as an agent of the police?" Dino's lawyer asked.

Huh? I leaned into the microphone. "No, sir." Maybe this wouldn't be so hard.

Dino frequently shook his head, seemingly disgusted at the state's flimsy case against him, and furiously took notes as I enumerated the identifying information he had collected on me.

The defense attorney tried to undermine the legitimacy of the computer evidence, on the basis that I'd left it with a friend to work on overnight. "So you don't know what your friend did, by your own personal knowledge?"

"I guess that's true."

"No further questions, your honor."

ON JUNE 3, 2005, based in part on evidence found on the computer he left behind, the jury convicted Dino Loren Smith, 55, on eight of eleven counts of robbery, false imprisonment, burglary, and conspiracy. On November 10, he was sentenced to 23 years in prison. He is now under processing at San Quentin, while authorities decide where to send him.

I still haven't figured out who ransacked Dino's room that time. Was it a would-be accomplice who'd been cut out of the jewelry-store job? Somebody who'd heard Dino bragging in the street? Was it Dino himself, trying to see how I'd react? Who knows? Nothing was what it seemed with my ex-roommate—the dead sister in Seattle never existed; the one he brought to the apartment was actually his wife.

An even bigger mystery concerns Troy, who's still on the lam despite the FBI's $50,000 reward. Every so often, I see a guy in the street who resembles his mug shot and I'm spooked into thinking it's *him*. I tell myself I'm just being crazy, but then I've said that before.

I've since moved out of the place where I lived with Dino, into an upper-Manhattan apartment that I share with a financial planner, a dance teacher, and their 5-year-old son. I found them on Craigslist.

Unlikely crime reporter BRIAN BOUCHER *is on the editorial staff at* Art in America *magazine, where he writes art criticism, exhibition reviews, and news items. He lives in upper Manhattan.*

Coda

March 6, 2006, the day my interview with Steve Inskeep aired on NPR's *Morning Edition,* Devin "Troy" Smith entered San Francisco's Hall of Justice and surrendered himself to the authorities after almost three years on the run. He was later convicted of involvement in the Lang heist. On May 8, 2007, he was sentenced to 26 years in prision. Dino Smith is now in residence at Pelican Bay State Prison, where he has not answered my letters as he prepares his appeal.

Douglas Preston

THE MONSTER OF FLORENCE

FROM *The Atlantic Monthly*

MY WIFE AND I had always dreamed of living in Italy. Six years ago we finally made the move with our two young children. We rented a fourteenth-century farmhouse surrounded by olive groves and vineyards in the enchanting hills south of Florence. There were two famous landmarks near us: the villa La Sfacciata, once the home of Amerigo Vespucci, the Florentine explorer who gave America its name; and the villa I Collazzi, said to have been designed by Michelangelo, where Prince Charles painted many of his watercolors of the Tuscan landscape.

The olive grove beyond our front door boasted a third landmark, of sorts. It had been the site of one of the most horrific murders in Italian history, one of a string of double homicides committed by a serial killer known as "the Monster of Florence." As an author of murder mysteries, I was more curious than dismayed. I began researching the case. It didn't take me long to realize I'd stumbled across one of the most harrowing and remarkable stories in the annals of crime.

I contrived to introduce myself to the journalist who was the acknowledged expert on the case, a former crime correspondent for *La Nazione* named Mario Spezi. We met in Caffe Ricchi, in Piazza Santo Spirito, overlooking Brunelleschi's last and greatest church. Spezi was a journalist of the old school, with a handsome if cadaverous face, salt-and-pepper hair, and a Gauloise hanging from his lip. He wore a Bogart fedora and trench coat, and, knocking back one espresso after another, he told me the full story. As he spoke, he had his pocket notebook open on the table and he sketched his thoughts—I later learned it was a habit of his—the pencil cutting and darting across the paper, making arrows and circles and boxes and dotted lines, illustrating the intricate connections among the killings, the arrests, the suspects, the trials, and the many failed lines of investigation.

Between 1974 and 1985, seven couples—fourteen people in all—were murdered while making love in parked cars in the hills of Florence. The case was never solved, and it has become one of the longest and most expensive criminal investigations in Italian history. More than 100,000 men have been investigated and more than a dozen arrested, and scores of lives have been ruined by rumor and false accusations. There have been suicides, exhumations, poisonings, body parts sent by post, séances in graveyards, lawsuits, and prosecutorial vendettas. The investigation has been like a malignancy, spreading backward in time and outward in space, metastasizing to different cities and swelling into new investigations, with new judges, police, and prosecutors, more suspects, more arrests, and many more lives ruined.

It was an extraordinary story, and I would—to my sorrow—come to share Spezi's obsession with it. We became friends after that first meeting, and in the fall of 2000 we set off to find the truth. We believed we had identified the real killer. We interviewed him. But along the way we offended the wrong people, and our investigation took an unexpected turn. Spezi has just emerged from three weeks in prison, accused of complicity in the Monster of Florence killings. I have been accused of obstruction of justice, planting evidence, and being an accessory to murder. I can never return to Italy.

IT ALL BEGAN one summer morning many years ago in the Florentine hills. The date was June 7, 1981, a Sunday. Mario Spezi, then thirty-five, was covering the crime desk at *La Nazione,* Florence's leading paper, when a call came in: a young couple had been found dead in a quiet lane in the hills south of town. Spezi, who lived in those same hills, hopped into his Citroën and drove like hell along back roads, arriving before the police.

He will never forget what he saw. The Tuscan countryside, dotted with olive groves and vineyards, lay under a sky of cobalt blue. A medieval castle, framed by cypress trees, crowned a nearby rise. The boy seemed to be sleeping in the driver's seat, his head leaning on the window. Only a little black mark on his temple, and the car window shattered by a bullet, indicated that it was a crime scene. The girl's body lay some feet behind the car, at the foot of a little embankment, amid scattered wildflowers. She had also been shot and was on her back, naked except for a gold chain, which had fallen between her lips. Her vagina had been removed with a knife.

"What shook me most of all," Spezi told me, "was the coldness of the scene. I'd seen many murder scenes before, and this wasn't like any of them." Everything was unnaturally composed, immobile, with no signs of struggle or confusion. It looked, he said, like a museum diorama.

Due to the sexual nature of the crime, it was assumed that the killer was a man. And yet the medical examiner's report noted that the killer had not sexually assaulted the woman. On the contrary, he had assiduously avoided touching her body, except to perform a mutilation so expert that the medical examiner speculated he might be a surgeon—or a butcher. The report also noted that the killer had used a peculiar knife with a special notch in it, probably a scuba knife.

Spezi's article caused a sensation: it revealed that a serial killer was stalking the countryside of Florence. In a sidebar, next to the article, *La Nazione* pointed to something the police had overlooked: this killing was similar to a double homicide that had taken place in the hills north of Florence in 1974. The article prompted the police to compare the shells recovered from both crimes. They discovered that the bullets had been fired by the same gun, a .22-caliber Beretta "long barrel" firing Winchester series "H" copper-jacketed rounds, which, according to ballistics experts, probably came from the same box of fifty. The gun had a defective firing pin that left an unmistakable mark on the rim of each shell.

The investigation that followed lifted the lid off a bizarre underworld, which few Florentines realized existed in the beautiful hills surrounding their city. Because most Italians live with their parents until they marry, sex in cars is a national pastime. At night, dozens of voyeurs prowled the hills spying on people making love in parked cars. Locally, these voyeurs were called *"Indiani,"* or Indians, because they crept around in the dark, some loaded down with sophisticated electronic equipment like suction-cup microphones and night-vision cameras. Following a quick investigation, the police arrested and jailed one of these *Indiani*.

A few months later the killer struck again, on a Saturday night with no moon, this time north of Florence, using the same Beretta and performing the same mutilation. This third double homicide panicked Florence and garnered front-page headlines across Italy.

Spezi worked nonstop for a month, filing fifty-seven articles. The excellent contacts he had developed among the police and the Carabinieri ensured he had the breaking news first. The circulation of *La Nazione* skyrocketed to the highest point in its history. Spezi wrote about one suspect, a priest, who frequented prostitutes for the thrill of shaving their pubic hair. He wrote about a psychic who spent a night in the cemetery where a victim was buried, sending and receiving messages from the dead. Spezi's articles became famous for their dry turns of phrase and that one wicked little detail that remained with readers long after their morning espresso. Florentines have a flair for conspiracy thinking, and the citizenry indulged in wild speculation. Spezi's articles were a counterpoint to the hysteria: understated and ironic in tone, they crushed one rumor after another and gently pointed the reader back to the actual evidence.

Late that November, Spezi received a journalistic prize for work he had done unrelated to the case. He was invited to Urbino to accept the prize, a kilo of the finest white Umbrian truffles. His editor allowed him to go only after he promised to file a story from Urbino. Not having anything new to write about, Spezi recounted the histories of some of the famous serial killers of the past, from Jack the Ripper to the Monster of Düsseldorf. He concluded by saying that Florence now had its very own serial killer—and there, amid the perfume of truffles, he gave the killer a name: *"il Mostro di Firenze,"* the Monster of Florence.

The austere savagery of the crimes preyed heavily on Spezi's mind. He began to have nightmares and was fearful for his young and beautiful Flemish wife, Myriam, and for their baby daughter, Eleonora. The Spezis lived in a converted monastery on a hill high above the city, in the very heart of the Monster's territory. What frightened Mario most of all, I think, was that coming in contact with such barbarity had forced him to confront the existence of a kernel of absolute evil within us all. The Monster, he once told me, was more like us than we might care to admit—it was a matter of degree, not kind.

Myriam urged her husband to seek help, and finally he agreed. Instead of going to a psychiatrist, Spezi, a devout Catholic, turned to a monk who ran a small mental-health practice out of his cell in a crumbling eleventh-century Franciscan monastery. Brother Galileo Babbini was short, with Coke-bottle glasses that magnified his piercing black eyes. He was always cold, even in summer, and wore a shabby down coat beneath his brown monk's habit. He seemed to have stepped out of the Middle Ages, and yet he was a highly trained psychoanalyst with a doctorate from the University of Rome.

Brother Galileo combined psychoanalysis with mystical Christianity to counsel people recovering from devastating trauma. His methods were not gentle, and he was unyielding in his pursuit of truth. He had, Spezi told me, an almost supernatural insight into the dark side of the human soul. Spezi would see him throughout the case; he would confide to me that Brother Galileo had preserved not only his sanity, but also his life.

THE NEXT KILLING took place eight months later, in June 1982, again on a Saturday night with no moon. The same gun was used and the same inexplicable mutilation performed. Twelve days later, an anonymous letter arrived at police headquarters in Florence. Inside was a yellowed clipping from *La Nazione* about a forgotten 1968 double murder—of a man and a woman who had been having sex in a parked car. Scrawled on the article was a bit of advice: "Take another look at this crime."

Investigators rifled through their old evidence files and found that, through a bureaucratic oversight, the shells collected in 1968 had not been disposed of. They were Winchester series "H" rounds, and each one bore on the rim the unique signature of the Monster's gun.

The police were confounded, because the 1968 murders had been solved. It was an open-and-shut case. A married woman, Barbara Locci, had gone to the movies with her lover; afterward, they had parked on a quiet lane to have sex. They were ambushed in the middle of the act and shot to death. The woman's husband, Stefano Mele, an immigrant from the island of Sardinia, was picked up the following morning; when a paraffin-glove test indicated he had recently fired a handgun, he broke down and confessed to killing his wife and her lover in a fit of jealousy. But Mele could not be the Monster of Florence: he had been in prison at the time of the 1981 killing, and had lived since his release in a halfway house in Verona.

Overnight, every crime journalist in Italy wanted to interview Stefano Mele. The priest who ran the halfway house in Verona was equally determined to keep them away. Spezi arrived with a filmmaker on the pretense of shooting a documentary on the halfway house's good work. Little by little, after taking generous footage of the priest and conducting a series of fake interviews with inmates, he reached Mele.

His first glimpse was discouraging: the Sardinian walked around in circles, taking tiny, nervous steps. An expressionless smile, frozen on his face, revealed a cemetery of rotten teeth. He mumbled rambling answers to Spezi's questions, his words defying interpretation. Then, at the end, he said something odd: "They need to figure out where that pistol is," he said. "Otherwise there will be more murders . . . *They* will continue to kill . . . *They* will continue."

Spezi grasped something the police would also learn: Stefano Mele had not been alone that night in 1968. It had not been a spontaneous crime of passion but a *"delitto di clan,"* a clan killing, in which others from Mele's Sardinian circle had participated. Investigators theorized that one of the killers had enjoyed the experience so much that he had gone on to become the Monster of Florence—using the same gun.

This stage of the investigation became known as the *"Pista Sarda,"* the Sardinian Connection. It focused on three Sardinian brothers: Francesco, Salvatore, and Giovanni Vinci. All three had been lovers in turn of the woman murdered in 1968, and one or more had been present at her killing.

The police first arrested Francesco.

In September 1983, with Francesco Vinci in jail, the Monster struck again. This was the killing that took place in the olive grove beyond our front door. A German couple had parked their Volkswagen camper in the grove for the night. It was only after killing the two lovers that the Monster realized he had made a mistake: both were men, one of whom had long blond hair. Instead of performing his usual mutilation, the Monster tore up a homosexual magazine he found in the camper and scattered the pieces outside.

The authorities refused to release Francesco Vinci. They believed one of his relatives had tried to throw them off by committing a new murder using the same gun—or at the very least, that Francesco knew who the Monster was. Investigators became suspicious of another member of the clan, Antonio Vinci, and arrested him on firearms charges. They grilled the two men relentlessly, but were unable to break them, and finally were forced to release Antonio. Francesco remained in custody.

Four months later the police electrified Florence with an announcement, and once again Spezi had the scoop. *La Nazione* carried the banner headline *"I Mostri Sono Due"*—"There Are Two Monsters." Two other members of the Sardinian group—both suspected of having been present at the 1968 clan killing—were arrested and charged with being the Monster of Florence. Francesco Vinci was released.

All winter the police worked on the two men desperately trying to extract confessions and develop their case—with no success. Summer arrived, and tensions rose in Florence, even though suspects were in prison. Then, in July, the Monster struck again. Again he left the empty shells, which had become, perhaps intentionally, his calling card. He mutilated the woman and, adding a new horror, amputated and carried away her left breast.

This killing, which had occurred outside Vicchio, the birthplace of Giotto, triggered a nationwide outcry and generated headlines across Europe. Six times the Monster had attacked, killing twelve people, while the police had arrested and then been forced to release a steady stream of suspects. A special strike team was formed: the Squadra anti-Mostro composed of both Polizia and Carabinieri. (Italy has two police forces that investigate crime, the civilian Polizia and the branch of the military known as the

Carabinieri; they opperate independently, and often antagonistically, especially in high-profile cases.) The government offered a reward of roughly $290,000 for information leading to the capture of the Monster, the highest bounty in Italian history. Warning posters went up, and millions of postcards were distributed to tourists entering Florence, advising them not to go into the hills at night.

For Mario Spezi, the case had become a career. His colleagues at *La Nazione* affectionately referred to him as the paper's "Monstrologer." He wrote a highly regarded book about the case that was made into two films. He often appeared on television, and his soft voice and highly developed sense of irony were not always pleasing to investigators, especially those with whom he disagreed. Spezi had a perverse passion for needling people in positions of power, and he developed a second career as a caricaturist for *La Nazione*, which regularly printed his outrageously funny cartoons of politicians, officials, and judges in the news.

At the same time, he continued to see Brother Galileo, who helped him make peace with the physical horror of the murder scenes and the metaphysical evil behind them. Galileo spent a great deal of time probing Spezi's nightmares and his childhood, forcing him to confront his own inner demons.

IN THE SUMMER OF 1985 the Monster resurfaced in what would be the most terrible killing of all. The victims were two young French tourists who had pitched a tent in a field on the edge of a wood, not far from the villa where Machiavelli wrote *The Prince*. According to the reconstruction of the crime, the killer approached the tent and, with the tip of a knife, made a twelve-inch cut in the fly. The campers heard the noise and unzipped the front flap to investigate. The killer was waiting for them and opened fire, hitting the woman in the face and the man in the wrist. The woman died instantly, but the man, an amateur sprinter, dashed out of the tent and fled toward the trees. The killer raced after him, intercepted him in the woods, and cut his throat, almost decapitating him. The young man's blood stained the tree branches above to a height of ten feet. The killer returned to his female victim to perform the usual ritual mutilation—and again, he carved out and carried off her left breast.

This killing occurred on either Saturday or Sunday night; the date would become a matter of the utmost importance. The bodies were discovered by a mushroom picker on Monday at 2 p.m. At 5 p.m. the police took a detailed series of photographs, which showed the bodies covered with centimeter-long blowfly larvae.

On Tuesday, one of the prosecutors in the case, Silvia Della Monica, received an envelope in the mail. It had been addressed like a ransom note, with letters cut out of magazines, and inside was the victim's left nipple. As with everything else, the killer had been careful not to leave fingerprints; he had even avoided sealing the letter with his tongue. The experience shattered Della Monica: she withdrew from the case and, soon after, abandoned her career in law enforcement.

This, so far as we know, was the Monster's last killing. Over eleven years, fourteen lovers had been shot with the same gun. But the investigation had hardly begun. A judicial storm was mounting that would change its course and perhaps guarantee that the truth would never be known—and the killer never found. There were two key players in the coming storm: the chief prosecutor in the case, Pier Luigi Vigna, and the examining magistrate, Mario Rotella.

VIGNA WAS ALREADY A CELEBRITY in Italy when he assumed his role in the Monster case. He had ended a plague of kidnapping for ransom in Tuscany with a simple method: when a person was kidnapped, the state immediately froze the family's bank accounts. Vigna refused to travel with bodyguards, and he listed his name in the telephone book and on his doorbell, a gesture of defiance that Italians found admirable. The press ate up his pithy quotes and dry witticisms. He dressed like a true Florentine, in smartly cut suits and natty ties, and, in a country where a pretty face means a great deal, he was exceptionally good-looking, with finely cut features, crisp blue eyes, and a knowing smile.

Mario Rotella, the examining magistrate, was from the south of Italy, an immediate cause for suspicion among Tuscans. He sported an old-fashioned mustache, which made him look more like a greengrocer than a judge. And he was a pedant and a bore. He didn't like to mingle with journalists and, when cornered, answered their questions with unquotable circumlocutions. Under the Italian system, the prosecutor and the examining magistrate work together. But Vigna and Rotella disliked each other and disagreed on the direction the investigation should take.

The two suspects had been in jail when the French tourists were killed, and Vigna wanted to release them. Judge Rotella refused. He remained convinced that one of the clan members was the Monster—and that the others knew it. For a while Rotella prevailed. His focus turned to Salvatore Vinci, who had been involved with Barbara Locci and Stefano Mele in an elaborate sexual threesome, and who appeared to have been the prime shooter in the 1968 killing. Salvatore had been forced to leave Sardinia after his nineteen-year-old wife, Barbarina, was found asphyxiated by gas in their home. The death, in 1961, had officially been determined a suicide—although everyone in town believed it was a murder. Someone had mysteriously rescued their one-year-old son, Antonio, from the gas while leaving the boy's mother to die. Rotella didn't have enough evidence to arrest Salvatore Vinci for being the Monster, so he had him arrested instead for the murder of Barbarina. His plan was to convict him for that murder, and leverage it against him to identify the Monster.

The trial was a disaster: witnesses were vague, and evidence had gone stale. Antonio Vinci refused to testify against his father, at whom he glowered silently in court. Salvatore was acquitted, walked out of the courtroom, and vanished, slipping through the hands of the police, apparently forever.

This was the last straw for Vigna. He felt that the Sardinian investigation had led nowhere and brought nothing but humiliation. There was enormous public pressure to make a radical break. Vigna argued that the gun and bullets must have passed out of the hands of the Sardinians before the Monster killings had begun. He demanded that the investigation be started afresh. Rotella refused. He was supported by the Carabinieri, Vigna by the Polizia.

It was an ugly fight, and, as is usual in Italy, it devolved into a personality contest, which Rotella naturally lost. The Sardinian Connection was formally closed, and the suspects—including the men who had participated in the 1968 killing—were officially absolved. The problem was that, if Rotella was right, the investigation could now proceed in every direction except the correct one. Officers in the Carabinieri were so angry at this turn of events that they withdrew the organization from the Squadra anti-Mostro and renounced all involvement in the case.

Vigna reorganized the Squadra anti-Mostro into an all-Polizia force under the leadership of Commissario (Chief Inspector) Ruggero Perugini, later fictionalized as Chief Inspector Rinaldo Pazzi in Thomas Harris's novel *Hannibal*. Harris had followed the case while writing the novel, and he had been a guest in Perugini's home. (The chief inspector was not altogether pleased to see his alter ego gutted and hung from the Palazzo Vecchio by Hannibal Lecter.) Perugini was more dignified than his sweaty and troubled fictional counterpart in the movie version of *Hannibal*. He spoke with a Roman accent, but his movements and dress, and the elegant way he handled his pipe, made him seem more English than Italian.

The new chief inspector became an instant celebrity when, on a popular news program, he fixed his Ray-Bans on the camera and spoke directly to the Monster in firm but not unsympathetic tones. "People call you a monster, a maniac, a beast," he said. "But I believe I have come to know and understand you better." He urged the Monster to give himself up. "We are here to help you," he said.

Inspector Perugini wiped the slate clean. He started with the axiom that the gun and bullets had somehow passed out of the hands of the Sardinians, and that the Monster was unconnected to the 1968 clan killing. The forensic examination of the crime scenes had been spectacularly incompetent: people came and went, picking up shells, taking pictures, throwing their cigarette butts on the ground. What forensic evidence was collected—a knee print, a bloody rag, a partial fingerprint—was never properly analyzed, and, infuriatingly, some had been allowed to spoil. Perugini viewed this evidence with skepticism; he was smitten by the idea of solving the crime with computers.

He examined tens of thousands of men in Tuscany, punching in various criteria—convictions for sex crimes, propensity for violence, past prison sentences—and winnowed down the results. The search eventually fingered a sixty-nine-year-old Tuscan farmer named Pietro Pacciani, an alcoholic brute of a man with thick arms and a short, blunt body who had been convicted of sexually assaulting his daughters. His prison sentence coincided with the gap in killings between 1974 and 1981. And he was violent: in 1951 he had bashed in the head of a traveling salesman whom he had caught seducing his fiancée, and then raped her next to the dead man's body.

Inspector Perugini had his suspect; all that remained was to gather evidence. In reviewing Pacciani's old crimes, Perugini was struck by something: Pacciani had told the police he'd gone crazy when he had seen his fiancée uncover her left breast for her seducer. This statement, he felt, linked Pacciani to the Monster, who had amputated the left breast of two of his victims.

Perugini searched Pacciani's house and came up with incriminating evidence. Prime among this was a reproduction of Botticelli's *Primavera,* the famous painting in the Uffizi Gallery that depicts (in part) a pagan nymph with flowers spilling from her mouth. The picture reminded the inspector of the gold chain lying in the mouth of one of the Monster's first victims. This clue so captivated Perugini that the cover of the book he would publish about the case showed Botticelli's nymph vomiting bloody flowers.

Perugini organized a twelve-day search of Pacciani's property. The police took apart the farmer's miserable house and plowed up his garden. The haul was pretty disappointing, but on the twelfth day, just as the operation was winding down, Perugini announced with great fanfare that he had found an unfired .22 bullet in the garden. Later, in court, experts said it "might" have been inserted into the infamous Beretta and ejected without being fired—the ballistics report was inconclusive. In Pacciani's garage, the police found a scrap of torn rag, which was duly cataloged. Not long afterward, the Carabinieri received a piece of a .22 Beretta wrapped in a torn rag, with an anonymous note saying it had been found under a tree where Pacciani often went. When the two rags were compared, they matched up.

PACCIANI WAS ARRESTED on January 16, 1993, and charged with being the Monster of Florence. The public, by and large, approved of his arrest. Spezi, however, remained unconvinced. He felt that a drunken, semiliterate peasant given to fits of rage could not possibly have committed the meticulous crimes he had seen. Spezi continued to feel that the Sardinian investigation had been prematurely closed. He laid out his views in a series of carefully reasoned articles, but few readers were persuaded: Pacciani's trial was being broadcast almost every night on television, and the drama of the proceedings overwhelmed all logic. Florentines have never forgotten the sight of Pacciani's violated daughters (one of whom had entered a convent), weeping on the witness stand as they described being raped by their father.

This was melodrama worthy of Puccini. Pacciani rocked and

sobbed during the proceedings, sometimes crying out in his Tuscan dialect, "I am a sweet little lamb! . . . I am here like Christ on the cross!" At other times he erupted, face on fire, spittle flying from his lips. Thomas Harris attended the trial, taking notes in longhand on yellow legal pads. The prosecutors presented no murder weapon and no reliable eyewitnesses. Even Pacciani's wife and daughters, who hated him, said he couldn't have been the Monster—he was home drunk most of the time, yelling, hitting them, and acting the bully.

Pacciani was convicted and sentenced to life in prison. During the mandatory appeal, the prosecutor assigned to handle the case did something almost unheard of: he refused to prosecute. He became Pacciani's unlikely advocate, decrying in court the lack of evidence and comparing the police investigation to the work of Inspector Clouseau. On February 13, 1996, Pacciani was acquitted. A higher court sent the case back to be retried, but Pacciani died in February 1998, before the new trial could begin.

On the very day of Pacciani's acquittal, the police brought forward new witnesses and dramatically announced that they had a confession in hand, in an attempt to salvage their case. The judge refused to allow them to testify, and excoriated the police for the last-minute maneuver. But the investigation was far from over, and eventually their story would emerge. The first surprise witness had actually confessed to being Pacciani's accomplice. He said that he and Pacciani had been hired by a wealthy Florentine doctor to "handle a few little jobs." These "little jobs," investigators later said, were to collect female body parts for Black Masses, to be used as offerings to the devil. The man made many odd claims and contradicted himself continually. He implicated a third man, and the two men were convicted, in a subsequent trial, of murder; one was sentenced to life in prison and the other to twenty-six years.

Thus began the investigation that remains open to this day: the search for the Florentine doctor and the other *mandanti* (masterminds) behind the killings. Inconveniently, the police's selfinculpating witness said he didn't know the doctor's name—he claimed that only Pacciani did. But Pacciani denied the whole story to his dying day.

With the death of Pacciani and the conviction of his accomplices, the investigation receded into the shadows. Most people felt the case had been solved, and Florence moved on. And perhaps it was just as well. For over time, thread by thread, the web of evidence began to unravel. The rag and gun pieces were found to have been a manufactured clue, although by whom was not established. The expert who had been asked to certify that the bullet found in Pacciani's garden might have been inserted into the Monster's gun complained of pressure put on him. On assignment from a television station, Spezi videotaped a police officer, present at the search of Pacciani's property, saying it was his impression that the chief inspector had planted the bullet. The television station refused to air the segment; Spezi published the allegation—and was promptly sued for libel. (He won the case, but not without further antagonizing the Squadra anti-Mostro and its boss.)

SPEZI WAS BY NOW EXHAUSTED—by the case, which he had covered for more than fifteen years, and by the grueling life of a crime correspondent. Brother Galileo had urged him to quit his job. Spezi's daughter was growing up, and he was feeling the pinch of his journalist's salary. When his wife's cousin offered him a lucrative partnership in his luggage business, he jumped. *La Nazione* agreed to keep him on a freelance contract. It would leave him time to fulfill a longtime dream of writing mystery novels, and to embark on his own counter-investigation, which became a hobby of sorts.

Around this time, Spezi received crucial help from a high-ranking official in the Carabinieri whose identity he has never revealed, not even to me. This man was part of a group of officers who had continued a secret investigation into the killings after the

Carabinieri officially withdrew from the case. His clandestine group had identified a possible suspect as the Monster, a man who had previously been arrested and released.

One of Spezi's big scoops had been the discovery of a report prepared for Inspector Perugini by the FBI's Behavioral Science Unit in Quantico, Virginia. It had been commissioned in secret and then suppressed, because it didn't describe Pacciani. The report cataloged the killer's likely characteristics, explained his probable motive, and speculated as to how and why he killed, how he chose his targets, what he did with the body parts he collected, and much more. Its conclusion was that the Monster was of a type well known to the FBI: a lone, sexually impotent male with a pathological hatred of women, who satisfied his libidinous cravings through killing.

The FBI report said that the Monster chose the places for his crimes, not the victims, and that he would kill only in familiar locations. The murders had been committed in some of the most beautiful landscapes in the world, over a large area encompassing the hills south, east, and north of Florence. The police had stared at pins in maps for years, never finding a pattern. But when Spezi mapped the life and movements of the Carabinieri's suspect to the locations of the killings, he found surprising overlaps.

AFTER THAT FIRST MEETING at Caffe Ricchi, Mario Spezi and I became friends. He often talked about the case, and I began to share his frustration at its unsatisfying conclusion. I cannot remember exactly when my curiosity became more than idle speculation, but by the spring of 2001, Spezi and I had agreed to write something together—a collaboration that would eventually take the form of a book. But first, I needed a crash course from the "Monstrologer."

A couple of days a week I would shove my laptop into a backpack and bicycle the six miles from our home to Spezi's. The last kilometer was a bear, almost straight uphill through groves of knotted olive trees. I would find him in the dining room, thick with smoke, with papers and photographs scattered about the table. Myriam, Spezi's wife, would check in on us every now and then and bring us cups of espresso or fresh-squeezed orange juice. Spezi was always careful to keep the strongest details—and the crime-scene photographs—well out of her sight.

He went through the entire history chronologically, chain-smoking all the way, from time to time plucking a document or a photograph from the heap by way of illustration. I took notes furiously on my computer, in an almost indecipherable mix of English and Italian (I was still learning the language then). *"Bello,* eh?" he often said when he had finished recounting some particularly egregious example of investigative incompetence.

We visited the crime scenes together and tracked down, where we could, the family members of the victims. We went to Vicchio to visit the mother of one of the female victims. She was living a hollow existence in what had once been an imposing house in the center of town. Her husband had squandered the family fortune on his futile search for the killer and had dropped dead of a heart attack at police headquarters during one of his many visits.

I began to understand, in a small way, the immensity of the evil that Brother Galileo—now dead—had helped Spezi to accept. And yet, despite the darkness of our hunt, my days with Spezi were my happiest in Italy. My wife and I enjoyed many elegant dinners with Mario and Myriam on their terrace overlooking the hills, where they gathered writers, photographers, countesses—even, one night, a woman who was half Apache, half Florentine. Spezi had a seemingly inexhaustible store of outrageous tales, which he recounted with the quiet delight of an epicure serving a mossy bottle of Château Pétrus. As he told a story, he often imitated the players, speaking in flawless dialect. Sometimes he would require each guest to bring a story to dinner, in lieu of flowers or wine.

Spezi's view of the case was not complicated. He had nothing but contempt for the conspiracy theories and heated speculation about satanic sects. The simplest and most obvious explanation, to his mind, was most likely the correct one. He had always believed—and I came to share his conviction—that the Monster of Florence was a lone psychopath, and that the key to finding him was the gun used in the 1968 clan killing. Every cop, Spezi often told me, knows that a gun used in a homicide—especially a clan killing—is never disposed of casually. It is either destroyed or kept in a safe place. One of the killers had taken the gun home.

Spezi believed that the Monster must either be Salvatore Vinci, the man Rotella had had his eye on, or someone close to him—someone with access to the gun *and* the box of bullets. It was that simple. He turned to the crime-scene evidence. It suggested that the Monster was a tall, right-handed man in excellent physical condition who acted with almost preternatural sangfroid (ruling out Pacciani, who was short, fat, old, and usually drunk). The killer was an expert shot and skilled with a knife.

When we had chased down every other person we could find with some connection to the crimes, I pressed Spezi on the subject of the Carabinieri's suspect, who he told me was the son of one of the original Sardinians. He was still alive and living in Florence. (I will not mention his name, since the evidence against him remains circumstantial.) The stumbling block was Myriam, who had begged her husband not to approach him. Alone, Spezi had heeded her pleas, but there were two of us now, and I goaded him on. Without telling Myriam, Spezi and I began to plan our visit. We developed a cover story—that I was an American journalist and Spezi my translator, and we were conducting a series of interviews about the Monster of Florence case. Out of deference to Myriam's fears, we decided to use false names.

FOR YEARS, the Sardinian had been living a quiet life in a working-class area west of Florence. We arrived at his apartment building at 9:40 p.m., when we would be most likely to find him home. His neighborhood was neat, even cheerful, with tiny garden plots in front of modest stuccoed apartment buildings. There was a grocery store on the corner, and bicycles were chained to the railings. Across the street, past a row of umbrella pines, lay the skeletons of abandoned textile factories.

Spezi pressed the intercom, and a woman's voice asked, "Who is it?"

"Marco Tiezzi," Spezi replied.

We were buzzed in without further questions.

A man greeted us at the door, wearing only a pair of tight shorts. He recognized Spezi immediately: "Ah, Spezi! It's you!" he said with a smile. "I must've misheard the name. I've wanted to meet you for the longest time." He invited us to be seated at a small kitchen table and offered us a glass of Mirto, a Sardinian liqueur. His wife, who had been washing spinach in a sink, silently left the room.

Our host was a strikingly handsome man with a dimpled smile. His curly black hair was lightly peppered with gray, his body tanned and heavily muscled. He projected a cocky air of working-class charm. While we talked about the case, he casually rippled the muscles of his upper arms or slid his hands over them in what seemed an unconscious gesture of self-admiration. He spoke in a husky and compelling voice that reminded me of Robert De Niro's.

Spezi casually slipped his tape recorder out of his pocket and laid it on the table. "May I?"

The man flexed and smiled. "No," he said. "I'm jealous of my voice."

Spezi took notes in longhand, slowly working his way from generic questions toward his real objective. (The quoted passages below are from his notes.)

"Your father had strange sexual habits," Spezi said. "Perhaps that was a reason you hated him?"

"Back then I knew nothing about it. Only later did I hear about his . . . tics."

"But you and he had some really big fights. Even when you

were young. In the spring of 1974, for example, you were charged with breaking and entering and theft."

"That's not correct. Since he didn't know if I had taken anything, I was charged only with violation of domicile. Another time we had a big fight, and I pinned him, putting my scuba knife to his throat, but he broke free and I locked myself in the bathroom."

"When did you leave Florence?"

"In the beginning of 1975. First I went to Sardinia, and then to Lake Como."

"Then you returned and got married."

"Right. I married a childhood sweetheart, but it didn't work. We married in 1982 and separated in 1985."

"What didn't work?"

"She couldn't have children."

Spezi did not mention he had learned that the marriage had been annulled for non-consummation. "Can I ask you a rather direct question?" he said.

"Sure. I may not answer it."

"If your father owned the .22 Beretta, you were the person in the best position to take it. Perhaps during the breaking and entering in the spring of 1974."

He didn't answer immediately. "I have proof I didn't take it," he said at last.

"Which is?"

"If I had taken it, I would have fired it into my father's forehead."

Spezi pressed on. He pointed out that our host had been away from Florence from 1975 to 1980, when there were no Monster killings. When he returned, they began again.

The Sardinian leaned back in his seat, and his smile broadened. "Those years were the best of my life," he said, "up there at Lake Como. I had a house, I ate well, and all those girls . . ." He whistled and made a vulgar Italian gesture.

"And so," Spezi said, "you're not . . . the Monster of Florence?"

There was only a brief hesitation. The Sardinian never ceased smiling, not even for an instant. "No," he said. "I like my pussy whole."

We rose to go. Our host followed us to the door. Just before opening it, he leaned toward Spezi and spoke in a low and casual voice. "Ah, Spezi, I was forgetting something." He leaned even closer and smiled. His voice took on a hoarse, gravelly tone. "Listen carefully: I never joke around."

SPEZI AND I agreed that we would publish our book first in Italian, and then I would rewrite it and publish it in English. The publisher of my murder mysteries in Italy, Sonzogno, a division of the Italian publishing house RCS Libri, gave us a contract and an advance. The book, which was titled *Dolci Colline di Sangue (Sweet Hills of Blood,* a play on the phrase *Dolci colline di Firenze),* was scheduled for publication in April 2006.

Meanwhile, the search for the hidden masterminds began to intensify. Time had passed, and the old investigators had retired or been promoted. Vigna was appointed head of Italy's anti-Mafia unit, while Perugini went on to become the liaison officer with the American FBI. A new investigator rose to the fore: Chief Inspector Michele Giuttari, who had organized and headed an elite police unit known as GIDES (Investigative Group for Serial Crimes), heir to Perugini's Squadra anti-Mostro. The newspapers dubbed him *"il Superpoliziotto,"* because he was, in practice, answerable to nobody.

In the summer of 2001, the case once again hit the front pages in Italy. GIDES had focused its attention on a villa in Chianti where Pietro Pacciani had worked as a gardener. This villa, which the papers dubbed the "Villa of Horrors," was suspected of being the meeting place for the cult of devil worshippers who had supposedly hired Pacciani to do their bidding. One important clue that a satanic sect was behind the killings was a rough, hexagonal stone in the form of a broken pyramid found at the site of one of the crimes. Only Giuttari realized its significance. "I hypothesized that it was an object connected to the occult," he would later explain in one of his many books on the case, "and that, for some reason, it had been left there deliberately."

Spezi ridiculed this conclusion in the media and produced a similar stone, which a friend had given him. He pointed out that it was not an esoteric object at all, but a type of doorstop commonly found in old Tuscan farmhouses. On May 14, he appeared on a popular TV show with an explosive allegation: he had shown the photographs of the murdered French tourists to one of Europe's leading forensic entomologists, and the entomologist had concluded, by examining the larvae on the corpses, that the lovers could not have been killed any later than Saturday night.

This determination, if true, was fatal to the satanic-sect theory: Pacciani's supposed accomplice swore the French tourists were killed on Sunday night. If the crime had occurred Saturday, all his claims would be thrown into question. What's more, Pacciani had an ironclad alibi for Saturday night.

Much to Spezi's dismay, Giuttari dismissed the entomologist's findings and pressed ahead with his investigation. Spezi's appearance on television had another effect entirely from that intended: it seemed to have inspired the chief inspector's undying hatred.

In June 2004, I moved back to the States with my family, into a house we had built on the coast of Maine. When I left Italy, Mario gave me a pencil drawing he'd made of Pacciani during the trial and a caricature of myself, spying on my wife through a keyhole. I hung both on the wall of my writing shack, in the woods behind our house, along with a photograph of Spezi in his fedora and trench coat, standing in a butcher's shop under a rack of hog jowls.

Spezi and I spoke frequently. I missed my life in Italy—but Maine was quiet, and quiet is what a writer needs. We continued to work on the book by e-mail and telephone. Spezi did most of the actual writing, while I made suggestions and contributed a few chapters, which he had to rewrite (I write in Italian at about a fifth-grade level). He continued to keep me abreast of the *"Pista Satanica,"* which, curiously, seemed to be heating up.

That summer, Spezi called me with a strange bit of news. An old friend of his, a pharmacist, was being investigated for the death of Francesco Narducci, a gastroenterologist whose body had been found floating in Lake Trasimeno some twenty years earlier. The original investigators had considered it a suicide—Narducci had been heavily into drugs and was known to be depressed—but GIDES suspected that the doctor may in fact have been murdered by the Monster's satanic sect. This brought into the investigation the public prosecutor who has jurisdiction over Lake Trasimeno: the *pubblico ministero* of Perugia, Giuliano Mignini.

On November 18, 2004, at 6 a.m., Spezi and his family were awoken by the sound of their door buzzer. *"Polizia!"* screamed a voice. *"Perquisizione!"* The police were from GIDES, Giuttari's squad. Their warrant gave two reasons for the search: Spezi had "materially damaged the investigation by casting doubt on the accusations through use of the medium of television," and he had "evidenced a peculiar and suspicious interest in . . . the investiga- tion." He was served with an *avviso di garanzia,* one step short of a formal indictment. It listed seventeen crimes for which Spezi was being investigated, all undisclosed.

For seven hours the police searched the apartment, while Spezi, Myriam, and their daughter looked on. Officers pulled books off the shelves and rummaged through photos, letters, and school- books, scattering things on the floor. They took everything Spezi had that related to the case: his computer, disks, archives, clippings, interviews, even our notes and drafts of the book. They found Spezi's old doorstop, which a document would later describe as having been "secreted behind a door." To Giuttari, this became one of the most important fruits of the search.

Twelve months later, Spezi opened the newspaper and read a headline about himself: "Narducci Murder: Journalist Investigated."

"When I read that," Spezi told me, "it was like a hallucination. I felt I was inside a film of Kafka's *Trial,* remade by Jerry Lewis and Dean Martin." Spezi had gone from journalist to suspect.

It was in this climate that I arrived in Florence on February 14 of this year. The kids were on winter vacation, and plane tickets were cheap. I was anxious to see my old friend. Our book would be published in two months, and Spezi hoped we might do some preliminary publicity and line up an evening presentation at Seeber, one of the best bookstores in Florence.

I visited Spezi on February 15. He told me he had recently heard from a source that during the Monster killings and afterward, a group of Sardinians had frequented a run-down outbuilding on the thousand-acre estate of a grand villa outside Florence. The source claimed to have a friend who had been at the building a few months earlier, with the Carabinieri's suspect (the man I've been calling "the Sardinian"). He had seen six locked iron boxes and two guns: a machine pistol and a .22 Beretta.

"What are those boxes?" the friend had asked.

"That's *my* stuff," the Sardinian allegedly said, slapping his chest.

Six locked iron boxes. Six female victims. A .22 Beretta. It was almost too perfect to be true.

I asked Spezi what he planned to do. He said he had been agonizing about this. He smelled a scoop—the scoop of a lifetime. He had driven past the villa a couple of times, but in the end he had decided that he had no choice but to call the police.

I had never seen Mario so excited. "This could be it," he told me. "The culmination of all my years on this case. And you'll be here to see it." He said the villa was open to the public for sales of wine and olive oil, and that it was rented out for parties.

I asked if I could see it. "Sure," he said. "Why not?" We couldn't go to the outbuilding, but we could at least see the part open to the public.

We decided to go the next day, accompanied by a friend of Spezi's who owned a security firm in Florence and from his days as a cop knew the source, an ex-con. Driving over to his friend's office, Spezi apologized for the state of his car: a few days earlier someone had wrecked the door and stolen his radio.

It was raining when we arrived at the villa. A woman leaned out a window and said the salesroom was closed for lunch. We took a desultory stroll along the drive and returned to the car. We had been there about ten minutes. It was a disappointing visit, at least to me; something about the whole story didn't feel quite right.

Two days later, Spezi called me on my cell phone. "We did it," he said. "We did it all." He didn't go into details, but I knew what he meant: he had given the information to the police. He also said, before I could ask too many questions, "The telephone is bad." For two years he had been complaining that the police were tapping his phones.

ON FEBRUARY 22, as I was heading out for a morning coffee, my cell phone rang. A man speaking Italian informed me that he was a police detective and that he needed to see me—immediately. No, it wasn't a joke. And no, he couldn't tell me what it was about, only that it was *"obbligatorio."*

I chose the most public place possible, the Piazza della Signoria. Two plainclothes detectives from GIDES took me into the Palazzo Vecchio, where, in the magnificent Renaissance courtyard, surrounded by Vasari's frescoes, I was presented with a legal summons to appear before Judge Mignini. The detective politely explained that a no-show would be a serious crime; it would put him in the regrettable position of having to come and get me.

I asked, "Is this about the Monster of Florence case?"

"Bravo," said the detective.

The next day, I was ushered into a pleasant office in the Procura della Repubblica, just outside the ancient city walls of Perugia. Present were one of the detectives from the previous day, a small and very tense captain of police with orange hair, a stenographer, and Giuliano Mignini, sitting behind a desk. I had dressed smartly—Italians judge harshly in such matters—and I had a folded copy of the *International Herald Tribune* under my arm as a prop.

Mignini was a small man of indeterminate middle age, well groomed, with a fleshy face and thinning hair. His voice was calm and pleasant and he addressed me with elaborate courtesy, bestowing the honorific of *dottore,* which, in Italy, denotes the highest respect. He explained that I had the right to an interpreter, but finding one might take many hours, during which time I would be unpleasantly detained. In his opinion, I spoke Italian fluently. I asked if I needed a lawyer, and he said that, although it was of course my right, it wasn't necessary; he merely wanted to ask a few questions of a routine nature.

His questions were gentle, posed almost apologetically. The stenographer typed the questions, and my answers, into her computer. Sometimes Mignini rephrased my answers in better Italian, checking solicitously to see if that was what I had meant to say. He asked me about Spezi's lawyer, Alessandro Traversi, and wanted to know what I could say about Spezi's legal strategy. He named many names and asked if Spezi had ever mentioned them. Most were unfamiliar. The questions went on like this for an hour, and I was starting to feel reassured. I even had a glimmer of hope that I might get out in time to join my wife and children for lunch at a nearby restaurant, which came highly recommended in the guidebooks.

At this point the conversation turned to our visit to the villa. Why did we go? What did we do there? Where exactly did we walk? Was there talk of a gun? Of iron boxes? Was my back ever to Spezi? Did we see anyone there? Who? What was said?

I answered truthfully, trying to suppress a damnable habit of over-explanation, but I could see that Mignini was not happy. He repeated the same questions, in different forms. It began to dawn on me that the previous line of inquiry had been nothing more than a few balls lobbed in the bullpen. Now, the game had begun.

Mignini's face flushed as his frustration mounted. He frequently instructed the stenographer to read back my earlier answers. "You said that, and now you say this. Which is true, Dottor Preston? *Which is true?*"

I began to stumble over my words (as I've noted, I am not fluent in Italian, especially legal and criminological terms). With a growing sense of dismay, I could hear from my own stammering, hesitant voice that I was sounding like a liar.

"Listen to this," Mignini said. He nodded to the stenographer, who pressed a button on her computer. There was the ringing of a phone, and then my voice:

"Pronto."

"Ciao, sono Mario."

Spezi and I chatted for a moment while I listened in amazement to my own voice, clearer on the intercept than in the original call on my lousy cell phone. Mignini played it once, then again. He stopped at the point where Spezi said, "We did it all," and fixed his eyes on me: "What exactly did you do, Dottor Preston?"

I explained that Spezi was referring to his decision to report to the police what he had heard about possible evidence hidden at the villa.

"No, Dottor Preston." He played the recording again and again, asking repeatedly, "What is this thing you did? *What did you do?*" He seized on Spezi's comment that the telephone was bad. What did he mean by that?

I explained that he thought the phone was tapped.

And why, Mignini wanted to know, were we concerned about the phones being tapped *if we weren't engaged in illegal activity?*

"Because it isn't nice to have your phone tapped," I answered feebly.

"That is not an answer, Dottor Preston."

He played the recording again, stopping at several words and demanding to know what Spezi or I meant, as if we were speaking in code, a common Mafia ploy. I tried to explain that the conversation meant what it said, but Mignini brushed my explanations aside. His face was flushed with a look of contempt. I knew why: he had expected me to lie, and I had met his expectation. I stammered out a question: Did he think we had committed a crime at the villa?

Mignini straightened up in his chair and, with a note of triumph in his voice, said, *"Yes."*

"What?"

"You and Spezi either planted, or were planning to plant, *false evidence* at that villa in an attempt to frame an innocent man for being the Monster of Florence, to derail this investigation, and to deflect suspicion from Spezi. *That* is what you were doing. This comment— *'We did it all'*—that is what he meant."

I was floored. I stammered that this was just a theory, but Mignini interrupted me and said, "These are not theories. They are facts!" He insisted I knew perfectly well that Spezi was being investigated for the murder of Narducci, and that I knew more about the murder than I was letting on. "That makes you an accessory. Yes, Dottor Preston," Mignini insisted, "I can *hear* it in your voice. I can hear the tone of knowledge, of deep familiarity with these events. Just listen." His voice rose with restrained exaltation. *"Listen* to yourself!"

And, for maybe the tenth time, he replayed the phone conversation. "Perhaps you have been duped, but I don't think so. You *know!* And now, you have one last chance—one *last* chance—to tell us what you know, or I will charge you with perjury. I don't care; I will do it, even if the news goes around the world tomorrow."

I felt sick, and I had the sudden urge to relieve myself. I asked for the way to the bathroom. I returned a few minutes later, having failed to muster much composure. "I've told you the truth," I managed to croak. "What more can I say?"

Mignini waved his hand and was handed a legal tome. He placed it on his desk with the utmost delicacy, opened it, and, in a voice worthy of a funeral oration, began to read the text of the law. I heard that I was now *"indagato"* (an official suspect under investigation) for the crime of reticence and making false statements. He announced that the investigation would be suspended to allow me to leave Italy, but that it would be reinstated when the investigation of Spezi was concluded.

The secretary printed out a transcript. The two-and-a-half-hour interrogation had been edited down to two pages, which I amended and signed.

"May I keep this?" I asked.

"No. It is under seal."

Very stiffly, I picked up my *International Herald Tribune,* folded it under my arm, and turned to leave.

"If you ever decide to talk, Dottor Preston, we are here."

On rubbery legs I descended to the street, into a wintry drizzle.

I left Italy the next day. When I returned to my home in Maine, which stands on a bluff overlooking the gray Atlantic, and listened to the breakers on the rocks below and the seagulls calling above, I felt tears trickling down my face.

BUT IT WAS NOT OVER—not at all.

After I left, Spezi brought his car to a mechanic to get the broken door and radio fixed. The mechanic emerged holding a few thousand dollars' worth of electronics: a sophisticated GPS, microphone, and transmitter, which had been carefully attached to the old radio wires. Spezi filed a complaint, and a week or two later, his crappy radio was returned to him by GIDES.

For Spezi, the wrecking of his car was the last straw. He asked his lawyer to file a civil lawsuit against Chief Inspector Michele Giuttari. The suit was dated March 23. Spezi wrote the introductory statement himself, every word perfectly pitched to infuriate his foe:

> For more than a year, I have been the victim not just of half-baked police work, but of what could be said to be authentic violations of civil rights. This phenomenon—which pertains not just to me, but to many others—brings to mind the most dysfunctional societies, such as one might expect to find in Asia or Africa.

Spezi proceeded to deliver an uppercut to Giuttari's soft underbelly—his literary talent. In February, Giuttari had published his second book (there had also been several novels) on the Monster of Florence case, *The Monster: Anatomy of an Investigation,* in which he had taken several jabs at Spezi and others. In the lawsuit, Spezi quoted extract after extract, savaging Giuttari's theories, his logic, and his writing ability.

On Friday, April 7, eleven days before the publication of our book, a squad of policemen arrived at Spezi's apartment, lured him outside under false pretenses, arrested him, and hustled him into a car. He was driven to GIDES headquarters and taken from there to prison in Perugia. The Italian papers reported the charges against him: "calumny," "disturbing an essential public service," and "attempting to derail the investigation into the case of the Monster of Florence." A number of other people were named by the police as being involved in these crimes; I was one of them. The final charge, the papers claimed, was complicity in murder.

The day of the arrest, Mignini asked for and received a special dispensation to invoke a law that is normally used only for terrorists or Mafia dons who pose an imminent threat to the state. For a period of five days Spezi was denied access to his lawyers, kept in a tiny isolation cell under conditions of extreme deprivation, and grilled mercilessly. It was noted in the press that Spezi's treatment was harsher than that of Bernardo Provenzano, the Mafia "boss of bosses" captured in Sicily a few days later.

Spezi spent three weeks in Capanne, one of Italy's grimmest prisons. On April 29, a three-judge panel in Perugia surprised everyone by annulling his imprisonment and setting him free. It was a decisive slap in the face for Mignini and Giuttari. A week later, Florence hosted a demonstration for freedom of the press, and Spezi was the guest of honor. That same day our book hit the best-seller lists across Italy.

When Spezi returned home from prison, a crowd of journalists greeted him. "No, I'll not deal with the Monster affair anymore," he told one. "I'll write books, but not about that." Twenty-five years after that perfect summer Sunday in June when the bodies of two lovers were first found, Mario Spezi had finally declared his emancipation from the Monster of Florence.

Spezi's legal problems will likely drag on for years. He has been summoned back for another round of interrogation, and fresh charges are reportedly in the works. And yet, the tide may be turning. Mignini's fellow judges have severely criticized his conduct of the case, and, in early May, Giuttari himself became the target of an investigation, accused of falsifying evidence in the case. And so the investigation grinds on, voracious in its appetite for new victims.

People have often asked me if the Monster of Florence will ever be found. I once believed that Spezi and I could find the truth; now I am not so certain. Any crime novel, to be successful, must contain certain basic elements: there must be a motive; evidence; a trail of clues; and a process of discovery that leads, one way or another, to a conclusion. All novels, even *Crime and Punishment,* must come to an end.

But life, I have learned, is not so tidy. Here were murders without motive and a trail of clues apparently without end. The process of discovery has led investigators so deeply into a wilderness of falsehood that I doubt they will ever find their way out. Spezi and I used to laugh at their elaborate theories, but ours may not be much better. It wasn't based on what a good criminal investigation should be: the nitty-gritty of blood, hair, fibers, fingerprints, DNA, and reliable eyewitnesses. In the absence of solid forensic police work— which, in the Monster case, was shockingly deficient—any hypothesis will remain like something dreamed up by Hercule Poirot: a beautiful story in search of a confession. Only this is not a novel, and there won't be a confession—and without one, the Monster of Florence will never be found.

DOUGLAS PRESTON *began his writing career at the American Museum of Natural History in New York City, which led to his first nonfiction book,* Dinosaurs in the Attic, *as well as his first novel,* The Relic, *which he co-authored with Lincoln Child. Since then he has published fourteen novels and four nonfiction books. Preston writes occasional pieces for* The New Yorker *and* The Atlantic Monthly; *he taught non-fiction writing at Princeton University.*

Coda

Immediately upon hearing of Spezi's arrest, the first call I made was to a close friend in Italy, Count Niccolò Capponi, whose family had been in Florence since the early 1200s and whose judgment in all matters Italian I consider impeccable.

All in a panic, I asked him: "What does it mean? What's going to happen?"

"Don't worry," he replied coolly. "This time they have gone too far. Something will happen soon, and it will be big. It's all about saving face, my dear Douglas, something you Anglo-Saxons will never understand."

Capponi's prediction came to pass. Immediately after the "Monster of Florence" article was published in *The Atlantic Monthly,* a series of extraordinary revelations blew the investigation wide open. The Monster of Florence case may have an end after all—which will be detailed in the book Spezi and I are writing.

The television show *Dateline NBC* picked up the story and flew me to Italy, with a promise that if I were arrested, NBC would do its damnedest to spring me from Italian jail. Spezi and I, along with Stone Phillips and a *Dateline* crew, spent a week exploring the scenes of the crimes, interviewing witnesses, investigators, and suspects. We had one close call with the police, but for the most part we managed to slip in and out of the country before the authorities got wise to our activities. The program will be aired in the spring of 2007.

The article also generated interest in Hollywood. Not long after the article was published I got a call from Christopher McQuarrie, who won an Academy Award for his screenplay of *The Usual Suspects*. McQuarrie felt the Monster story would make an outstanding movie and offered to write the screenplay himself—an offer that Spezi and I accepted with alacrity, *The Usual Suspects* being one of our favorite films. The film will be produced in partnership with the Jinks/Cohen Company, which also produced *American Beauty* and other movies.

Our book on the case, *The Monster of Florence,* will be published by Warner Books in 2008.

Permissions

THE BEST AMERICAN CRIME REPORTING SERIES

Otto Penzler and Thomas H. Cook, Series Editors

THE BEST AMERICAN CRIME REPORTING 2007
Linda Fairstein, Editor

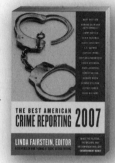

ISBN 978-0-06-081553-0 (paperback)

Edited by Linda Fairstein, bestselling crime novelist and sex crimes expert, *The Best American Crime Reporting 2007* is another must-have for the true crime reader, featuring smart, controversial, and suspenseful stories by the masters of the genre.

THE BEST AMERICAN CRIME WRITING 2006
Mark Bowden, Editor

ISBN 978-0-06-081552-3 (paperback)

"Solid and diverse. . . . Anyone interested in true crime should find something to enjoy in this wide-ranging collection." —*Publishers Weekly*

THE BEST AMERICAN CRIME WRITING 2005
James Ellroy, Editor

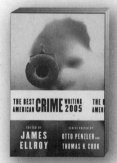

ISBN 978-0-06-081551-6 (paperback)

"Mixes the political, the macabre, and the downright brilliant." —*Entertainment Weekly*